Teaching Reading in the Middle School

Common Core and More

Anna J. Small Roseboro

ROWMAN & LITTLEFIELD EDUCATION

A division of
ROWMAN & LITTLEFIELD
Lanham • Boulder • New York • Toronto • Plymouth, UK

Published by Rowman & Littlefield Education
A division of Rowman & Littlefield
4501 Forbes Boulevard, Suite 200, Lanham, Maryland 20706
www.rowman.com

10 Thornbury Road, Plymouth PL6 7PP, United Kingdom

British Library Cataloguing in Publication Information Available

Library of Congress Cataloging-in-Publication Data

Roseboro, Anna J. Small, 1945-
  Reading in the middle school : common core and more / Anna J. Small Roseboro.
    pages cm
  Includes bibliographical references.
  ISBN 978-1-4758-0533-8 (cloth : alk. paper) — ISBN 978-1-4758-0534-5 (pbk. :
alk. paper) — ISBN 978-1-4758-0535-2 (ebook) 1. Reading (Middle school)—United
States. 2. Language arts (Middle school)—Curricula—United States—States. 3.
Language arts (Middle school)—Standards—United States—States. I. Title.
  LB1631.R633 2014
  418'.40712—dc23

                                                              2013034336

∞™ The paper used in this publication meets the minimum requirements of American
National Standard for Information Sciences—Permanence of Paper for Printed Library
Materials, ANSI/NISO Z39.48-1992.

Printed in the United States of America

To my husband, William Gerald Roseboro,
and children Rosalyn, William II, and Robert

To Dr. Robert Infantino for his sage advice to me
and other educators eager to contribute to the profession

To Alison Taylor, a dear friend, respected colleague,
and enthusiastic cheerleader

To early career educators who accept the challenge
of a lifetime and to veterans who remain and mentor them,
demonstrating the wisdom of balancing personal
and professional lives, showing and sharing the
joys of teaching young adolescents

Contents

Foreword

Amazing Grace

If you don't know where you are going, any old way will do.

—Lewis Carroll

I started teaching middle school because I didn't know what else to do. Though born into a family of teachers, I had always said "Not me!" when asked if I planned to take my degree in English and teach. But a combination of crippling student loans and a dearth of other plans pushed me toward the Education Department at the University of Southern California. After what I recall as the briefest of interviews, the advisor told me to show up the next day at Lincoln Junior High to start my student teaching. I arrived expecting to take a couple of weeks getting my bearings, but the master teacher was out sick and his substitute told me to start teaching.

It was not an auspicious beginning. There were no textbooks, no standards, and no curriculum that I could find, just 36 eager, fresh-faced eighth graders waiting for me to do something. I shudder to remember the lessons I offered my young charges, students who most certainly deserve a refund for their first semester of eighth grade. But I was trying hard: typing up short stories on purple dittos, writing discussion questions, grading papers, and going through the motions of what I thought English teachers did. Of course I struggled with classroom management, but the bigger problem was that I didn't know where my instruction was supposed to be heading. A line from Alice in Wonderland kept echoing in my dreams, "If you don't know where you are going, any old way will do."

Those students from long ago deserved better than what I was able to offer. If only I had had a mentor like Anna Roseboro to ease my way into the classroom. If only someone had handed me *Teaching Reading in the Middle*

School: Common Core and More to help me plan a coherent year of learning for them. The middle school scenario I describe is unfortunately more common than educators would like to admit. Data on teacher attrition demonstrates that we are a profession that eats its young. Between 40 and 50 percent of teachers leave the profession in the first five years. Anna Roseboro's book can help turn these numbers around by helping new teachers be successful right from the first year. It also provides a much-needed tonic for experienced teachers who may have lost their way and are wondering if there isn't an easier way to make a living.

The Common Core State Standards have set new guidelines for what students should know and be able to do in order to be prepared to meet the literacy demands of college and the workplace.[1] When teachers read in the Common Core that students in grade 8 should be able to "Delineate and evaluate the argument and specific claims in a text, assessing whether the reasoning is sound and the evidence is relevant and sufficient," they sometimes throw up their hands in despair. "My kids? You must be kidding!" Authors of the Common Core and developers of Common Core–aligned assessments are not kidding. Eighty to 90 percent of the reading standards at every grade require text-dependent analysis. Making the shift to more rigorous and at the same time more relevant instruction is not going to be easy.

Teaching Reading in the Middle School: Common Core and More lays out a plan for approaching a school year that is both student centered and Common Core aligned. Anna Roseboro's lessons employ a gradual release model designed to offer strong support and extensive guidance in the first months of the school year and then, week-by-week, month-by-month, greater opportunities for independent learning as students acquire the skills and habits of mind needed for 21st-century literacy. Roseboro answers common questions new teachers have, providing practical answers of the kind only someone who has spent a lifetime in the classroom could offer. Covering everything from choice of texts to the arrangement of desks, *Teaching Reading in the Middle School* presents a pedagogy grounded in sound theory and effective practice.

Rather than fighting middle school students' buoyant natures, Anna Roseboro revels in her students' enthusiasm. In lesson after lesson, she demonstrates how a wily teacher can use young people's energy for educational purposes, capitalizing on their eagerness to know one another and know more about the world around them. She also shows how to put their love of talk to work. Calling her lessons "benevolent athletic training sessions," Roseboro artfully leads her charges in the direction she wants them to go. There is no doubt in her students' minds who is the coach. At the same time, they seem to draw strength from this knowledge.

I was particularly struck by the manner in which Anna's instructional plan treats every minute of classroom time as golden. Again and again Anna limits the time students have to work on a project, plan their writing, or prepare for a presentation—sometimes using a timer to drive home the message. This technique sends students the message that their work has urgency. There is no time to waste. We have stories to read and papers to write and so much—so much—to tell one another.

But how can a young teacher manage all that middle-school energy and talk? My first classroom was located on the second floor just above the principal's office. I received more than one note from Mr. Steinman's secretary querying the noise level and wondering why the furniture had to be moved quite so often. Anna offers readers not only explanations about how putting students' desks together facilitates the collaborative process (I wish I had had this defense in hand 30 years ago) but also provides helpful hints for students. She tells her charges when working in pairs to use "six-inch voices."

Teaching Reading in the Middle School: Common Core and More will be a valuable resource for both new and experienced teachers whatever the particulars of their school or district curriculum. It will also be of great help to teachers working to align their district's curriculum to the Common Core. We can't make excuses for not teaching well. Whatever our resources, we need to serve the children who have been entrusted to our care. Anna urges teachers working with middle school students "to challenge them to think deeply, critically, and broadly—but also charitably—toward those who are different, whether in the classroom or in the literature."

I do not know a single teacher who doesn't want to be more effective in the classroom. Most teachers are eager, often desperate, to help students become better readers and writers. They agree with the authors of the Common Core that success in school and in the workplace depends upon literacy. They want their eighth graders to be able to "Produce clear and coherent writing in which the development, organization, and style are appropriate to task, purpose, and audience." They sweat to make this happen. But if media reports are to be believed, our schools are full of underprepared, uninspired, and relatively unqualified individuals collecting full-time pay for part-time work. Such reporting is dispiriting, particularly for teachers who know they could be doing a better job but don't know where to find the help they need.

Of particular interest to teachers of middle school "digital natives" are the many examples of 21st-century technology applications included in this text. The average student spends six hours a day plugged into a digital communication device, often several simultaneously.[2] Linda Stone, a former Microsoft executive, describes this habit of mind as "continuous partial attention."[3] No wonder teachers have difficulty making students attend to their lessons.

Fortunately Anna Roseboro has powerful ideas for engaging preoccupied youngsters in their learning so that they can "Use technology, including the Internet, to produce and publish writing and present the relationships between information and ideas efficiently as well as to interact and collaborate with others."

What I never guessed those 30-odd years ago when I faced my first group of middle school students was how seductive teaching could be or how the work itself could be so rewarding that I would never want to leave the classroom. In *I Want to Thank My Brain for Remembering Me*, Jimmy Breslin writes that "Grace appears when you don't expect it and have asked for nothing. It comes out of the mists to help people at their work. Grace comes to those who teach." Every good teacher knows what it feels like to be on the receiving end of this gift of grace. It doesn't appear on the check stub but is the best payment of all. Thank you, Anna Roseboro, for sharing this grace, your grace, with us.

CAROL JAGO

Carol Jago has taught middle and high school English for 32 years and serves as associate director the California Reading and Literature Project at UCLA. She is a past president of the National Council of Teachers of English.

NOTES

1. *Common Core State Standards for English Language Arts and Literacy in History/Social Studies, Science, and Technical Subjects.* www.corestandards.org/ELA-Literacy/RST/introduction (accessed May 14, 2013).

2. Don Tapscott, *Growing Up Digital: The Rise of the Net Generation* (New York: McGraw-Hill, 1998).

3. Linda Stone, "Continuous Partial Attention." *Linda Stone.* www.lindastone.net/ (accessed May 14, 2013).

Preface

Getting to the Core of Language Arts Instruction

Over the past few decades, education has been moving in all kinds of curricular and pedagogical directions. Language arts, in particular, has undergone tremendous changes, primarily because of new technologies, multiple-intelligence teaching and learning, and multicultural opportunities. But it's time again in the history of education to focus on the core; the core becomes our agreed-upon nonnegotiables in our field. States and provinces are rightly involved in helping educators define what all faculty must teach and what all students must learn. National initiatives are helpful, too. But we all know that educational standards are always evolving. States differ; normatively speaking, some states seem to be ahead of others in establishing core curricula amid social and cultural changes.

Teaching in the Western world has always addressed agreed-upon standards. Moreover, language arts educators, from the ancient Greek and Roman rhetoricians forward, have continually tried to define such standards at the intersection of ancient and modern *literacies*—that is, at the intersection of older means and methods of gaining communicative comprehension.[1] Why? Because every educator and every school has to teach both tried-and-true and the newly emerging information and practices. I still teach basic public speaking along with PowerPoint; essay writing along with blogging; library research along with online Internet searching. Each instructor is a medium, a go-between, who teaches at the intersection not only of "text" (broadly speaking, the "material") and student but also of traditional and contemporary cultures. This is why developing a common core is so critically important, especially in times of great social change. Somehow we have to define and teach both traditional and contemporary methods and content. So I use low-tech, lobby-based conversation to teach my smartphone-toting students! Most fun of all, they don't necessarily see the conversation as education. Little do they realize how much I teach while they are hanging out with me.

The traditional–contemporary intersection often leads to disagreements among educators and between educators and the communities they serve. Who will set the standards? What do we give up when we define core competencies? Who is to say that speech communication is still as important as written communication? This tension goes back at least to Plato, for whom the word *poetry* referred to all language arts, but especially to the most popular forms of artistic expression. Plato feared that the poets promoted undesirable passions, failed to pursue truth, and wasted students' time with impractical instruction.[2] Poets were eloquent teachers, but they didn't care about truth, let alone anyone else's definition of common standards. The poets were careerists who wanted job stability.

The Common Core State Standards Initiative, which focuses primarily on using standards to help students prepare for college, included particular standards "only when the best available evidence indicated that its mastery was essential for college and career readiness in a twenty-first-century, globally competitive society. The standards are intended to be a living work: as new and better evidence emerges, the standards will be revised accordingly."[3] So we set standards in the midst of social, cultural, and technological shifts constantly occurring in our communities and the world. Standards are never perfect, but they help us together to define and to understand the needs of our students in a changing world. When it comes to defining a common core, we educators are in a pickle; we can't entirely live with the resulting standards, but we can't live without them. So we move ahead as a community of educators, setting, assessing, and revising standards. We wish we had more time, better pedagogies, wiser mentors. Just when we seem to have figured out how to teach to the standards with flair and distinction, the curriculum has to be adjusted again. But this problem has always been true of teaching. In fact, when we don't feel the anxiety of having to change what and how we teach, we are probably losing our passion to be outstanding educators. The gift of knowing our discipline's core offers educational traction and focus. We don't have to teach all things to all students. We can say "no" to some things while affirming those in the core.

Common standards in the language arts rightly focus first on language, the most basic form of human communication. The primary and most lasting media were—and still are—mass languages. Languages were the original viral media, millennia before social media like Facebook and Twitter. After addressing language skills, standards address how to apply such skills to other disciplines. In other words, we language arts educators teach our discipline in order to help students learn in other disciplines. Of course, we expect colleagues in history or the sciences to teach things like writing and speaking along with their core disciplines. But we also know that they tend not to be quite as good at it as we are because we teach communicative competencies all day long. Nevertheless, we and our colleagues in other subjects together have to teach the use of newer technologies or media, such as PowerPoint, video, and audio—all of which have their own "languages" that students and teachers need to understand.

My wife says she doesn't like to watch movies with me because I'm always commenting on how and how well the movies are communicating, not just on what the movies are saying. I don't just get into the storyline. I have the same problem watching and listening to other teachers teach. And I wonder if I should have gone into a field like chemistry so I wouldn't be so conscious about how people communicate! "Language arts" seems to be part of everything human beings do. That's the rub. Our curricular standards and core competencies are especially important because they shape how our students communicate in all of life. Our teaching is "metacommunication"— communication about communication. It's not easy. But what fun! What a joy to teach about the core of what it means for us to be human beings. We humans are creatures of language. Other creatures communicate, too, but there is no solid evidence in the research that they communicate about their communication. We do it all the time—sometimes probably too much.

The College and Career Readiness (CCR) Standards highlight "Reading, Writing, and Speaking and Listening Standards" as the "backbone" for language arts. Those are worthy of being at the core of our work. But then the CCR Standards statement adds, "The Standards set requirements not only for English language arts (ELA) but also for literacy in history/social studies, science, and technical subjects. Just as students must learn to read, write, speak, listen, and use language effectively in a variety of content areas, so too must the Standards specify the literacy skills and understandings required for college and career readiness in multiple disciplines."[4] There is much wisdom in that interdisciplinary conclusion. I would just hope that our colleagues in other disciplines would include some of our core competencies in their standards, too. In my school we teach writing across the curriculum. It's not just the job of the English Department.

At its best, language arts instruction invites students into rich, multimedia communion with persons and cultures, with those nearby and far away, with people who lived before us and now live among us on Earth. We learn with students and colleagues what others have thought, believed, and done; how others have told and still tell us about themselves through various art forms; how we can identify with their life stories; and ultimately how we can share our own stories with others. The language arts are also the cultural and social arts.

Some of this sociocultural communication is highly practical, such as writing a complex sentence, reading poetic alliteration, establishing a speech thesis, or memorizing vocabulary. Other aspects of language arts focus both explicitly and implicitly on character-building, heart-opening, mind-sharpening practices. These are among the many deeply human literacies that have existed across time and through geographic space. Good standards help us to focus on such fundamental aspects of what it means to be virtuous as well as skilled communicators. I know that when I am hanging out with my students in the lobby, they are learning partly through my modeling of right, fitting, and kind communication. So I need to integrate the core of my discipline into the very core of my life. Otherwise both I and my curriculum lack integrity.

Our professional lives are multimedia parables. We language arts educators are living texts. There is something refreshingly old and new about that vision. Thanks to Anna for inspiring us to live up to the standards of great language-arts instruction. May her wisdom stir us to listen well to her words in this book with graceful hearts and open minds.

QUENTIN J. SCHULTZE

Quentin J. Schultze, PhD, is a professor of communication at Calvin College and author of many books, including *An Essential Guide to Public Speaking* and *Resume 101: A Student and Recent-Grad Guide to Crafting Resumes and Cover Letters That Land Jobs.*

NOTES

1. As Kylene Beers suggests, reading theorists and researchers generally agree that the "point of reading is comprehension." See Beers, *When Kids Can't Read: What Teachers Can Do: A Guide for Teachers 6–12* (Portsmouth, NH: Heinemann, 2002), 59. We could expand Beers's insight, considering that all human communication primarily is for the practical purpose of comprehension, not for the other purposes of personal expression—romanticism—or impact—behaviorism. If humans don't understand one another, they invariably create unhealthy conflicts.

2. Plato, *Republic*, especially books II, III, and X.

3. "The Standards—English Language Arts Standards," Common Core State Standards Initiative, www.corestandards.org/ELA-Literacy.

4. "The Standards—English Language Arts Standards."

Acknowledgments

Colleagues who have collaborated with me and the students who inspired me when I taught in Michigan, Missouri, New York, Massachusetts, and California, especially those from The Bishop's School.

Critical Readers: Christine Berry, Shayna S. Costello, Delores Geter, Marilyn Gross, Nancy Perkins, Verneal Mitchell, Alan L. Sitomer, Brooke Suiter, and Joan Williams, whose feedback heartened me to revise and massage the manuscript with confidence.

Teachers of middle school students Lindsey Lautenbach and Michelle Shepherdson and their students from the Excel Academy in Kentwood, Michigan.

Contributions to annotated book lists by Bethany J. Kim and by the Kent District Library Teen Services Staff, Comstock Park, Michigan.

Donna Lynn Russ and Tamara Swafford for their assistance.

Poems "Finalists," "Evening Cicadas," "A Kiss," and "The Pond," used by permission of the poet Nancy Genevieve.

Poem "My Poems Have Holes Sewn into Them," used by permission of poet Quincy Troupe.

Poem "Unfolding Bud" by Naoshi Koriyama, used by permission of *Christian Science Monitor*.

Poetry T.I.M.E. cartoons used by permission of artist Linda Hargrove.

Student writing used by permission of students named.

Colleagues from the California Association of Teach.ers of English, the Greater San Diego Council of Teachers of English, the San Diego Area Writing Project, the Michigan Council of Teachers of English, and Conference of English Leadership of the National Council of Teachers of English, and members of the online social networks for educators, like the English Companion Ning, Making Curriculum Pop Ning, and the National Council of Teachers of English Connected Community.

Introduction

> If a child can't learn the way we teach, maybe we should teach the way they learn.
>
> —Ignacio "Nacho" Estrada

Few careers in education are more exciting and rewarding than teaching middle school English/language arts. Sure, some of your friends shake their heads and maybe even feel sorry for you when they hear about your work with young adolescents. Unless they have worked with this age group, however, they won't understand your enthusiasm. You and I get to spend our days helping young adults develop the reading, writing, viewing, speaking, listening, and study skills they need for success wherever their career path takes them. Our work is challenging but also lots of fun; we get to share our love of language and literature, speaking and writing—and to cultivate such love in our students. We not only must know, understand, and love the language arts content, but we must also know, understand, and love our learners in all of their remarkable diversity.

TEACHING AND WRITING ABOUT TEACHING

When a candidate for National Board Certification for Early Adolescent/English Language Arts, I reflected seriously about what, why, and how I teach. When others inquired about that certification experience, they requested more explanation. From those conversations and from feedback to workshops presented at local, state, and national conferences and conventions, it became clear that I have valuable experiences to share with my colleagues. So began the writing—putting into words some of my rationales, ideas, lessons.

In other settings, during receptions for new teachers held as part of the annual meetings of the California Association of Teachers of English and Michigan Council of Teachers of English, I recognized how thirsty novice teachers are to learn about the solid, structured lessons that successful experienced teachers use. Concerns that those starting out in the profession without the benefit of local mentors, that many states offer emergency credentialing to satisfy the rising demand for new teachers especially in growing ethnic communities, and because most states can ill afford special courses for such new teachers, I felt compelled to record and share my experience.

Many novice teachers begin enthusiastically but soon face tough standards and accountability; although eager to do a good job, they are not sure how to serve their early adolescent students well in an increasingly multicultural, assessment-driven, 21st-century environment and one that has specific long-range goals for middle school students that prepare them for college or careers similar to the Common Core Standards for English Language Arts.

GROWING PROFESSIONALLY

None of us can become an effective middle school teacher on our own. We need active mentors. We need professional colleagues and wise administrators. We all must continue to grow professionally during each school-year journey throughout our years of service. Why? Pedagogies change. So do students. Of course, so do standards of and standards for assessment. When it comes to middle school, the technological environments that our students live in are shifting continuously. It is critical that we constantly learn from one another how to tap into these cultural and technological dynamics. We have to admit that the differences in our ages, even generations, are factors in making such adaptations successfully. As Quentin J. Schultze reminds us in the preface, we teach at the constantly changing intersection of old and new.

I have benefitted for decades from formal study; involvement in professional organizations, conferences, and workshops; journal articles; online conversations; advice from generous colleagues; and years of experience teaching students from middle school to graduate college—and on that experience ground my lesson planning. Consequently, the lessons in this book are informed by the philosophies and theories from a variety of sources as well as my four decades of experience as an English/language arts teacher and college instructor.

Publications by the National Middle School Association and the National Research Council have proven invaluable. Chris Stevenson asserts that middle school curricula must be challenging, integrated, and exploratory.[1] His perspective goes along with Howard Gardner, who "proposed the existence of seven relatively autonomous intelligences: linguistic, logical, musical, spatial, bodily kinesthetic, interpersonal, and intrapersonal."[2] The views of both are reflected in lessons described in this book.

SERVING STUDENTS ARTFULLY

These and many other currents in educational research have shaped my daily pedagogy. The writings of Louise Rosenblatt and Fran Claggett inspired me to incorporate assignments to accommodate many of Gardner's multiple intelligences. Rosenblatt encourages educators to allow students to respond to the reading in their own ways—that students should rely on their prior knowledge to help them make sense of the literature.[3]

This approach to reading and interpretation of literature frees us from the burden of focusing with students only on what the book means. It gives us permission to let the literature speak to the students, and it helps us to trust the students' own responses about what it says to them in their own cultural contexts and developmental stages. Nevertheless, the "literature" does have to be taught, standards must be met, and students must demonstrate academic proficiency, so you need to plan lessons that require students to ground their responses in the texts to show their grasp of the knowledge, understanding of the concepts, and acquisition of the skills. Otherwise they can stray too far afield during class discussions or while writing about the literature.

Here are theory-based lessons to help you plan units for the range of students you teach. Specific assignments for the course of a school year, a journey of learning, take into account myriad ways that adolescents can be taught and assessed based on their specific age and maturation as well as their individual learning styles. Keeping in mind the grade-level standards and incorporating technology helps, too. I readily admit that such a variety of lessons is developed this way to maintain interest myself because I thoroughly enjoy learning from my students.

You may find that you gain greater insight into the fiction and nonfiction works each time you offer your students the option to demonstrate their understanding of literature and life as you study together. You also form a deeper understanding of the students and their ways of looking at text and at the world around them. At the same time, you have confidence that you are on the road to fulfilling the charge of preparing students for success in the years to come.

LOOKING FOR THE CURRICULUM?

Unless you have taken a college course in or are a devotee of young adult literature, chances are you are not familiar with much of the literature that you are being asked to teach. You may discover that the literature in your own middle school curriculum is very different from that which you read as a student. My advice? Do not worry about your lack of background in this genre. Although it is important for you to read all the literature in the curriculum, it is not crucial for you to have studied all of the academic texts you are using.

Most middle school curricula require students to learn about different kinds of writing, how to read it, how to recognize its structure, how to identify the function and understand the purpose of literary structure and devices, and, of course, how to talk and write about it intelligently. The schools often are less concerned about the specific titles used in a class than they are about students' ability to read and understand any kind of writing—fiction and nonfiction, in print or digital formats. Therefore, it is important to develop a range of strategies for teaching any kind of literature so that you can adapt to the reading lists in schools or districts that employ you.

CHOOSING ALTERNATIVE WAYS
TO TEACH AND ASSESS

Reading is not the same as comprehension. Once the students have read the assigned stories, plays, articles, essays, and poems, you have to determine how well the students understand them. Fran Claggett, a pioneer in the use of graphics in teaching literature, recommends that teachers employ art—either via graphics to help plot out the structure before or after the students read, or assignments for which students may use art to show what they know.[4] Today the word "graphics" seems anachronistic. So do the terms "visuals" and "media," let alone "audio-visual."

Twenty-first century students are more versed in digital, computerized media. Yet the basics of literature as art and story have not changed. There still is skillful use of language and imaginative use of arrangement. Therefore, lessons in this book incorporate old and new media to show students a work's traditional devices, such as structure and plot lines, images, and symbols. With proper guidance, students can use their artistic interests and digital talents to demonstrate their comprehension of specific works of even the most traditional literature and sophisticated essays.

What I also like personally about using art and digital media is the fact that I am neither an artist nor a techy, so my students get to see me at my mediocre best. They seem more inclined to risk being vulnerable when they see me somewhat inartfully expressing what literature means to me. Students see they can produce something better because drawing definitely is not one of my strengths; they often are more adroit than I at working with the current digital media from PowerPoint to Prezi, podcasts to movie making.

Artistic diversity goes beyond linguistic modes of reading, writing, and speaking. You can discover in this book that such diversity can help a wider range of students to shine before their peers, building self-esteem among some of those who need it most. Yet, at the same time, such variety saves you time. Generally speaking, written assignments take more time to grade even when they may not be as conducive to assessing particular types of learning. You soon realize that incorporating art and technology enhances your instruction, improves student engagement, and increases learning.

In other words, seek to reduce your students' insecurities and strive to design lessons that build their confidence and develop their strengths. Let students use music or dance to express the mood of a literary work or characters in those works, and even the tone of an article they are reading or video they are viewing. Invite your students to act out scenes, partly to assist kinetic learners and partly to give all your energetic adolescents an opportunity to get out of their seats and move around. When auditory and visual learners see the work of their peers, they too are learning at a deeper level.

All of this is to say that language arts learning is more than demonstrating competence in traditional linguistic modes of reading, writing, and speaking. Notice as you read that the assignments in this book give more students an opportunity to shine individually before their peers by employing the range of their own multimedia abilities to specific language arts learning. Several of the assignments are designed to provide a variety of assessment opportunities that are not nearly as time consuming to grade as a written assignment yet are equally revealing and authentic.

TEACHING PRESERVICE TEACHERS
AND GRADUATE SCHOOL STUDENTS

When I moved from California to Michigan and became an adjunct education professor at a state university, I noticed that preservice students were keen to the study literacy assessment. They eagerly leaned forward to hear about instructional practices useful in guiding developmentally appropriate learning. These students recognized through their internship assignments in classrooms in local schools that being able to provide instruction is only half the responsibility of teachers. The other half is choosing or developing formative assessment tools that demonstrate what students are learning and then designing subsequent lessons based on the data revealed in these assessments.

After working years in the classroom, graduate students found it beneficial to spend their summer examining research and theories, differentiated instruction, and assessment practices appropriate for the literacy needs of their students and crafting curricula to meet these needs. When it comes to assessing for 21st-century literacies, however, few of us can be well versed in the research, because it is still being done; still, we do our best based on what it is we are trying to measure and what our measurements tell us about our students. Some of the lessons that follow can stretch you, maybe even pull you further along than you thought possible into the world of teaching with technology and working toward reaching Common Core standards without teaching solely for the tests. That is fine. We teachers have to be students ourselves, learning by doing and assessing.

UNDERSTANDING WHAT IS APPROPRIATE FOR MIDDLE SCHOOL

Perhaps the notion that most influences effective instruction for middle school students is that they tend to work well in groups, yet you must design such group lessons to maximize individual student learning. In the early weeks of the semester, you recognize the importance of using more teacher-directed instruction, demonstrating manners, modeling lessons, and giving students opportunities to develop a set of behaviors for successful group activities throughout the year.

For this reason, a rule of thumb is "student choice, teacher control." This may be another way of applying Vygotsky's notion of the zone of proximal development or what Pearson and Gallagher call the "gradual release of responsibility."[5] You are responsible for planning lessons that provide opportunities not only for students to learn in different ways from different sources but also for teachers to design lessons that deliberately lead to meeting the standards set forth by their schools, districts, and states in ways that students become increasingly independent learners.

Bethany J. Kim, an early career teacher who contributed to some of the lists of supplemental book titles, says that one of her greatest challenges as a new middle school teacher is appropriately and effectively assessing her teaching and then maintaining the right classroom atmosphere. In a sixth-grade charter school that focused on building character as well as strong academics, Bethany found it difficult to set the right tone at the beginning of the year. Student choice began to swamp teacher control. When it came time for formal assessment, she realized that it would have been better to phase in the student choice more gradually during the first semester. She loved the students and the students loved learning from her, but she had not tied the pedagogy to assessment as well as she would have liked. That need not be a problem for you.

KNOWING WHAT YOUNG ADOLESCENTS ENJOY

Young adolescents enjoy talking and often learn well from each other. As *Turning Points 2000: Educating Adolescents in the 21st Century* puts it, "Cooperative learning . . . can be a successful technique both to teach content and to raise self-esteem among all students particularly those whose, native language is not English."[6] Adolescents are very sensitive to perception of their peers. "A Safe and Healthy School Environment"[7] requires cooperative learning and project-based learning in order to enhance relationships among different social and ethnic groups. This is why it is good to structure frequent lessons that give the students permission to do what they love to do: talk to one another. The key words here are *structure* and *talk*.

Once the students begin working together, regularly circulate among the groups, listening in, giving assistance as needed; you will begin to discover in an informal but intentional way what ideas they have grasped, what areas need further instruction, and whether the students are ready for more formal assessment to demonstrate individual readiness to move on the next level of instruction. Tryon Edwards writes that "Thoroughly to teach another is the best way to learn for yourself."[8] As often as appropriate, include assessments where pairs and small groups of students can use the new technologies, even if they are more familiar to your students than to you. By teaching each other how to "do" language arts via newer as well as older media, students teach themselves and often the teacher as well.

While students prepare together for group or student-led discussions, they are also reviewing the lessons in more depth than they might have if they were working solely on their own. Students are then able to participate in the necessary preconditions for quality: content, collaboration, and choice. When the researchers finally determine the educational value of "new" media, they might conclude along with all of the other benefits for 21st-century literacies is an age-old truth: Collaborating on projects can produce mutual learning.

APPLYING NATIONAL WRITING PROJECT CONCEPTS

After becoming a writing fellow of the San Diego Area Writing Project, I began incorporating the National Writing Project's strategies into my lessons. In particular, I followed the project's sequence of fluency, form, and correctness and soon noticed that both my students and I were more enthusiastic about learning. Sequencing lessons this way gives students the time to write frequently, to conduct peer editing, to revise, to edit, and to publish in a variety of ways for a variety of audiences. With more ready access to technology, it is easier to publish regularly to real audiences—who may be parents logging onto the class website or students in classes across the ocean who are participating in a collaborative reading and writing project. The lessons in this book are similarly flexible. In the chapters that follow are suggested assignments for different purposes, such as to explore, to explain, to expand, and even to entertain.

The lessons described in this book also show ways to reduce the time-consuming burden of grading each piece of writing for correctness. Following the recommendations in the lessons, you will begin to see the benefits of reading some students' writing or viewing their media projects just to discover whether your young students comprehend a specific text or just what they think about a particular topic. As a result, you can enjoy the freedom to read or view some assignments only for the ideas presented.

These kinds of writings and media productions become no-stress assessments. As you determine what students think, know, understand, and are able to do, you begin to adjust your instruction based on what you have observed and read. When the students realize that every word they write or image they project is to not be evaluated for correctness, your otherwise self-conscious young teens become more fluent. They are willing to write more often; and they also appreciate that you give them some choice about what writing, print, or digital media they wish to submit to peer editing, evaluation, and publication.

BALANCING STRUCTURE WITH CHOICES

Although offering students lots of choice in their reading, writing, and responding is important, the key to becoming an effective teacher is to establish structures and routines on which the students can depend. These structures and routines foster important habits: using time efficiently; maintaining useful notebooks and digital files for test and exam preparation; reading and writing efficiently; and participating cooperatively in small-group or full-class discussions, using technology with a critical eye and creative bent. The good habits help students learn the basics of language and forms of literature, including essays, novels, poetry, and drama. When students know the daily class requirements and routines, they have something against which to rebel without rejecting it completely. As Anne King declared in a presentation titled "You Are Not Going Crazy, This Really Is Normal Behavior," once adolescents know the boundaries, they frequently challenge them, but they usually comply.[9]

Experience has shown that even though middle school students love to try the system and test the rules—just to see how teachers respond—they also appreciate the predictability and structure. For some of the students, a dependable pattern gives them a sense of control and power. They know what to expect and how to perform in the midst of their own physical and emotional changes.

For these reasons, the lessons early in the school year are designed like benevolent training sessions in an athletic program, providing opportunities for participants to learn the rules of the games and to develop the knowledge and skills to be successful. The effective, experienced teachers you observe only seem to handle this training period effortlessly; such veterans know how to offer student choices within a fair but firm classroom structure.

REMOVING THE SCAFFOLDS

As the school year progresses, you can step aside and become more of a coach than an instructor. If all has gone well, students already know the kinds of reading, writing, media, speaking, and listening skills that they must learn. You have shown them the Common Core Standards for English Language Arts to which you all are striving to achieve. The goals of the course should not be a secret to them. As with fellow travelers, if everyone knows where you are going, all can be alert and supportive along the road. Even backseat drivers come in handy sometime.

You can then increase the number of choices to practice these skills more independently and to demonstrate their growing knowledge and skills even more creatively. As you move on along the way, the students soon learn how to act and what to do because they develop the habits of mind as well as the confidence and competence to handle the tasks set before them. They rise to the challenge of future goals as they see evidence they are meeting earlier ones. Happily, they begin to enjoy the learning. When adolescents feel secure, they are able to function more effectively, bringing joy to all involved.

Although I tend toward student choice over teacher control, my goals are always student-centered. What is it that the students want and need to know and do by the end of the school year? What kind of nurturing environment must be developed and experiences offered to ensure the students reach these goals? For a young adolescent and for a novice teacher, this may mean a little more visible structure than would be evident in the classroom of a veteran teacher. So, although I recognize that many approaches to teaching can be effective, the ideas I share are those that have worked well for me and the new-to-middle-school teachers I have mentored.

In this book, then, are comments both about my experiences teaching young adolescents and descriptions of specific lessons you can use throughout a full school year. These lessons are structured to allow you to get to know the students and introduce the course's main concepts, while permitting the students to demonstrate their understanding of what they read through various methods. You can find interdisciplinary lessons that encourage students to use the knowledge they are learning in social studies, science, music, and art. Some lessons are designed to increase students' understanding and ease with library and online research while meeting the language arts standards you are required to address.

ACKNOWLEDGING PHYSICAL AND EMOTIONAL CHALLENGES

The primary challenge in teaching middle school is that physical, emotional, and social issues often overwhelm and distract students. Both your male and female students can be manically mischievous one day and dismally depressed the next.

Be prepared by designing lessons to keep them excited about learning to use the receptive and expressive language arts that can help them succeed personally and academically. You could view yourself as a ship's captain whose charge is to chart a course that provides safe passage through the tumultuous preteen and early teen years. As the captain, you recognize the need for balancing structure and choice. Though you already know the standards you are expected to meet, as the year goes by you develop a clearer vision of where you are going and how you may get there.

You learn more specifically what this year's students need to know and be able to do. You also discover that they prefer to contribute to the journey. You may even begin to envision the curriculum as the ship, the units as the decks, and the lessons as the rooms. Within the ship, upon the decks, and inside the rooms, there are choices the students can make regarding specific assignments.

As you become better acquainted with your traveling companions, you find yourself adapting and adopting strategies that best keep them and you engaged, moving progressively from port to port. Eventually more and more of your students complete the journey ready to step onto the firmer, more solid ground of the high school territory with self-assurance and proficiency, prepared for the challenges awaiting them.

ADAPTING THE LESSONS AND IDEAS IN THIS BOOK

An equally significant teaching challenge in middle school is the fact that the readings in the curriculum vary greatly from school to school. Few teachers arrive in their middle school classrooms having studied all of the literary works and all the specific kinds of writings they are expected to teach. So rather than being a manual for teaching only specific texts, this book provides general background for teaching the primary genres generally taught in middle school, so that you can adapt the approaches in this book to the reading and writing you are asked to teach. The lessons in this book are designed to

- Be inviting and vigorous
- Help students connect their own lives to the literature through their speaking and writing
- Challenge students to think deeply, critically, and broadly
- Help the students write clearly, correctly, and creatively
- Encourage students to work independently, in pairs, small groups, and as a whole class
- Expand their understanding of themselves and their world
- Develop ways to express themselves in a variety of modes by reading, writing, and discussing a variety of fiction and nonfiction literature and on issues in life
- Use digital technologies effectively for research, writing, and communication
- Meet the curriculum standards of most middle school English Language Arts (ELA) programs

In order to accomplish these goals, look here for ideas to help with introductions to the various units of instruction; for assignments that build on students' understanding of the elements of fiction, literary terms, and poetic devices; and for ideas for teaching specific communication skills, including learning vocabulary, using appropriate grammar, giving public speeches, and critically viewing and using electronic and print media. Provided are sample lessons, student study aids, rubrics, and lists of resources, along with practical ideas for engaging students in the digital world.

For the veteran educators looking to revive or revise their instruction or the novice looking to rev up for the first year of teaching, here are proven ways to manage grading and assessments, and strategies for students to reflect and assess their own work. Throughout the book, note connections to the language arts standards of the National Council of Teachers of English and International Reading Association that reflect curriculum standards in most states.

According to the National Council of Teachers of English, 21st-century readers and writers need to:[10]

- Develop proficiency with the tools of technology
- Build relationships with others to pose and solve problems collaboratively and cross-culturally
- Design and share information for global communities to meet a variety of purposes
- Manage, analyze, and synthesize multiple streams of simultaneous information
- Create, critique, analyze, and evaluate multimedia texts
- Attend to the ethical responsibilities required by these complex environments

The Common Core Standards for English Language Arts address the basic goal of applying traditional literacies to new literacy contexts while challenging educators to design lessons that equip students with the knowledge and skills to be college and career ready when they complete their first 12 years of schooling. Managing both charges requires time and talent, effort and efficiency.

INTEGRATING 21ST-CENTURY LITERACIES AND COMMON CORE STATE STANDARDS FOR ELA

For these reasons, some chapters have suggestions for using technology tools to help your students develop the knowledge, skills, and understanding of these 21st-century literacies, while serving as informal assessments to reveal how closely students have read their fiction and nonfiction texts or used the range of skills called for in the Common Core Standards for English Language Arts.[11]

To incorporate opportunities for your students to learn and hone their skills to become ready for the demands of college and the challenges of careers, choose from options to:

- Look for information on the Internet and learn to evaluate validity of sources.
- Use the digital camera to capture images for use in reports or simply to show understanding of vocabulary, literature, or life experiences.
- Use computer software to make word clouds or collages.
- Create online communities for students to post and edit their own and others' work, to collaborate with peers in the class or with students across the continent.

These simple ideas give you jumping off points to create assignments that interest you and your students. Other ideas are on the companion website for this book, http://teachingenglishlanguagearts.com.

Some of the chapters include examples of students' written responses to assignments and comments on what that writing reveals about student learning. They may help expand your insight and prepare you for what to expect as you accept the challenge and come to value the privilege of teaching English language arts to young teenagers.

REACHING THE ULTIMATE GOAL: TO ENJOY TEACHING

To support you in your early years and sustain you along the road and to enable you to remain an engaged, enthusiastic, and effective teacher of English language arts in the middle school, here are ideas to develop and present lessons that meet students' emotional and intellectual needs while challenging them to complete increasingly complex tasks. When students are learning and you can document that learning through appropriate assessments, both you and your students enjoy more of your times together. It is my goal with this book to offer you practical and proven practices that bring you the kind of pleasure in teaching that I have experienced these past 40 or so years.

NOTES

Epigraph: Ignacio "Nacho" Estrada, *Think Exist*. http://thinkexist.com/quotes/ignacio_estrada/ (accessed May 31, 2012).

1. Chris Stevenson, "Curriculum that is challenging, integrative, and exploratory," *This We Believe . . . and Now We Must Act I*. ed. Thomas O. Erb (Westerville, OH: National Middle School Association, 2001), 63.

2. John D. Bransford, Ann L. Brown, and Rodney R. Cocking, eds., *How Children Learn, How People Learn: Brain, Mind, Experience, and School-Expanded Edition* (Washington, D.C.: National Academy Press, 2000), 109.

3. For further information about Louise Rosenblatt's research on teaching reading, see the article "Louise Rosenblatt and theories of reader-response" by Carolyn Allen, published in 1988, www.hu.mtu.edu/reader/online/20/allen20.html (accessed April 3, 2004).

4. Fran Claggett and Joan Brown, *Drawing Your Own Conclusions: Graphic Strategies for Reading Writing, and Thinking* (Portsmouth, NH: Heinemann, 1992).

5. Quoted by D. Ray Reutzel and Robert B. Cotter Jr., "Classroom reading assessment," *Strategies for Reading Assessment and Instruction: Helping Every Child Succeed*, 2nd ed. (Upper Saddle River, NJ: Merrill-Prentice Hall, 2003), 26.

6. Anthony W. Jackson and Gayle A Davis, "Curriculum and assessment to improve teaching and learning," *Turning Points 2000: Educating Adolescents in the 21st Century* (New York: Teachers College Press, 2000), 48.

7. Jackson and Davis, "Curriculum and assessment," 176.

8. Edwards quoted by Suzanne Siegel Zenkel, *For My Teacher* (White Plains, NY: Pauper Press, 1994).

9. Anne King spoke at the middle school conference on "Teaching the Good Stuff in the Middle," Grand Valley State University, February 2006.

10. www.ascd.org/research-a-topic/21st-century-skills-resources.aspx (accessed August 26, 2013).

11. "NCTE definition of 21st-century literacies," *National Council of Teachers of English*, 2008, http://ncte.org (accessed 13 May 2013). "Writing in the 21st Century, a report from the National Council of Teachers of English, NCTE Past President, Kathleen Blake Yancey, Florida State University, Tallahassee," February 2009, *National Council of Teachers of English*. Reprinted with permission.

Chapter One

Scoping Out the Year in Preview

Plan Now to Be Effective and Efficient

The mediocre teacher tells. The good teacher explains. The superior teacher demonstrates. The great teacher inspires.

—William A. Ward

Each school year is a journey, somewhat like leading an extended tour with young people you have just met. You want to be ready for the unexpected, learning and adjusting as you go, but you also want them to know you are in charge. In the era of standardization, it still is important to customize the trip and personalize instruction, keeping in mind what you are required to teach and who you will be teaching, and never forgetting that you are a professional in the classroom. One way of making the trip an effective one for all involved is to keep in mind the features of the trip you can control and those you cannot.

Even with a curriculum or an itinerary handed to you, as a professional, you can incorporate personal touches based on your own interests and experiences to reflect your unique qualities.

It may seem odd, but a good place to begin planning and personalizing instruction for a whole school year is to zoom in on school holidays, breaks, and vacations. Aha! You do recall from your own days as a student how challenging it was to be attentive the few days before and after any of these three! Among the ways you can ensure that you stay on course for your course is to consider ways to maximize instruction time on such potentially lost days.

Take into consideration the ethnicities and cultures of the students in your classes. Consider what holidays they share in common, which are unique to a few, and most of all, how you can integrate into your lessons the wealth of information, experience, and passion surrounding holidays, breaks, and

Figure 1.1.   Spring break calendar.

vacations. More subtle to think about is the emotional and physical drain that these holidays may cause—say, on your Jewish and Muslim students, who for cultural or religious reasons may be fasting on a day you may have scheduled a major test. Many Asian families observe their calendar's new year with days of celebrations that may run late into the evening, making it difficult for students to attend to homework.

One way to connect with your students in a personal way is to let them know that you know, without making them subject to censure by peers who may not understand. What about rodeo and sports tryouts, dance recitals, bar and bat mitzvahs, school extracurriculars, and religious confirmations? The middle school years are when students are more easily sidetracked by such out-of-school events. What kind of lesson plans can you organize to redeem the time and channel the energy of sure-to-be-distracted students?

In addition to knowing the cultures and ethnicities of your students, it also is important to learn a little more about them, their families, and the circumstances in which they live. How much do you know about the resources available in the community in which your school is located or from which your students come? Are there local libraries with technology available to the middle school students? Once you have your class lists, take a look at any notices regarding special physical or emotional needs. Early in the first week, you could ask students to tell you privately those needs they are comfortable sharing. Some have learned to speak up about vision and hearing issues, for example.

What are you learning that may affect the way you set up your classroom or design lessons? In your conversations with veterans at the school, what can you learn about the most efficient ways to initiate and maintain communication with the families regarding languages spoken at home and access to technology? What is required at your school? Do you have a choice of contacting families by phone or e-mail? Just as a tour company would gather this information before the trip begins, so should a teacher commit to being prepared for those inherent eventualities. Like scouting, you want to be prepared.

One of the best things you can do for your students is to learn to pronounce and spell their names. Consider getting someone to help you with pronunciation or use online sites like www.pronouncenames.com on which you can hear names from many nationalities pronounced. Can you imagine what a pleasant surprise it will be for students who seldom hear their name said correctly to hear it from you on the first day of school? Even if you do not say them all perfectly, the fact that you care enough about each individual student as a person will gain their respect. The students will see that you are trying, and they may be open to doing the same.

PERSONALIZING THE CLASSROOM

All right, on to personalizing instruction for the journey. Think about ways you can:

- Reflect you and your students
- Display a list of acceptable standards of conduct
- Shape guidelines for grading
- Devise ways to tailor lessons for the combination of students who make up the classes each particular year
- Select efficient ways to measure learning in ways that provide valid information without swamping you with minutiae
- And most important, preplan ways to stay healthy until journey's end

But, even before preplanning a trip, one must know the destination. As soon as possible, review the requirements for the course set forth by your school, district, or state. What specific ways are you expected to prepare your students for ultimate success in college or careers based on the Common Core State Standards for English Language Arts or the specific curriculum in your school? Know these well enough to be able to state in your own words the definite portions of the school curriculum you will be required to teach in the grades assigned to you. Then work backward. You will want to include answers to questions such as:

- What do students need to know and be able to do at the end of the school year?
- How will I learn what they know and are able to do by the end of our time together?
- What do they know already?
- How can I learn what they know and are able to do already?
- How can I provide opportunities for them to show me what they know already, to learn from one another, and ultimately, to acquire the knowledge and develop the skills they need to have by the end of the school year? (In other words, how will I know we have arrived at our destination?)
- What resources are available to me in my classroom and in my building or school site? To my students in the classroom, in the building, or at home?
- How can I collaborate with other teachers to design lessons that link what the students are learning in their other classes to what I am required to teach or am able to teach? Most people think of social studies and science for collaboration but consider other opportunities, such as in the arts, physical education, and health classes.
- What will make teaching this course fun and interesting for me?

Once you can answer these questions—in writing—you can begin to select from the resources you have on hand and then request or assemble those needed to meet the needs of the students you are assigned to teach.

The physical space in which you teach should support your instruction. Think about ways you can make your classroom an attractive and inviting place to be, knowing that one does not need to be wealthy or have artistic skills to do so. It is possible to begin the school year with a bulletin board, covered only with an attractive neutral color, and labeled "Student Work," a welcome sign, and an inspiring thought for the week; leave the rest blank.

Then, during the first week, have lessons that call for small group or individual art work that you can post on your bulletin boards. You will have the control of designing the lesson to show what you would like to know about the young men and women you will be teaching this school year. And the students will know from day one that the classroom is for them and reflects them. Then keep the bulletin boards up for Fall Parents' Night of Classes or Open House or whatever event your school schedules early in the school year.

ASSEMBLING A CLASSROOM LIBRARY

Begin building your classroom library by collecting new and used books right away. Many libraries have monthly book sales and you can find books at reasonable costs. Visit garage and yard sales in your community. Invite graduates to donate books before they move on to the next stage in their lives. Ask relatives to help. Some may be traveling and want to bring back something you can use.

Contact local service organizations like Kiwanis, Lions, and Rotary for contributions. Many such groups encourage support of educational endeavors. See titles to consider from those recommended by Goodreads on their website at "Top 100 Middle School Must-Reads." Consider picture books, too. They are particularly effective for creating interest and providing background information as you start a general unit or begin teaching a specific work of fiction or nonfiction. Your school may qualify for programs such as that offered by BookMentors.org, a nonprofit, that uses micropatronage, making donations to help supply teachers, students, and librarians in high-needs schools with books.

Check offices and hair salons with waiting rooms. Managers and owners would be glad to have a dependable place to pass along old magazines when new ones arrive. (Of course, you know to add to your library only those that are appropriate for middle school students.) Invite students to bring their self-selected reading to class every day to pull out and read silently whenever they complete assignments before the period ends.

One of your most valuable teaching tools can be a classroom library stocked with books your students can borrow and magazines they can read, scan, skim, and cut up for art projects. Do not get too attached to the books, though. Some will disappear but will be read by someone.

SCHMOOZING THE LIBRARIANS

Your librarians or media specialists can be your most precious human resources. These respected professional colleagues interact with teachers across the curriculum and with students from all grades; they know the school curriculum very well. Moreover, librarians know their collection of materials and can work with you to utilize them in ways that support your lessons with culturally relevant and age-appropriate selections. As soon as you have an idea of what and when you plan to teach particular units of study, make an appointment to meet with your school librarian, who often will volunteer to reserve books, magazines, journals, and newspapers and identify online sites that students can use. The librarian also may be willing to prepare a talk to introduce your students to the specific media available in your school resource center.

Equally important, librarians usually know when the science and social studies teachers assign their big projects and can help you avoid student overload by recommending alternative due dates. Of course, it is good if you work in a school setting in which those who teach the same grades work together to coordinate the scheduling of major assignments. It is better when there is interdisciplinary collaboration and common projects that students do for two classes, with the teachers from both classes sharing the grading. However, if that is not yet the case at the school where you teach, befriend the librarians and welcome the wealth of experience and knowledge they can add to your lesson planning and implementation.

GUIDING PRINCIPLES TO MANAGE MAYHEM

Middle school students can be marvelous and mischievous. Think about ways to maximize the former and minimize the latter. Reflect on what you can and cannot stand in terms of classroom behavior, homework deadlines, movement and noise in the classroom, and flexibility in assignments. Prepare notes on how you will outline acceptable classroom behavior for your students. Experienced teachers often have three or four general principles that can be applied in specific situations. Consider, as a start, those that refer to attendance, homework, and student behavior in class, such as:

- Be present.
- Be prepared.
- Participate courteously.

Once you decide your three or four guiding principles, include them on your class handouts, on your website, on the wall in your room, on all major assignments, and in beginning of the school year in a letter to parents/guardians. It is essential for all to know the basic principles by which you plan to conduct the class. It also is good for students to be reminded throughout the course. When they understand the reason for the rules, students usually respond with compliance rather than adolescent sarcasm. Some schools have building-wide behavior statements and expect you to teach and follow them. You may find them sufficient or needing a little tweaking.

ASSESSING PRIOR KNOWLEDGE

Your students are young adolescents, not new travelers along the road of life. They are just joining you for this portion of a lifelong journey of living and learning and therefore come to you already familiar with some experiences that can enhance their time with you. As a teacher, fellow traveler, and tour guide, you want to do all you can to prepare them for the weeks and months ahead, perhaps warn them of possible landslides that can occur and inclement weather they may experience, all the time assuring them that you all are in this together.

You are there to help them climb the rock walls of new tasks that seem unscaleable; to work with them, eager to observe them open their hearts and minds to see and appreciate the beauty of reading, writing, discussing, and thinking about new kinds of writing, novel narratives—both fiction and nonfiction; to be ready to explore with them the natural wonders encountered along the way; and most of all, to guide their practice and use of skills as they strive to achieve their own personal goals.

You may find it helpful to use online resources to discover the range of learning styles among the students you have in each class on sites like Edu-topia.org where you can find an online quiz called "What's Your Learning Style?"[1] Keep in mind, however, that this information provides just one component of the range of information you need to know about your students. You also need to pay attention to their age, readiness, and interests.

So, now you know to learn what students know and are already able to do in the first couple of weeks. This could be collecting reading comprehension and writing samples, conducting interest surveys, or as described in chapter 2, observing small-group activities during which students work together on a common project using the kinds of skills they should be bringing to the new class.

Begin the school year the way you would like it to continue throughout the school year. For example, consider homework deadlines. Be informative and be firm from the beginning, while knowing that it is normal to make adjustments as the school year unfolds. Of course, students understand that firm and fair do not mean inflexible. Middle school students can deal with special circumstances, so do not be afraid to be merciful. However, beginning with a few general rules helps to establish the groundwork for the upcoming year. In the metaphor of the school year as a trip, you are working on the rules for the road.

DECIDING RULES FOR THE ROAD

Among the rules for the road, decide procedural matters like how you can organize and keep your lesson plans and master copies of handouts, as well as how you can collect and where you can store student work. Consider using color coding as often as possible. For example, you could have different colored loose-leaf binders for each grade or sturdy folders in assorted hues for each period. If you have access to colored paper for photocopying, you could use a single color for assignments in the same unit. It would be helpful to students if you were to say, "Sylvia, will you bring me the folder for your class? Yes, the purple one in the second shelf on the left corner of my desk," or to the class, "Take out the blue assignment sheet for our unit on poetry," or to Horace who has come for extra help, "Did you bring the yellow sheet with the academic vocabulary list?"

If you really are uncomfortable with lots of noise but understand the value of small-group discussions, think about ways to design lessons that include specific instructions that you explain ahead of time, and then plan to circulate among the students as they work in small groups. When students know exactly what is expected and you are present among them, they usually can discipline themselves enough to work in a focused manner and maintain a lower noise volume. It is helpful to write or project the class outline and steps for assignments right on the board.

GRADING GUIDELINES

Just as you like to know what is expected of you, the same is true for students. On a road trip, you look for signs to indicate how near or far you are from your ultimate destination. When you see familiar topography or promised landmarks, you relax a bit and breathe a little easier. The same can be true about grading as it relates to you and to your students.

Grading becomes less stressful when you understand what you are looking for in each assignment and share these expectations with the students. They can review their work before turning it in, using your guidelines as a checklist. Some students, because of other commitments, may settle for a B rather than put in the time to earn the A. That's okay. It is their choice.

Fewer students challenge their grades when they have had a clearly written set of printed instructions to which they can refer before submitting their work. So consider a set of general grading principles that can be applied to most graded assignments. Explain these guidelines in the first couple of weeks, but not on the first day of school. Students already will be overwhelmed with the newness of everything! You can, however, have something like the following posted on your website and on any general handouts you distribute on opening day.

C = Complete (includes all components of the assignment)
B = Complete and Correct (minimal errors in mechanics, usage, grammar, and spelling)
A = Complete, Correct, and Creative (something original, fresh, and special that enhances final performance or product)

Plan to include rubrics with each graded assignment, especially those that are weighted heavily enough to have a major impact on reported grades. Providing students with lists of the standards and the semester goals fulfills

General Grading Guidelines

A = complete, correct and creative
B = complete and correct
C = complete

C = THE SEA – *Complete* (includes all components of the assignment)
B = THE BOAT – *Complete and Correct* (rides on the sea with minimum errors in mechanics, usage, grammar and spelling)
A = THE SAIL – *Complete, Correct and Creative* (demonstrates something above and beyond the boat; original and fresh elements enhancing final performance/product)

Figure 1.2. Image of a boat.

comparable purposes and provides the same comfort as a map or the voice on the GPS when you travel in unfamiliar territory.

UNDERSTANDING BRAIN DEVELOPMENT AIDS IN LESSON PLANNING

New teachers of middle school students often are surprised at how literal their students are, especially in the earlier grades and at the beginning of the school year. You may be disappointed that these young teenagers just seem so very immature; few are able to see the subtleties in literature and seem inept at writing clever imagery. The fact is, few young adolescents are mentally ready for this kind of thinking. No need to despair.

As the year unfolds, some students may display a leap in development of the brain's frontal cortex that occurs in early teens.[2] Others only get taller and wilder. Usually at the beginning of the school year, young teens still are pretty literal, thinking in concrete terms, but as the year progresses and their frontal lobes mature and they gain practice and experience under your tutelage, these youngsters begin looking at literature and life more abstractly, recognizing and using more subtle metaphors in their speech and writing. They are growing physically, emotionally, and cerebrally. Plan with that knowledge in mind.

LEARNING THE LANGUAGE OF THE LAND

You know the value of a broad, rich vocabulary, even if you just visit a different area of the nation and not some exotic country on a different continent. The same is true for your students. For many of them, the language of school may seem just as foreign to them. Students will need to understand some basic terms to be able to follow directions and stay on task. You can plan from the very beginning to teach vocabulary intentionally. If they use it, they won't lose it.

Consider levels of vocabulary. As you choose and prepare lessons around specific readings, you know to pull and give definitions for words that are specific to a particular book/article and also to pull out some of the published academic vocabulary words students will need to know across the content areas. You may recognize these levels as Tier 1, 2, and 3 words, referring to the vocabulary based on how practical the words are for everyday speaking, reading, writing, and/or academic use. In your area of the country, you may hear about the 40/40/40 rule. Decide what words students need to know for 40 days, for 40 weeks, and for 40 years; then allot teaching and study time accordingly.

Think about dedicating space for a Word Wall so students see words daily during particular units, and can refer to and draw from this list when they write or talk about the literature. This can be a poster to which you add words all through the school year or one that you change to coordinate with specific units of instruction. If space is available, it may be better to have one permanent poster with general words and a changing posting with specific words. Fresh lists create new interest just as the changing road signs you notice along the highway revive interest in the trip.

Among the academic words to begin defining and using in early lessons are those having to do with instructions: explain, diagram, evaluate, describe, analyze, discuss, and so forth. If your students are new to middle school, they may have different ideas about what is required when asked to do these tasks. Help your travel-mates get off to a good start by clarifying what is expected when they see or hear these terms. You can find lists of academic words on websites describing Bloom's Taxonomy verbs to help you measure students' level of knowledge, comprehension, application, analysis, synthesis, evaluation, and creativity.

TEACHING TEST-TAKING LANGUAGE

Administering standardized tests probably will be a part of your responsibility as leader of this educational expedition. Just as you find it comforting to know how to read the basic language of the land when you visit a foreign country, prepare your students to read the signs that direct their work on a test. Teach your students the language of academic assessments long before students take these tests, and use these terms on the tests you give all year long.

Once you have settled into your classes, you may want to have a lesson on the different definitions the same word may have in different content areas— words like "plot": in English, *plot* is an element of fiction; in history/social studies' map reading, it refers to a *plot* of land or to *plot* a course of action; and in science or math, a student might *plot* a graph. "Draw," as seen in the above paragraph, is another of those multidefinition words.

REWARDING LANGUAGE LEARNING

To speed up students' acquisition of vocabulary, encourage and reward them for using words from the English vocabulary lists in the writing they do in other classes. A maximum of 10 points per marking period, one point for each word in a graded assignment for other classes should suffice. All extra credit work should be due one week before the end of the marking period to avoid last-minute papers when you need time for computing grades to be turned in or posted for report cards.

Promote active learning by inviting students to bring in samples with the vocabulary words used in their reading outside of class. You could simply put up a blank poster board and ask students to bring in highlighted photocopies of passages from other published writing where students find words from the current vocabulary. (No duplicates from same source.) If you keep it low key, this should not escalate into a contest but remain a way to raise their awareness of language use outside their academic setting.

You also could set aside a day in class when students are asked to include correct use of vocabulary words in their conversation in pairs, small groups, or even full-class discussion. It could be great fun . . . especially if you let peers give the feedback, instead of you. This is another strategy to encourage close listening. You may recall those days when you were studying a foreign language, say Spanish or French, and the teacher announced, "¡*Hoy día, sólo se habla español aquí!*" or "*Aujourd'hui, seul le français est parlé ici!*"

Rather than waiting for a test to measure the understanding of vocabulary, you may find it more effective to require the correct use of vocabulary from current lists in their writing assignments instead of spending time making up weekly quizzes. During journal writing, students can be asked to use different words from the list in sentences that include definition, synonym or antonym, or some context clue to the meaning of the word. They can work in pairs to "check" these writings, and by the time students have an assignment that is to be graded, most students will be confident about using the vocabulary words. Then, on the full-length writing for the week or biweek, students are expected to incorporate vocabulary from recent lists.

KEEPING UP WITH LEARNING WITHOUT OVERTESTING

Current education theories proclaim the value of conducting both formal and informal assessments all year long. Such measuring informs both students and teachers about what is learned and taught successfully. The question is: When and how should we test?

Since you, the teacher, have very definite content matter you are asked to teach, and you are expected to guide the students across tempestuous seas to learn and show what they know about good writing, efficient reading, effective speaking, courteous listening, and skillful use of technology, it may be useful to work backward by asking yourself questions like the following:

- What specific skills am I trying to develop or measure in this assignment?
  - Is it how well students understand the text we've studied together?
  - Is it how well they can show they can analyze a character?
  - Is it how well they can write an organized response in a timed setting?
- What will I need to see in their work to know their level of understanding or skill?
  - Is it reference to the text?
  - Is it correct use of literary language?
  - Is it organization?
  - Is it development of ideas?
  - Is it correct use of vocabulary and grammar?

Some of these skills are revealed in student journal writing, in conversations during small-group and full-class discussion, and may not need to be measured again on a formal test. As you become more experienced, you will design more lessons to measure student learning, become a more efficient listener and a close observer, and develop the habit of taking brief notes based on what you see and hear during regular class meetings. You may even find it practical to write reflective journal notes at the end of each school day. You will stay attuned, attentive to what students say, do not say, respond, and react.

You can become adept at using what you learn through formative assessments to reshape lessons, then reteaching when necessary. This would be like backtracking on a trip, a time when passengers notice details they might have missed the first time passing by. In some situations, based primarily on informal assessments of student learning, you may choose to speed up the pace and move on to the next unit of study. You know ahead there could be potholes that may trip them up and quagmires that may bog them down; having extra time to negotiate them may be necessary. Still, you do not whiz on by.

You take seriously your charge to teach, knowing you are more than a tour narrator who simply points out and names landmarks you pass along the way.

Making formative assessments and deciding what to do about the results takes practice. You may find it is like taking a break in the trip to check the map, to assure yourself that you have not drifted off the trail and been distracted unduly by the foggy, damp weather of students complaining that the terrain is just too rough! But the more proficient you become at recognizing learning and adjusting instruction, the less overwhelmed you and your students become at summative testing time. Although both may be disappointed, neither the student nor the teacher should be surprised at the results of a formal test.

It's important to do what you can to ensure that all those on the trip with you reach the destination safe, secure, confident, and competent with the knowledge and skills they need to have continued success when you pass along this tour group to the next year's tour guide.

PREPARING TO ASSESS FOR UNDERSTANDING

Test-taking skills are important for students to learn, especially as they prepare for high school. You can serve your young people well by reviewing ways to take these tests and then formatting tests in a student-friendly way. Your young teens not only appreciate less-stressful testing but also perform better on tests they understand. This can be as simple as creating a "Prepare for the Test" handout that includes the test format and suggestions on how to study for each kind of question. Possessing a map that shows the topography of the hike can be comforting to a teen trekker.

For example, if you plan to test their understanding of vocabulary from the book, tell your students whether they need to know definitions, synonyms, antonyms, or how to use the words in a sentence. Or, if you have had students copy select passages from the book into their reading journals, you should be able to test successfully for quotations simply by reminding students to study the text material in their journals.

If you have test questions that require answers in a complete paragraph or short essay, remind students in advance to review the structure of each one. A test prep handout can also include the number of points allotted for each section of the test. Such information saves time and angst. Students do not have to use valuable test time trying to figure out the format of the exam or how best to allot their time. On the test review day, remind students to spend the most time studying for the sections with the highest value. Your preparation of these handouts provides time for you to reflect on what you have taught, what you are expecting the test to measure, and how this test will show student learning. With such thinking before the test, grading these assessments usually takes less time.

KEEPING RECORDS OF INFORMAL ASSESSMENTS

Do you know any regular travelers who do not keep some kind of written, photo, or video record of their trip? Many of the more intrepid ones do all three. The same is true for you as a teacher–tour guide. As you work with the young people, offer different ways for them to show what they are learning, assessing sometimes with quizzes, essays, art, music, drama, video, and as often as appropriate, inviting students to choose. Then include in what they submit for evaluation a written page to explain how their choice of product or performance will prove to anyone reading or viewing that the student knows the content and has the skills required for them to meet the standards. Keep a checklist in each of their classroom folders so students can view them regularly.

You could schedule biweekly in-class reading days on which you meet with the individuals for three to five minutes to review their progress for the week and plan for the next. It may be useful to plan to meet with half the class one week and the other half the next week. As students learn to draw from their wealth of knowledge and apply it in new situations, they become more competent and confident learners.

Yes, teaching this way can create a little more uncertainty on your part, but with practice on both sides, your students will be more motivated and self-assured if they know where they are supposed to be by the end of the school year and have some choices in as many ways as are appropriate in your school setting. On a tour, the guide knows the passengers need to eat and offers restaurant options within the framework of the time or budget. As you consider the year as a whole, keeping an eye on the goal, you will see there is much room for flexibility and personalization in ways that lead to effective and efficient teaching and consistent and satisfactory learning.

RETEACHING IN DIFFERENT FORMATS

A fact of teaching is that students do not always treasure the pearls of wisdom that flow from your lips. They do not always remember exactly how to do everything you present them, even things they have done well in the past. It is imperative to solidify that knowledge and hone those skills by asking students to use knowledge and skills in different settings. You can help increase retention by designing lessons that require your students to use what they learned when reading a short story or news article, preparing a speech, or writing an essay.

On Friday, for example, you could ask students to choose a passage they particularly enjoy in their self-selected book and pattern that passage about something the student has recently experienced or observed. Then have the student quietly turn to a partner and read the original passage aloud and then their patterned writing. Ask the students to pay attention to the rhythm of the sentences. Each listener could be asked to note closely to see how well their partner has followed the sentence syntax of the original writer. Exact duplication should not be required; coming close enough to show attentive reading and an attempt to pattern a published writer's style should suffice. Trust the students to know what works but circulate among them to confirm their analyses.

You could have the students do scavenger hunts in their self-selected books, looking for whatever grammatical structure or reading strategy you have taught most recently. For example, ask them to find examples of complex sentences, sentences written in passive voice, subjunctive voice, the use of complementary conjunctions, different text structures, and so on. How many different kinds of sentence starts do they notice on a single page in their book? What does this suggest about interesting and effective writing?

Grading? Just have groups check one another's work. Anything they cannot figure out together, discuss as a class. Circulate, taking notes on levels of participation, assessing informally, planning the next lessons, and continue down the road intent on completing the trip together.

INCORPORATING MOVEMENT, COLORS, AND SHAPES TO ENHANCE LEARNING

From your own experience traveling, you know how easy it is to get bored when you have to sit a long time or when nothing interesting can be seen out of the windows. As the leader of the educational journey, you can keep your charges engaged if you spice things up a bit with lessons that include movement and personal decision making.

Learning Actively

Think about ways to incorporate kinesthetic games and active learning as a regular part of your instruction. Consider lessons that invite students to get up from their seats for reasons as simple as moving into groups or as sophis-ticated as expressing an opinion by the corner in which one chooses to stand. It will be like getting up and walking down the aisle while on a transatlantic airplane trip. Sometimes you just have to get up and move. In the classroom, movement can lead to learning.

Do you have access to an overhead projector and a whiteboard? If so, you can project games, puzzles, and diagrams onto the whiteboard. This way all the students can see but have to get up and write, draw, circle, or indicate a choice. Instead of worksheets students complete at their seats, you could cre-ate some on transparencies where students have to walk up and write answers "on the board."

You can plan lessons where students have to express their opinions by getting up and going to one or another corner of the room to indicate their position on questions about literature or about life. For example, after reading about a choice the protagonist has made, you could ask students to go to the front corner or back corner depending on their opinions or predictions about the story. "What do you think Alfonso should or will do? Four different sup-positions? OK, Sal and those who agree with him, stand over there. Those who think Hamera is right, stand with her, back there. Gerald stand right here and Felicia right there, and those who think their predictions are right, join them."

Ask each group to sit together and find evidence from the text to support their thinking. Choose a spokesperson to explain. Then, having heard the evi-dence and reasons for opposing opinions, invite students who wish to change places to do so. Thinking, moving, talking, referring to texts, speaking, listen-ing, moving, learning. Good teaching.

Using Shapes and Colors

You can plan now to increase critical thinking and appeal to students who learn in different ways. Adapting lessons for the visual and spatial learners to think about which color or shape is appropriate will add to something you have projected for all to see. For example, some students may benefit from seeing the structure of an essay and how each part of an essay has a specific function. This works when you compare an essay to a train and have different geometric shapes to represent the different kinds of train cars.

- Right-facing triangle for the introduction: the engine, moving the essay forward
- Rectangles for the body: cargo or box cars, containers carrying the facts, explanations, and reasons

- Left-facing triangle for conclusion: caboose, looking back on what has been said
- Ovals: the couplings to represent transitions that connect the parts of the essay

Use colors to show the patterns of essay construction, with different organizational patterns for various paragraphs within the body of an essay. This visual activity can be done with photocopies of an essay, and students use colored pencils or markers to show in color the way parts of an essay should blend to explain, explore, and expand on the statement of purpose or thesis sentence. Your art students probably already know that red and blue make purple, or that blue and yellow make green. They will understand the concept of blending to create something new.

- Thesis statement in purple (or green)
- Topic sentences in red (or blue)
- Supporting sentences in blue (or yellow)

Seeing colors also can help students understand both the function of parts of speech and the impact of syntax on sentence structure when you ask them to circle, underline, and draw arrows as part of a grammar lesson.

Use different colors for parts of the speech or parts of the sentence.

- Green for action verbs
- Brown for linking verbs
- Same color for subject and predicate noun/adjective to show the relationship
- Dark color for noun/lighter version for pronoun to show agreement

Draw arrow from the modifier (word, phrase, or clause) to the word modified. If there are dangling modifiers, students will see how out of place the dangler is.

Keep the movement in the lesson by inviting students to work on sentences written or projected onto the whiteboard or on swaths of white butcher paper. You could project a sentence with a dangling modifier and have students draw what they "see" based on the wording of the sentence. If you have space in your room, you could have groups of students working on the floor with posterboards and markers. There will be giggling, but that's OK. It releases tension.

Showing Patterns in Fiction

If students are not allowed to write in their books, print out or project so all can see a section from the exposition of a story you are teaching. Then invite one student at a time to come forward to mark on the projected passage, asking individuals to

- Draw an oval around main characters when first introduced (different color for each one)
- Underline in the matching color words/phrases that describe each of the main characters
  - Character A: Red, words describing him/her underlined in red
  - Character B: Blue, words describing him/her underlined in blue
- Mark word(s) that identify the setting
  - Rectangle for place where story or scene is set
  - Circle for time of day, year, or period in life (childhood, teens, adult) story is set

Just as noise and movement outside the window of a bus or train attract the attention of travelers who may have dozed off, these kinds of verbal and visual activities capture students' attention and reengage them in the lesson of the moment. They teach and reinforce concepts, showing students that writers of fiction usually introduce main characters early in the story and very soon afterward include words and phrases to help elicit an image of the character and their personality in the minds of the reader.

Since the time and place of a story often are critical to the action that follows, that information is presented in the exposition as well. Seeing features together will remind your students to look for these patterns when they read themselves. Recognizing these expected patterns will help students as they begin writing stories of their own.

SENSING SURROUNDINGS AS SOURCES FOR WRITING

How about including time for side trips in your plans for this extended journey? Consider taking the students outside to explore their environment as an alternative journal assignment. They can take along their notebooks or tablet computers, cell phones, and plastic grocery bags and then have them write what they experience through their senses. You also carry along your kitchen timer.

Depending on your school setting, this could simply mean finding a grassy area and asking students to sit on their grocery bags and close their eyes for two minutes, alternate between sensing and writing as they listen, smell, touch, taste, and then look. If your school permits students to have cell phones in class, students who have a camera feature can take photos to add to their journal entries. First sense, then write, then photograph. (It helps to keep eyes closed as they experience the first two senses.)

- Close eyes for a couple minutes and LISTEN and then write what they hear.
- Close eyes for a couple minutes and SMELL, inhaling deeply, paying attention to the different fragrances/odors/aromas and then describe them with vivid adjectives and figurative language.
- TOUCH, pick up a stick, a rock, touch the bark of a tree, some pebbles, a clump of soil, describe that or just what it feels like to be sitting on the ground on top of a plastic grocery bag.
- TASTE, if it is safe. If not, bring along hard candy in different flavors and ask students to describe the taste sensation and the feel of the candy in their mouths, on their teeth, and so on. Or bring a bag of those baby carrots, radishes, or celery sticks to have something more healthy.
- SIGHT. Ask students to look around, paying attention to something they may not have noticed before, and describe it. (Save sight for last. By that time, students will have calmed down a bit and are ready to look at something other than one another.)

To make the excursion more active, you could have students walk around, stop, sense, write, then walk to another spot. You also could have them do

Figure 1.3. Writing sensory experiences.

some gentle calisthenics, then sit and write as though they were a character in a story describing what that exercise felt like. The notes from this outing can be used right away in poetry or to flesh out a scene in a short narrative piece. Yes, you will have students who find it difficult to attend at each step in the lesson, so that means saving this kind of adventure until you have established rapport and can depend on students to respond promptly with appropriate classroom behavior standards. In fact, this kind of outing can be a goal for you and a reward for them.

From the very beginning of the school year, it is beneficial to create and nurture an environment in which the students feel comfortable writing personally. However, it takes time for students to trust you enough to do so. No need to give up. Writing about something they do as a class may make them feel less vulnerable because it is a shared experience. This kind of side-trip adventure may be just one way to scaffold the writing where the students begin writing fictionally but are encouraged to use their own experiences to lend authenticity to their writing, whether poetry, short story, or narrative essay.

If it is not realistic to take a local field trip outside the school building, obtain permission from the administrator and from the person in charge of the cafeteria, auditorium, or library to schedule a field trip to those spaces. If you have several sections of the same class, you may end up taking different classes to different places depending on the weather, time of day, and places available. It is surprising what students notice when they tune in to experience a place through their senses.

Even though all of these strategies do not require all the students to be moving at the same time, what movement there is helps create and retain interest. Having to select colors and shapes gets them thinking. Sensing their space focuses their attention inward; then writing and photography move things outward into the public realm. Those sitting and watching also are checking to see if they would have chosen the same colors or shapes had they been called to go to the front of the class. Those reading and viewing their classmates' notes and photos relive the experience from a different perspective.

Whatever you decide to do, know that it is important to create a safe and nurturing environment so students will not be reluctant to step up and show what they know. If they are wrong, they should not be embarrassed by anyone in the classroom. Invite them to share their journals and pictures. Being realistic—no one attends all the time. But if lessons are varied, vigorous, and energizing, sometimes fun, and consistently supportive, more student-travelers remain tuned in for longer periods of time throughout the whole journey.

No matter how engaging the intellectual outings you plan or how enthusiastically they respond to the jaunts you schedule for this school-year trip, the fact of the matter is you are a teacher responsible for seeing that the majority of your students attain the standards set for the course. Evaluation time comes and the students must be ready.

STAYING HEALTHY ALONG THE JOURNEY

Totally exhausted after a thoroughly exasperating week, you may begin to wonder, "How do great teachers stay on top of their game and retain the energy and enthusiasm to return to the classroom year after year?"[3] Sipping a soothing cup of green tea, you ponder, "Why are so many long-term educators still healthy and happy, successful and satisfied with their career choice?" Another sip. Ah, that's better.

The knot in your lower back may loosen a bit. A little calmer, a little less stressed, you smile and envision the faces of those experienced teachers whom you would call "great" and you even try to see yourself among their ranks. However, you glance at the stack of papers still to be graded and you sigh, "Never. Not me. Errrr. Not I!" Whatever.

Whether a novice or veteran in the field, you know that no matter how much time you give to schoolwork, there always is more to be done. "How do they do it?" stays in the front of your mind. Myriad answers swirl as you pick up your pen, readying yourself to get back to work. One reason may crystallize when you consider what you have observed over the years. Great teachers somehow manage to achieve personal/professional balance.

You probably are familiar with the idea of a Sabbath. True, Sabbath has religious connotations, but observing Sabbath also is an attitude toward work that schedules regular breaks. Plan now to rest regularly. No, rest is not necessarily sitting with one's feet up, a cold drink in one hand and the television remote in the other. Rest can be a brief respite from the demands of the classroom.

You may decide to set aside at least one day a week to do no schoolwork— a regular date night with a spouse or children, with a parent, friend, or significant other. If you happen to take on an extracurricular assignment as a coach or club sponsor, you still can observe Sabbath by focusing attention on the team or club and not on lesson preparation and paper grading. I coached and traveled with competitive speech teams for 12 years and resisted the temptation to take along papers to grade. It is surprising how efficiently one can prepare for Monday, rested and refreshed! Try it.

Those colleagues whom you admire for their balanced lives participate in activities completely unrelated to the specific subject of their teaching. One may cultivate roses and enter them in the state fair; another may serve on a church or community committee. They serve on the board of their neighborhood library or take gourmet cooking classes. Some play in a chamber orchestra or sing in a community chorus. Like Langston Hughes, they "laugh / And eat well / and grow strong." Will you?

CONCLUSION

As the instructional tour guide in charge of the educational journey, plan now take some time off regularly, just for yourself. When you are little more relaxed and have reliable and healthy ways to renew yourself, you will be able to tackle these challenges with much more energy and creativity. Although you cannot automatically embed what you know into the hearts and minds of your students, you can inspire them to embrace new knowledge as you model doing the same.

And you, too, can enjoy the trip.

NOTES

Epigraph: William Arthur Ward, "Quotes about teaching," *National Education Association*, 2012. www.nea.org/grants/17417.htm (accessed March 8, 2012).

1. "What's Your Learning Style," 2012. www.edutopia.org/multiple-intelligences-learning-styles-quiz (accessed April 17, 2012).

2. "Adolescent brain development," *ACT for Youth Upstate Center of Excellence*, May 2002, a collaboration of Cornell University, University of Rochester, and the NYS Center for School Safety. www.actforyouth.net/resources/rf/rf_brain_0502.pdf (accessed April 6, 2012).

3. "Staying Healthy" section based on ideas from my article "Professional and personal lives," *California English* 16, no. 1 (September 2010): 8–9, and used here with permission.

Chapter Two

Networking Socially at
the Start of the School Year

Getting to know you, getting to know all about you.
Getting to like you, getting to hope you like me.

—Oscar Hammerstein[1]

Even in the age of electronic social networking, in-person relationships are the most meaningful for teachers and learners. The classroom itself becomes a "site" for social networking among increasingly diverse students and teachers. Learning, as encouraged by the Common Core State Standards for English Language Arts,[2] is grounded in social connections. The best way to nurture students toward high-level thinking is to design low-tech interactions.

The following opening-of-the-school-year projects show how to get your eclectic, energetic young teens working together so that you can assess how well they are reading, writing, speaking, listening, and using technology already. Such knowledge will be useful as they begin to explore, explain, and express themselves in writing and as you and your students get to know one another in the classroom and online.

You could think of the first week of language arts classes as the staging ground for the semester, preparation for your school year journey together. As you get to know individual students, you can map out personalized approaches to student activities. In this case, "personalized" need not mean the same thing as "individualized"; here, it means drafting lessons that more closely match the personalities of the specific students assigned to you in a particular class.

The five-day collage-making activity is based on group and personal responses to a shared reading, and it works well with an older, more established class. The one- or two-day scavenger hunt using the course anthology may be more fitting for shorter class periods during the first week and works well with a younger, less-experienced group of students who are new to the school or who may be using a literature anthology for the first time.

RESPONDING TO A SHARED READING: SMALL-GROUP COLLAGE ON BOOK OR STORY

If your students have read a specified book over the summer, you are in luck. You can use a few opening days of the semester to have students work in small groups to make poster or digital collages that reflect various perspectives on the summer reading. You can even organize groups around the elements of fiction: character, setting, conflict, plot, theme, and literary devices or specific writing genres.

If your students have not already read a common book, assign them to read a short story (Gary Soto's "Seventh Grade" is a great choice), silently, aloud together in class, or for homework. You might even ask for volunteer readers so that you can begin to identify some of the eager or hesitant readers. Avoid insisting that all students read aloud. Accept a "pass." Cold reading scares and shuts down some students. You want to keep them open to learning,

A collage is created from lots of words and pictures and reveals a message about the book or story. Each group can be responsible for finding pictures and cutting out words and letters to create a collage focusing on one of the following: main characters, setting, plot, conflicts, themes, others. The collage can be hard copy on poster board or created digitally using photos, clip art, and graphics students locate online. If technology is available to do it efficiently, students could take photos, upload them, and integrate them into their collages. Survey the skills and release the students to choose as often as it seems appropriate. This assignment can be extended to include writing about the collage-building experience, too.

The idea here is to get students involved in an activity that enables them to get to know one another and enables you to get to know each one. Assemble the following:

1. poster board
2. scissors
3. glue sticks
4. magazines
5. colored markers
6. envelopes
7. access to enough computers for at least one per group

8. index cards
9. a timer (kitchen timers work well)
10. blank sheets of address labels (e.g., Avery 5160)
11. a clipboard

These lessons are designed for a fifty-minute class period, but you can adapt them as needed to fit your schedule. See "Teacher Resource A" in the appendix for a sample collage assignment based on *The Circuit* by Francisco Jimenez, a novel assigned for summer reading.

ORIENTING TO AVAILABLE TECHNOLOGY

If your students have ready access to computers in the classroom, you could assign students to create a brief movie from the still shots or slides or Prezi or PowerPoint presentations that incorporate the same elements, including the oral presentation at the end. If your students are new to the available technology, you may need to adjust the schedule of lessons to allot time to introduce them to the equipment and to get signed in with usernames, passwords, and a tutorial on the basic program you plan for them to use right away. Consider inviting the school tech aid to help you plan this orientation.

Day One: Groups Conceive their Collages

Students need instructions, especially on the first few days of class! They want to know what is expected. Therefore, project, post, or print copies of instructions somewhere in the classroom where everybody can refer to them. Inform students that while they are working together you may be roaming around the room, listening in, observing, enjoying their conversations. Inform them that there are no "right" or "wrong" answers. Consider giving each group a name based on a literary term—or let them select their own names from a list. Be open and helpful. Define the literary terms as needed. Answer students' questions about the assignment.

Finally, before they begin working, distribute name tags—or tags for them to write their own names with the markers, perhaps color-coded for each group or literary term. Set the kitchen timer to ring ten minutes before the class period ends so that you have time to collect supplies, clear up the room, reflect on what they have been doing, and give the assignment for the next class meeting.

Once groups begin working, it is time for you to begin observing and listening. If you are not working with your own tablet computer, use the

Figure 2.1.   Students Working on the Floor

clipboard and mailing labels to jot down notes about individual students. If possible, write specific words that particular students say during group activities. Listen for their pithy comments, not lengthy quotations. Jot down exact words, phrases, or short sentences that can help you to structure future lessons. Note whether students understand and use literary terms or synonyms that make sense. Indicate positive/negative language toward group members. For example, "You've got that right, Lindsay," or "You dummy! Don't you know what conflict means in a story?"

BOX 2.1: PROJECT IT! MAKING TIME FOR TIME

Language arts is all about culture and communication. Since every culture has its own sense of time, using a timer in class is an opportunity to address how meaningful time varies from place to place. Project on the screen, while the students work, an image of one of the websites around the world that count local time on a digital clock, preferably a twenty-four-hour clock situated on a website in a language other than English. Note the time you begin and the time you end the session.

Also, make short notes about student behavior. Who is talkative? Who is articulate? Involved? Pensive? Easily distracted? Who is having the most fun? Who likes asking tough questions? How are the various groups and members "doing" in their groups?[3] Most groups progress naturally from forming, to storming (arguing over roles), to norming (settling down and accepting the skills brought to the group), to performing (getting down to business.[4] Be sure to avoid looking like a severe disciplinarian. Smile.

The kitchen timer is visual as well as aural. It can help get you and the students into the rhythm of time-crunched class sessions. Students, right at the beginning of the school year, need to start thinking about completing projects by deadline. So do you. And the classroom needs to be cleaned up on time, especially if a colleague has to teach in the room shortly after your class is over. The timer also signals time for cleanup. Tell your students that when a timer goes off at the end of class, you need their help in straightening out the room so that they can mess it up the next day. They smile.

At the end of the class session, ask the students to bring in pictures, from magazines or printed out from websites, that can be used to represent people, places, events, conflict, and literary devices in their particular piece of literature. Be sure that you have your own supply on hand for those unable to bring pictures or magazines to the next class meeting. For those who have access to the Internet at home, encourage them to search and save images onto a site students can access from school the next day. If the group is making a hard-copy poster, the students may decide to print out pictures and bring them to the next class meeting.

Day Two: Groups Compose Their Collages

Briefly repeat instructions for the assignment, tell students how long they have to create a layout for their collages, and set a timer to signal the last ten minutes for cleanup. Since some of the collages are not likely to be finished, provide envelopes for groups to store their unused pictures. Remind those working online to save their work on the class site you already have set up for use this school year.

Invariably, during this second class meeting, some groups wish they had the images that other groups are using or discarding. So if day one was not overly chaotic, you can encourage covetous groups to swap a few pictures. Still, be careful that cross-group racket doesn't replace intragroup collaboration. You can always institute a couple of one-minute swap sessions to limit as well as encourage picture trading—call it "Picture Jeopardy." If possible, download the TV show's theme song from the Internet and play it while students make their changes. Once the music stops, swapping ends, and groups return to work with the pictures they have on hand.

Next, begin testing the validity of your observations about students from the previous day. See whether the behavior you observed the first day continues, changes, improves, or devolves. Also start looking for additional information about your crew. Who comes prepared? Who acts like the "artistic coordinator"? Which students seem to be more concrete or philosophical in group discussions? Which classmates invite in group members who may have been on the periphery of the discussions? Do any students seem overwhelmed, suggesting that you might need to provide additional encouragement and support as they board the ship for another school year? Remember to jot down brief comments by particular students, such as "Can't you do anything right?" and "I like that picture."

Day Three: Groups Complete Their Collages

By now, students are wondering what they have gotten themselves into—through no choice of their own! They might be noting that this class is going to be a lot of fun as well as a lot of work. It is time for them and you to face the reality of school deadlines, including those for collaborative work. Students do have to demonstrate what they have learned. So keep smiling but also start acting like the benevolent taskmaster you really are.

First, refresh their memories about the assignment. Tell them that the collages have to be completed that day. Finally, joyfully deliver the news that during the next class meeting, the groups are to give oral presentations based on their collages—and that each student is expected to contribute. Even your overachieving groups with already-completed collages now have plenty to do. A few of your students might be thinking uncomplimentary thoughts about school and especially about you. As Huckleberry Finn put it, "All I say is, [teachers] is [teachers], and you got to make allowances. Take them all around; they're a mighty ornery lot. It's the way they're raised."[5]

Hand each student a three-inch by five-inch index card. Inform the class that each group should jot down a couple of comments answering questions about its collage, such as "What does a particular image or group of pictures signify to them with respect to the story?" and "What does the collage reflect about different parts of the story or book?" Again, emphasize that there are no right or wrong answers. These presentations are not graded. Stress the fact that you are looking for creative responses to the reading. After all, this is language arts.

Undoubtedly, a few students become preoccupied with the stressful fact that they have to make an oral presentation already on the fourth day of class, when they are still anxious about their relationships with their classmates and teacher. Some students are relieved to know that they get to present in groups. Remind them that they can refer in their presentations to the ideas that they have already jotted down on their index cards. Even just a few key words or phrases should help each student follow through with her or his part of the presentation.

Day Four: Students Individually Convey Their Group Thoughts

Provide ten or fifteen minutes at the beginning of the period for groups to meet briefly to determine their intragroup speaking order and to recall what each member is going to say on behalf of the group. Ask a member of each group to write the speaking order on the class board so that each one can see when to present to the rest of the class.

To aid in smooth transitions between presentations, ask students to arrange the poster boards on the chalk or marker tray in the order of the presentations, but with posters facing away from the audience. When group members rise to share their collage, one of them can turn their board to face the audience. When the group finishes, the board turner should place their board behind all the others. If you have decided to have digitized presentations, have all files open so that students only have to toggle to open their files.

Whatever their final projects look like, you will be able to determine fairly quickly where they are in terms of reading standards as occur in most curricula, such as their ability to "Analyze how and why individuals, events, and ideas develop and interact over the course of a text"[6] as well as what this group of students' ease is in using the literary terms they will be expected to know by the end of the school year.

If the room has space, invite the class members to sit on the floor close to the collages so that students can see more of the details on the collage, as individual pictures are too small for most to see clearly if they all remain in their seats. For now, smaller-than-optimal collage details are acceptable since the purpose of making these posters is primarily to provide opportunities for students to work together and for you to get to know more about

Figure 2.2.   Daily Journal Writing Need Not be Graded

them, rather than to require polished speeches with equally professional-looking visual aids.

After the presentations, you can display the poster boards for a few weeks, giving group members more opportunities to examine other groups' posters up close. If the resources are available and the classroom is equipped, digitally photograph each collage and project the resulting images on a screen on day five or to show other classes who have a similar assignment. The digital photos also could be posted on your class website for families to view at home.

Day Five: Students Individually Compose Their Reflections

At the beginning of class, with the group posters in sight or projected onto the screen, ask the students to prepare to write a short reflection piece about their experience in class during the first four days. While you take attendance and review your label notes about students—associating your notes with their faces—they can be writing their first journal entries for the course. They get to practice metacognition (think about their own thinking) in their responses to the collage-creating experience. Here are sample prompts.

BOX 2.2: PROJECT IT! USING WORD CLOUDS

Numerous websites create a word cloud or word collage based on words entered by a user. Ask each group to enter ten to fifteen words that describe the images in its picture collage. Then project the resulting word collages and compare each image collage for the respective groups. Which collages are more meaningful to each group? Why? Students soon see that the result is more than words and that interesting and revealing results occur when students create together.*

*Wordle, http://www.wordle.net/ (accessed June 3, 2013).

- What did you have to consider about your story before creating a collage?
- How did you decide which picture worked better than others for your collage?
- Why did your group organize pictures and words a particular way?
- What would you have done differently if you had been working alone?
- Why do you think this is a useful activity to start the year?
- What did you learn about yourself as you worked on this collage?
- What did you discover about your reading skills while working on this collage?

Ask students to write neatly while assuring them that their personal reflections are not to be graded like exams or evaluated as though they were formal papers. Then collect and simply read the journals, thinking about what you learned as you observed them working together and as you read what they have written about the experience. These students' journal entries are now baseline writing samples—not for grading, but for future comparisons along with additional samples forthcoming in students' own journals.

SCAVENGER HUNTING IN THE COURSE ANTHOLOGY

Most middle school students are oblivious to the range of resources in language arts anthologies. Some students are unaware that an anthology is a treasured collection of words, literary passages, similar to the idea of a collection of flowers.

As you explain the concept of anthology to your students, ask them to mentally store an anthology image in their minds by picturing a bouquet of a variety of beautiful, fragrant flowers. If you have access to fresh-cut flowers, bring in a vase full of different varieties and colors and label the vase "anthology." If not, simply project a lovely bouquet of familiar intermixed with exotic flowers. Meanwhile, ask students to prepare for a scavenger hunt inside their anthology. They are likely to look at you askance. That is simply curiosity and is exactly what you want to create.

Planning the Hunt for Pairs of Students

Some publishers may include a scavenger hunt handout with their textbook resources. If yours does not, you can easily prepare fifteen to twenty questions with clues to help students know where to find various elements—using the helpful journalistic method of asking the "five Ws and an H" (who, what, when, where, why, and how). You may be surprised at how much you learn yourself if this is your first time using this particular textbook. Here are helpful categories:

General Content

1. Who is the author or publisher (explain the difference)?
2. What does the title mean or suggest about the contents?
3. When was it published—and when were various pieces written?
4. Where is the table of contents? How is it organized?
5. Where is the index? How is it organized—and why?

Graphics and Graphic Design

1. What is on the cover? Does it make the book seem interesting? Inviting?
2. Is there an introduction? If so, what is in it? Are the introductory pages in roman or arabic numbers (iii or 3)?
3. What kinds of design elements or text features are included (subheadings, captions, lines, colors, text boxes, drawings, maps, photos)?
4. Is the artwork acknowledged? Ask students to find the name of the artist of a particularly interesting piece of artwork. (This information may be found in a separate index or is simply identified in a special font within the complete index to the anthology.)

Organization

1. How is the table of contents organized? Genre (category of artistic composition, similar to types of flowers, such as roses), theme, time, nation or country? Chronologically? Other?
2. Use the table of contents to find . . . an author who has a name beginning with the letter of one of the students' names. Is it a short story, a poem, or a play?

3. Use the index to find a short-story title that includes words beginning with letters of your first name and your partner's last name.
4. How is each literary work introduced? (Devise a question that sends the students to this reader aid.) Some anthologies include background information on the author, historical period, genre, or literary device featured in the particular story, poem, essay, or play.
5. Where in the book is information about authors of individual works or the editors of the anthology? (Send the students to a particular page to learn something unique about an author whose work you may teach later in the school year.)
6. Does the anthology have questions following the text of each literary work, after several related pieces, or at the end of a unit? Send students to one such page and ask them to list the kind of questions found there—such as facts or interpretative responses, maybe even connecting the literature to their own lives.
7. Some anthologies include vocabulary and grammar and links to useful websites. Does yours?

Supplementary Resources

1. If there is a glossary of literary terms, ask students to locate and read the definition of a term that may be new to them but that you plan to teach them during the year—For example, onomatopoeia, pantoum or limerick. Middle schools students like the unusual sounds of these words.
2. Does the anthology include vocabulary definitions? If so, ask students to find the definition of an interesting new word—maybe in a story they may soon read.
3. Or is vocabulary defined in footnotes or side notes? If so, devise a question that requires students to use this text feature.
4. Does the anthology include grammar or writing resources—why or why not? (Question: Why would the publisher put such resources in a book about literature instead of in a book about writing?)
5. Are there lists of suggested readings? Website links? Other resource references?

Of course, it is best to avoid pressing students into feedback about the various social, ethnic, and national groups represented in the book. No anthology is completely diverse or thoroughly unbiased. Focus on the resources available in your anthology rather than on its deficits.

Time to go hunting. The student pairs now can complete the hunt by exploring the book for answers to the questions and then listing three to four literary works they hope the class is to study during the year. Circulate, listen,

---

BOX 2.3: SURVEY IT!

If you have an online blog or school website with a "polling" feature, create a list of the readings and ask students to vote for their top choice to read first. When you present the results to the class, ask students what seemed appealing to them about the top choices. Was it the title? Familiarity with the author? Length of the piece? Peer influence? Then explain that anthology entries are not popularity contests as much as hard, imperfect decisions that publishers and educators make about the educational as well as artistic value of a work.

---

and learn. As you hear them talking about what they notice in the book and hear the stories they mention, you begin to get a sense of what interests them. When possible, modify your lessons to include works that seem to draw their attention. Each pair of students also could be asked to come up with a couple of challenging scavenger questions to stump the panel of other classmates once the preliminary worksheet is completed.

If students take their textbooks home, assign the last question as homework. This gives individual students a reason to review the book on their own and possibly introduce the book to parents or guardians. You might even ask the students to show their book to other family members and ask them which pieces of literature they have read or would like to read.

It would be worthwhile to conclude this scavenger hunt by assigning a one-page summary or reflection. Ask students to write a letter to their parents or guardians explaining what they have learned about their textbook during this exploration. You can then save this ungraded, one-draft writing as a preliminary assessment demonstrating the writing skills the students have at the start of the school year, keeping in mind that they all probably would do better if there were time to revise. Just from reading these one-pagers you will have a sense of students' organization skills, quickly accessed vocabulary, sentence structure, and use of MUGS (mechanics, usage, grammar, and spelling).

Finally, for each of your classes, end the first week of meetings by reviewing some of your personal objectives for the school year that may include

- to increase their appreciation, understanding, and enjoyment of reading
- to improve their understanding and use of the writing process
- to help them become more at ease when speaking in front of a group
- to help them increase their knowledge and use of sophisticated vocabulary
- to review and extend their knowledge of correct grammar
- to discover more ways that technology can help them learn

CONCLUSION

Keep in mind that the first week of class needs to be both task oriented and relational. While introducing students to the work, be sure to help them get introduced to one another and to you. Middle school students are some of the most creative people on the planet. Half of your job as teacher is to keep from squelching their bubbling personalities and literary imaginations. They love using language to express themselves. They especially enjoy telling stories. They probably have been telling their families stories about you and your class. Now you get to tell them about how written language works. That is the focus of the chapters that follow.

NOTES

1. Oscar Hammerstein, "Getting to Know You," quotation from Sound Track Lyrics, http://www.stlyrics.com/lyrics/thekingandi/gettingtoknowyou.htm (accessed April 2, 2012).

2. "English Language Arts Standards » Anchor Standards » College and Career Readiness Anchor Standards for Language," Common Core State Standards Initiative, http://www.corestandards.org/the-standards/english-language-arts-standards/anchor-standards-6-12/college-and-career-readiness-anchor-standards-for-language/ (accessed March 15, 2012).

3. For more on observation strategies and record keeping, see "Royce Sadler: Conversations about the Learning Record," *Learning Record Online* March 31, 2004, http://www.learningrecord.org/sadler.html (accessed April 3, 2012).

4. Bruce W. Tuckman, "Developmental Sequence in Small Groups," *Psychological Bulletin* 63, no. 6 (1965): 384–89, available at http://aneesha.ceit.uq.edu.au/drupal/sites/default/files/Tuckman%201965.pdf (accessed March 16, 2012).

5. Mark Twain, *Huckleberry Finn*, quotation from Literature.org, http://www.literature.org/authors/twain-mark/huckleberry/chapter-23.html.

6. "English Language Arts Standards » Anchor Standards » College and Career Readiness Anchor Standards for Reading," Common Core State Standards Initiative, http://www.corestandards.org/ELA-Literacy/CCRA/R (accessed July 5, 2013).

Chapter Three

Unpacking the Story and Understanding the Genre

The best of my English teachers taught us literature because they wanted the art of it to expand our minds and help teach us new ways of seeing the world. I was taught to both see a work of literature as a way to understand the time it was written, and the people who produced it, and to find the parts of that work that spoke to me in my time and place.

—Sybylla Yeoman Hendrix

This chapter explains how to introduce students to the basic elements of fiction by reading stories, analyzing plot structures and characterization, and eventually coaching them in composing their own short story to submit to a school journal or to publish online. Notice that the approaches work well on lessons teaching short stories, novels, poetry, and plays. But, equally, know that as students learn the language of literature and come to appreciate how the elements work to construct stories, your young teens also come to see themselves and the world in new ways. In much the same way that veteran world travelers learn some of the basic words and phrases for countries they visit, so they will be able to read signs and navigate in new territory and enjoy the trip. Your challenge is to teach the language of literature without diluting that appreciation.

In this chapter are options for presenting or reviewing the definitions of literary terms that adolescents are expected to know and use by the time they complete those middle-level grades. Depending on the elementary schools from which your students come, some may be very familiar with the terms; others may be learning them for the first time.

At the same time, as a professional, you know you also must develop and present lessons that help your students meet the Common Core State Standards for English Language Arts or the curriculum goals in your school that include close reading, making logical inferences, citing specific textual evidence in speaking, and writing to support conclusions drawn from the text.[1]

INTRODUCING THE ELEMENTS OF FICTION

Here is a way to get your middle school students started. They need a journal, such as a spiral notebook, or an electronic device to which they have daily access. This study aid can be taken home daily, but if more appropriate for your school setting, set up labeled boxes or bins to store on classroom shelves so students can pick up their journals at the beginning of each class meeting and return them at the end. If students have access to computers in the classroom every day, help the youngsters set up files and folders they can access easily. Show them the link on the school server or Internet you have vetted for preteen use and that connects them to a safe place for them to save their files so they can access them in class, on the school site, or at home.

Ask students to set up their own journal section for short stories by folding a page in half vertically, forming a half-page bookmark titled "short stories" or creating a digital file for this purpose. So begins their own story in this unit—the opening of their files or turning of their page (not a bad metaphor!). Every new life story is a chance to begin again.

Then ask students to write on the next clean page in their journals the current date in the upper right-hand corner and, as you introduce them, the elements of fiction on the top line. Remind the students that all writers start with blank pages even if they use computers, as few students ever think about the fact that most of what they read was first written on blank paper, typed on a typewriter, or word-processed on a keyboard. Next, point out to your students that writers use proven techniques to engage readers—just as musicians use notes, chords, and rhythms. Writers do not just write to quickly express themselves—like many bloggers do. Knowing the different facets of fiction helps writers write and readers read. In fact, understanding the structure of literature can assist in all kinds of human communication, from interviewing for a job to making a movie.

If you are comfortable doing it, start this unit on unpacking stories by telling your own story about something that happened in your life—something students find humorous, unusual, or particularly revealing about you. Be a bit transparent to engage the students. Then ask a couple of students if they like listening more to stories or lectures. Students usually admit that they like listening to stories more than lectures. Moreover, they acknowledge that they prefer lectures that use stories to illustrate points, rather than lectures that just give information. Hmmm.

Normally it is best to teach those literary terms that are covered in your student textbook. If the text does not define terms, you can use those below or write your own. Wikipedia generally includes different definitions and a brief history of each of the terms.

Many of the following lessons follow the same basic order:

- Teach or demonstrate the literary term (an element of fiction).
- Assign reading a story that clearly illustrates the term.
- Encourage students to pay attention to how the story reflects the elements.
- Invite students to read for fun so they do not focus so much on identifying the elements that they fail to enjoy the story.

Consider assigning students to read several stories quickly, since multiple examples can be more effective than one. Below are ways of teaching each of the basic elements of fiction. You can do a pretest to discover what terms your students already know by simply creating a list of terms students are expected to know by the end of the school year, distributing the list, and asking the students to put a star next to the terms they know and could explain; a check next to the terms they recognize; and a minus sign next to the terms that are completely new to them.

As students are marking the lists, circulate, peeking over the shoulders to see if you notice a pattern among terms starred and checked. If time permits, ask students to turn and talk to a partner, explaining to their peer the words they starred and their partner checked. Again, listen as they talk. By this time, students realize that they have more knowledge than they imagined but still have much to learn. Commend them for their candid responses and helpful conversations. Collect their lists, tally the results, and decide how best to use this formative assessment to adjust upcoming lessons.

Remember, it always is appropriate to review, so if students already know many of the basic terms, you may just speed up the pace of the lessons that follow. Or assign the book report or project for quarter one at the end of this chapter and allot a class period to visit the library to locate and check out their books and in-class time to read them. Sometimes a special side trip during a tour is just the thing to reenergize those committed to a long trip. These self-selected books also provide fine fodder for feeding their minds and expanding their understanding about ways authors use the literary devices you are teaching.

Lesson 1: Plot

1. Ask students to turn to the short story section of their journals. Explain first that stories are about characters faced with solving a problem, confronting a conflict. The first term is *Plot*, the series of events that make

PLOT LINE

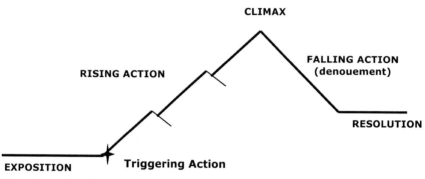

Figure 3.1. Plot line.

up a story. Plot usually includes six parts: an exposition, triggering action, rising action, climax, falling action, and resolution.

2. Draw a diagram of a plotline on the board or use one prepared on a poster or for a projector. See your class anthology or an online source for sample plotline.

3. Fill in the six parts of the plotline as you explain the purpose of each part:

- *Exposition*: Introduces the main characters, the setting, the conflict, and the point of view. (*Ex*= out, *position* = places. Exposition + places out for the reader…).
- *Triggering action*: That story point when the main character decides to do something about the problem.
- *Rising Action*: A series of events during which the main character attempts to solve the problem introduced in the exposition. Usually there are three attempts:
  - the first very simple
  - the second more difficult, often requiring the help of another character
  - the third most complex, often requiring the main character to make a moral or ethical decision
- If students are familiar with classic fairy tales, ask them to consider how often this three-part rising action occurs—"Three Little Pigs," "Goldilocks and the Three Bears," "Three Billy Goat's Gruff," and so on. Ask for examples of stories with which they may be more familiar in their culture or language; consider storylines from movies or TV shows.
- *Climax*: The highest point of suspense in the story, when the reader, viewer, or listener wonders whether the main character has gotten into such trouble that she or he cannot get out. But then the turning point occurs and the reader can see that the problem can be solved or (tragically) that the character has given up or been permanently overcome.

- *Falling Action*: The issues raised during the rising action begin to fall into place, the complications of the rising action seem to unravel, and the action begins to wind down. Some texts call this the *dénouement* (day-noo-mon).
- *Resolution*: The action stops and the readers see that the main character either has solved the problem or given up (not all stories have happy endings).

Adding Plotline Sound Effects—Play It!

Talking about a plotline is not nearly as engaging as telling the story itself. Therefore, it helps students to make your plotline lecture into a story by adding appropriate sound effects. After all, over 50 percent of the emotional impact of a movie is the soundtrack. If you have software like PowerPoint, create a diagram of a plotline (step #2) in which each step in the plot appears on the screen with appropriate sound effects. The "transition" feature in PowerPoint allows you to vary the effects and their loudness. This activity can also serve as a course project using images as well as words. Consider making or adding the sounds a roller-coaster car emits as it begins, ascends, lurches at the top, descends, and then slows at the end of the ride.

Close the session with the reading assignment, asking students to identify the plot parts in the story you assign. Encourage them to draw and label the plotline in their journals.

If you are teaching with block scheduling, you can use the additional time to start or complete a short story so students can begin identifying parts of the plot. Reading a story aloud and asking students to raise their hands when they recognize an element is a way to focus their attention on the elements and is also a no-stress assessment for you to determine whether they "get it." But be sure to stop reading at a critical plot point to entice the students to continue reading the story themselves just to find out what happens next.

The Limits of PowerPoint for Visual Learners

When humans think visually, they imagine how to associate images with one another using their own experiences. For instance, when we think of what we would like to accomplish, we imagine ourselves doing the things necessary to complete the task. Even if we make a list of the steps, we imagine ourselves doing verbs in the list (nouns like "store" imply actions, such as "go to" or "buy").

Many visual learners prefer to picture their creativity concretely in a medium; they will draw pictures and symbols, even when creating a list, adding underlines and uppercase letters, or combinations of cursive handwriting and block letters. Visual learners think in terms of special connections, too—arrows, boxes, circles, personal sketches, and the like.

The fact is, high-tech visual tools can be restrictive for relatively simple visual tasks. For instance, visual learners may prefer paper and pen to PowerPoint when it comes to brainstorming. PowerPoint is difficult to use for freehand drawing and doodling. However, a technology like PowerPoint can help visual learners express their ideas effectively to others, but usually only after they have expressed it on paper first. For many visual learners, thinking creatively with PowerPoint can be inefficient, if not totally aggravating.

Lesson 2: Conflict

In fiction, conflict is the problem the main character(s) must resolve as a result of a struggle against opposing forces. The main character may face internal conflict (a struggle for dominance between two elements within a person) or external conflict (against an outside force)—and often both.

Once you introduce the topic of conflict, students should be ready to work in pairs for 10 minutes to identify plot elements in the story they have just read. They can work together, referring to the definitions that they wrote in their notebooks and identifying specific examples from the text. Sharing desk space is a psychological reminder to students that they are sharing what they are learning, so encourage the students to collaborate by pulling their desks together and talking with one another. Circulate during discussions to learn:

- What students recall about the previous day's lesson and from the story they just read
- What needs to be retaught or clarified before continuing the lesson
- Who has and has not done the homework

Next, lead a classroom discussion of student conclusions for about 15 minutes. This discussion/response format reveals to the students that there is often more than one right response to a question, it allows you to determine students' understanding of the material, and it is excellent practice for writing fully developed essays. Students should follow this format in their responses:

- State their opinion: "I think that the climax of 'The Three Little Pigs' is when the wolf comes down the chimney."
- Support their opinion with an example from the text: "On page three it says, 'Finally, the wolf got so hungry that he jumped down the chimney.'"
- Explain how the chosen passage illustrates the definition of the term: "This seems like the high point of the story because the reader really wonders if the pigs will be okay. Also, the action of the story starts to fall after this event."

Internal conflict occurs when a character struggles within himself or herself to decide what is the right, moral, or safe action. It is something like the

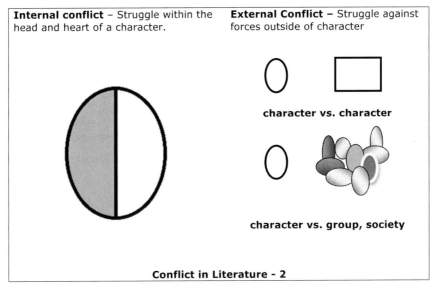

Conflict in Literature - 2

Figure 3.2.   Conflict 1. Designed by author.

cartoon of the devil and angel sitting on opposite shoulders of a character, trying to persuade the character to take certain actions.

External conflict occurs when the main character struggles against forces outside of himself or herself. The students may need to be reminded that even an animal or alien protagonist demonstrates a humanlike struggle. Examples of external conflict are:

- Person versus person—when the struggle is with another character
- Person versus nature—when the struggle is against a force of nature—weather, thirst, illness, or topography (desert, mountain, roiling rapids)
- Person versus society—when the struggle is against a group of people acting as one—a team, racial group, pack of peers, political party, social club, or ethnic tribe, etc.
- Person versus technology—when the struggle is against a machine, like a car, tractor, tank, or android or computer in science fiction
- Person versus the supernatural—when the struggle is against a ghost, an alien, the gods, or a Supreme Being

Ask students to identify the conflict in the story they have just completed and reply using P.I.E. response structure. This simply means make the *point*, *illustrate* it with examples from the literature, and then *explain* the link between the illustration and the point. Students use "because" statements to clarify their answer, illustrate it with an example from the text, and explain why that example fits the definition of the term they have just studied. Yes, insisting on P.I.E. may slow down the rate of responses, but P.I.E. necessitates deeper thinking and allows those who process information more slowly the time they need to do so.

Using Cartoons to Illustrate Stereotypes—Play It!

Thanks to YouTube and similar video websites, there are thousands of downloadable, copyright-free cartoons available for classroom use. The old Warner Brothers cartoons, in particular, have wonderfully illustrative, simple plotlines and relatively simple characters that tend to be entirely good or evil. They demonstrate static, flat characters who have to be the same at the beginning and end of every episode. Caution: Some early cartoons are extremely stereotypical with respect to gender, ethnicity, and race.

Creating a Plotline

Assign another short story to read for homework. If time permits, read aloud the opening passages. This often is enough to get students hooked so they are more likely to complete the reading on their own. Ask the students to draw

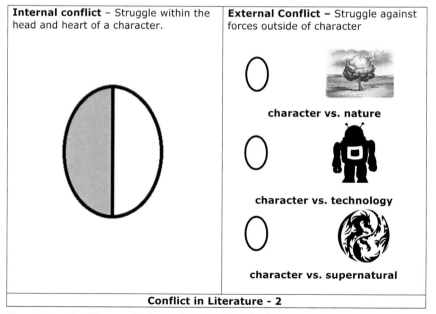

Figure 3.3.   Conflict may be internal, external, or both.

a plotline that represents the relative length of time it takes for each section of the story to unfold. Some stories have long expositions and precipitous falling action and minimal resolutions. Let the shape of the plotline show that relationship. "The Most Dangerous Game" by Richard Connell is an excellent choice for illustrating the types of conflict and an interesting plot structure. Ask students to label the incidents in the rising action. This can be fun for them and you to see how consistent they are in identifying those events of plot.

Lesson 3: Setting

The setting of a story is the time and place in which the action occurs. In a short story, the setting is particularly limited—sometimes just a single day or a few hours and a single location. Here is a suggested schedule for engaging students in a review of what you have taught and an introduction to this other basic element of story structure:

1. For 10 minutes, review the elements of plot and the story the students read. Ask them to work in pairs to identify the elements and the kind(s) of conflict.
2. Conduct a 10–15 minute, full-class discussion for students to share observations about the new story. This can be a think-pair-share format, or just turn and talk. It's important to build in time for students to talk, using the terminology you are teaching.
3. For the remaining time, guide the students through these new definitions:
   a. Setting in terms of time
      • Time of day: dawn, morning, afternoon, evening, night
      • Time of year: winter, spring, summer, fall
      • Time of life: childhood, teen years, adult, old age
      • Time in history: prehistoric, medieval, Elizabethan Age, future
   b. Setting in terms of place
      • Area of place: inside, outside, porch, roof, basement or cellar
      • Locale: city, country, mountains, sea, valley, forest
      • Continent: Africa, Asia, Europe, North or South America
      • Galaxy: Earth, another planet, another galaxy
4. Finally, assign a short story to read and ask students to pay close attention to the ways that the author establishes setting. Ask them to consider how the setting makes them feel or how setting creates a mood. Wait until the next period to remind them of the typical impact of daytime versus nighttime when good or bad things happen, rural versus urban places when the characters may be relaxed versus tense.

If students are permitted to write in their textbooks, ask them to pencil-in rectangles around words or phrases that reveal setting and then write "T" in the margin for "time" and "P" in the margin for "place." If the students are not permitted to write in their books, ask them to keep notes in their journal or use sticky notes. This active response to reading affirms for students what they are learning or reminds them about what they need to ask about during the next class meeting.

Lesson 4: Characters—Act I

Be sure to remind students to write lecture-discussion notes in their journals. As needed, remind students to write a particular definition or other material in their journals—even hinting that a specific key concept might be on a quiz or test.

Some notes about characters:

- The *protagonist* is a human or other humanlike character who struggles to overcome conflict. A story's suspense develops as a reader gets to know more about the protagonist and the ways the protagonist responds to obstacles.
- The *antagonist* is the opposing force (external forces include another character, a group, nature, technology, or even supernatural forces; internal forces include conscience).
- *Characterization* describes how authors reveal characters' personalities and motivations. Authors reveal such traits and motives directly or indirectly.

Here is a direct, expressed motive about a character, Claude: "Claude is a popular guy but is feared by most of the students in the school." However, if the author merely has other characters steering clear of Claude, then readers soon infer that characters in the story are afraid of Claude even though the readers are not told so directly through a statement by the author.

After introducing or reviewing the material about characters, ask the students to identify the kinds of characterizations the authors have used in stories read so far, giving students time to find specific examples in the text to support their responses and encouraging them to talk quietly as they search for text clues. Once again, circulate among them. At the end of the session, summarize the terms and assign a new story.

Lesson 5: Characters—Act II

Character development is complicated and involves an additional day of study. Explain how some characters develop and change during the course

---

Characters: People who are faced with solving a problem in a story. (Could be animals or robots acting as humans)

Flat: one dimensional, predictable, one-sided character
Round: one reader learns more about as story unfolds
Static: does not change as story unfolds
Dynamic: changes as a result of involvement in the conflict

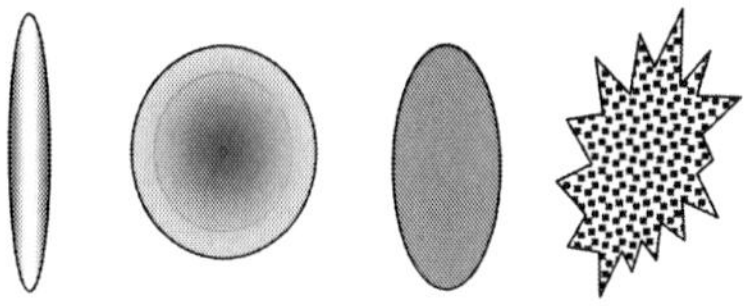

CHARACTERIZATION

Figure 3.4. **Kinds of characters.**

of the story. One option is to ask students why people do something right or wrong. The point would be that everyone is complex; every person acts on the basis of mixed motives. Real "characters" are not simple. In this regard, more complex fictional characters are like readers—and readers are like them. Show or reproduce the diagram on characters and explain that for fictional purposes, authors use a range of character types.

Dynamic and static characters: Usually the protagonist is a dynamic character who changes as a result of attempting to solve the conflict. Most minor characters are static; they change very little or not at all.

Round and flat characters: Round characters learn more as the story progresses but might not change (like a balloon that grows larger as it is blown up but does not change its basic nature). Flat characters are usually one-dimensional (like a paper doll), static, and often stereotypical (e.g., the pudgy best friend, the tough sidekick, the shy and bespectacled nerd, the bully, and the fairy tale's evil stepmother).

Since this is the good stopping point for introducing new literary terms, review each one using all previous stories for examples. Then assign a more challenging story with more fully developed characters and a more complex plot, like "The Most Dangerous Game" by Richard Connell. Edgar Allan Poe's short stories often fit this description but may be taxing for younger students or inexperienced English readers. Later lessons are designed to introduce more literary devices.

Now that you know your students better, it may be an appropriate time to differentiate your instruction. Set up groups of four or five students based on common interests or reading levels. Guided by what you have learned about your students so far, assign the groups to read different stories from the anthology. If it suits your situation, two groups can read the same story. During the next class meetings, those who have read the same stories could meet in small groups to discuss their findings using the vocabulary of literature they are learning. Again, observe, listen, and take notes about who is confident using the new terms, who finds accurate examples to validate his or her claims about the story, who is encouraging and supportive, who sits and listens first but responds with comments that show he or she knows what is going on, who hasn't a clue. This information can help you plan the next set of lessons tailored to meet the needs of the students you currently are teaching.

WRITING ABOUT SHORT STORIES

After you complete the series of lessons is a good time for a writing stress-free assessment that follows up their talking about the stories. Here is an idea to help guide students in summarizing a story in three to five sentences using the basic journalistic questions: Who, What, When, Where, Why, and How? First model for the students a way to glean this specific information from a story:

- Who? List main characters—protagonist and antagonist
- What? List 7–10 verbs that identify plot events. For example, choose a common fairy tale (or movie) and ask the students to list verbs, using only the verbs for "Little Red Riding Hood," "Goldilocks and the Three Bears," or a different but well-known tale. For example, Goldilocks:
  1. walks
  2. sees
  3. peeks
  4. tastes
  5. sits
  6. sleeps
  7. awakens
  8. fears
  9. flees
- When does the action occur—or from when to when?
- Where does the majority of the action take place?
- Why do the protagonist and antagonist act the way they do—what drives or motivates them to act? Students may need help with vocabulary of motivation. You could offer ideas like fear, love, hunger, hate, power, greed, jealousy, sense of adventure.
- How do the main characters accomplish their deeds—physically, mentally, both?

After you introduce students to the basic reportorial story categories, use the fairy tale or movie plot to write a three-to-five sentence summary with the students so they get the idea.

Then you can be ready to assemble students into brainstorming groups to gather facts (in 8–10 minutes) about one of the stories they just read for class. Two groups can work on the same story, as needed. Tell them that they are to report their findings to the rest of the class. When someone from each group reports to the rest of the class, point out that groups sometimes identify different Ws or Hs in their reports. Be open with students about the fact that two different interpretations can both be correct because stories and their characters are often complex—unlike simplistic TV commercials or cartoons with stereotypical characters. Continue your focused observation as students work independently, then in small groups, and finally as a whole class.

Pique students' interest in writing story summaries by showing them one or two online book listings—maybe even a blurb for a currently popular young adult fiction book. Note how the blurb uses the Ws and H but usually refrains from giving away the dénouement (no "spoiler").

After group brainstorming, permit students to work independently to write their own summaries for 10 minutes or so. If time permits, conclude the period by having one student from each group read his or her summary aloud while the rest of the class decides whether each reader has included all six requirements. What's missing? Who can add the missing information?

This reportorial activity provides a good appraisal of the class's readiness for a test or quiz on literary terms and story elements. If the students are ready, give them a test or quiz in a day or so. If not, take a couple of days to work with simpler stories and to practice identifying elements and using text evidence to support opinions and observations. See your own anthology or see Language Arts Resources on this book's companion website for a sample quiz on literary terms. Writing summaries about short stories will come in handy when you teach students how to conduct research and want them to write summaries of their findings.

DIGITIZING STUDENT OBSERVATIONS

What fun! Collaborate, review, produce, reinforce, decorate, learn, and teach with online cloud generators. For a whole class, in small groups, or as individuals, you can invite students to use online generators to create artwork

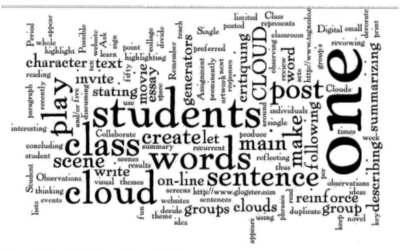

Figure 3.5.   Digitizing student thinking.

reflecting student responses to reading. Ask the students to write a paragraph describing a character, summarizing the events in a scene, discussing the theme of a novel or play, highlighting the main ideas in an essay, or critiquing a movie, and then make a cloud using a website like wordle.com, tagxedo. com, or gloster.com. Or you could make a class cloud by having the students write one of the following:

- Ten words describing one of the main characters
- One sentence summarizing a recently read scene from the literary work
- One sentence stating one of the main ideas
- One sentence stating in their own words the main idea of the story
- One sentence critiquing the literary work

Then in groups of five, invite the students to post their group's lists (keep duplicate words so that each cloud represents all 50 words), or all the sentences into one of the cloud text screens; next, create and print their group cloud. If reviewing a longer work or play, divide the book or play up and let students sign up for their preferred scene. Remember, the more times a single word appears in the text, the more prominently it will appear in the cloud. That's the point.

Then, create a class collage of all the group clouds—should make for an interesting visual summary of what the students are thinking, observing, concluding. When these word clouds are projected, recurrent words and phrases will highlight and thus reinforce the key observations. Then post the results around the classroom and/or on class website. If space is limited, let the class decide which one(s) to post or post them one per week.

APPLYING NEWLY LEARNED SKILLS—
BOOK REPORT #1

The end of the first quarter is a great opportunity to have students independently apply what they are learning about the elements of fiction, but in a work they are reading on their own. If it is not realistic to expect your students to complete a book outside of class, allot 20 minutes daily for the next couple of weeks for students to read in class. To make efficient use of class time, set up a schedule so that all students study grammar for about two-thirds of the period. Check your class textbook for ideas about teaching grammar, directly or indirectly as part of your writing instruction.

You can make that determination based on the grade and skill level of the students as revealed in the writing you already have seen them do on earlier assignments. See the Teacher Resource B for ideas for a first-quarter book report. This book report asks students to make connections between the story in their self-selected work of fiction and the stories they have studied together in class. It also includes a speech component to get students acclimated to giving more formal speeches later in the school year. Informal speaking activities conducted early in the semester can help students develop confidence for longer speeches in class. You can see how close they are to meeting the Common Core State Standards for English Language Art or curriculum standards for your course that ask students to demonstrate how well they can "present information, findings, and supporting evidence such that listeners can follow the line of reasoning."[2]

DISCUSSING AND WRITING
SHORT STORIES: WHERE STORY MEETS GENRE

To read without reflecting is like eating without digesting.

—Edmund Burke (www.quotegarden.com/books.html)

Some of your students may have heard of literary terms such as "omniscient" or "theme," but chances are your young teens just experience stories without thinking about who is talking to whom about what. Once they begin discussing and writing about literature, however, students soon see that learning the literary language leads to better understanding and eventually to an appreciation for how stories work.

Reading and talking about compact works of fiction provide opportunities to enhance skills at recognizing key ideas and details, appreciating craft and structure, and understanding ways that fiction writing reflects the integration of knowledge and ideas called for in the Common Core State Standards for English Language Arts.[3] Short stories are great teaching mediums for seeing literary devices at work because these short pieces provide manageable examples that students come to enjoy and even appreciate as they discover ways to see beyond what the text says to what it means and why it matters. Students can transfer these deeper reading skills to longer works as the school year unfolds.

Having completed lessons about literature already like those offered in Lessons 1 through 5, the students probably are curious and eager to begin exploring more subtle aspects of fiction, but it is always a good idea to conduct interim, no-stress assessments to assure yourself that students are ready for more.

One quick and easy assessment is to have students turn to the list of literary terms in their anthology and ask the students to put a plus sign next to terms they know and could explain to another student, put a check mark next to terms they recognize but are not sure how to use in conversation or writing, and a minus sign next to words that are completely new to them. If writing in their texts is verboten, print out a list of the terms on paper on which they can write. Include all the terms you plan to teach for the school year. This has a dual purpose. Seeing the whole list lets them know what they are expected to know by the end of the year; marking the terms they know shows them what they already have learned.

As you circulate among the students, peeking at their marking, you get a sense of their level of familiarity with the terms. If you notice lots of plus signs, commend the class for the knowledge they already have, and then move more rapidly through the lessons, using the ideas presented as a refresher; on the other hand, if you see more checks and minus signs, you know to move with deliberate steps through the lessons. As you discover increased student confidence in their oral and written conversations, just pick up the pace and move on. Consider the results of these kinds of formative assessments as speed limit signs. You are the one in charge of the trip, the professional in the classroom who knows what your students know and what they need to learn. Until students can show they know, go slow. You have much to teach.

Lesson Six: Point of View

Point of view (POV) is the perspective from which an author tells a story. The various points of view include:

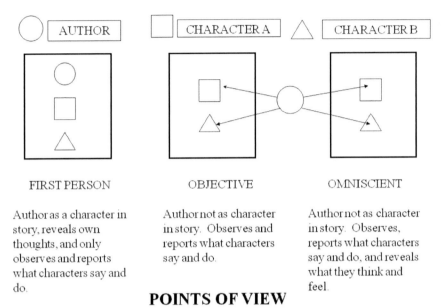

FIRST PERSON

Author as a character in story, reveals own thoughts, and only observes and reports what characters say and do.

OBJECTIVE

Author not as character in story. Observes and reports what characters say and do.

OMNISCIENT

Author not as character in story. Observes, reports what characters say and do, and reveals what they think and feel.

POINTS OF VIEW

Diagram adapted from work of Blair and Gerber, 1959

Figure 3.6. Point of view.

- First-Person POV: The author writes as though he or she is a character inside the story, using first-person pronouns and commenting on his or her own thoughts and feelings about the incidents in the plot. For example, if Charles Dickens had written his classic story about Scrooge as though he, Dickens, were the character Scrooge, the reader would know only what Scrooge sees and hears, thinks and does. With the limitations of first-person POV, the reader would not know what has gone on in Tiny Tim's house before Scrooge arrives.

- Objective or Third-Person POV: The author writes the story as though he or she is outside the story, limited to listening and observing what characters say and do—like a reporter. The author uses third-person pronouns (he, she, they—not we or I) to report the speech and actions of the characters in the story. The objective POV offers a broader perspective than first-person POV because the author stands outside of the story and can observe characters in different settings. The characters can speak in the first person, but the author is reporting only on what is heard. Speaking frankly, you know that no writing is completely objective because the author's attitude (tone) always shines through the choices of words, images, structure, and time spent on the topics. But, for purposes of introducing POV, this term can suffice.

- Omniscient POV: The author writes the story as though he or she is outside story but also can see into the hearts and minds of the characters inside the story. The author not only listens and observes what characters say and do but also relates what these characters feel and think, like an all-knowing Supreme Being. The author not only uses third-person pronouns but also words like "ponders," "gloated," "feared," and "worried" to show the inner thoughts and feelings of the characters. This is the broadest POV because the author gets inside the heads and hearts of the characters and comments on their thoughts and feelings as the story unfolds.

• Limited Omniscient POV: An author limits the revelation of thoughts and feelings to just one character, often the protagonist. To understand this, imagine being able to read the mind of one of your friends but not the mind of a different friend. This is the way Dickens wrote *A Christmas Carol*. The reader knows what Scrooge is thinking and feeling but can only infer that information about other characters based on what they say and do.

If you show your students the graphic depiction in figure 3.6 as you review points of views, those who are more visual learners are likely to be able to follow your explanations a little better.

Helping Students Picture Point of View—Shoot It!

Perhaps no contemporary media genre illustrates point of view better than the news. Modern news is not just factual; someone has to decide what to report, how to cover it, whom to interview, what text, and which images or sounds to include in the final version. During the week that you introduce the concept of point of view, ask interested students in groups of two or three to "cover" a school sports event with a digital camera, using no more than three photos and 30 seconds of vocal "copy" to summarize the game.

As long as at least two groups participate, the class should be able to compare the points of view of different reporter-editors as they read their copy and show their images to the class. Hint: Don't tell them in advance whether to use any first-person or objective copy in describing the event. See what they come up with on their own. After watching student presentations, ask students what they notice about the different points of view they have seen.

WRITING ASSIGNMENT FOR
UNDERSTANDING POINT OF VIEW

Challenge students. Ask them to imagine a minor automobile accident has occurred at a busy intersection during the lunch hour. State objectively that Car A failed to come to a complete stop at the intersection and rear-ended Car B, causing it to enter the intersection and hit a pedestrian crossing the street. No serious injuries occurred. Diagram the crash in PowerPoint or on the board but, like a reporter, give only the facts.

Divide the students into story-related personae:

a. Driver of Car A or B in the accident
b. Driver of any of the other cars stopped in the intersection
c. The pedestrian who was struck by Car B
d. One of three pedestrians who observed the accident
e. TV reporters in their station's helicopter who happened to be flying over while returning from a fire in the next county

Of course, you can use a different situation depending on what may be easier for your students to imagine: an accident at a horse show, a robbery in a shopping mall parking lot, a brawl on school grounds, or a scuffle in the cafeteria. Key: have similar roles as the car accident.

1. Invite the students to write, in first-person POV, a one-paragraph description of what happened from the perspective of their chosen or assigned persona.
2. Have them assemble in groups of five (representing each of the personae) to read their paragraphs aloud within their groups.
3. Then, ask students individually to describe the same accident from limited omniscient POV, choosing another person who observed the incident. This time, have them read their paragraph to a partner.

About 10 minutes before the class period ends, invite volunteers to read aloud to the class their writing from either perspective or point of view. Encourage the students to articulate what they learned from doing this exercise. They are likely to mention that the details seemed different depending on the position of the speaker in relation to the accident. They probably notice that using the omniscient POV provides more information for the reader and reveals bias in a character that can influence the readers' opinion of the events that occur in the story.

Lesson 7: Theme

Theme is the universal message of a story—what some textbooks call a story's central meaning or idea. To be universal, themes must reveal what is true about human nature or the human condition regardless of time or place. Life itself is an adventure in learning, and the best literature focuses on the themes that help us to understand life in all times and places.

Consider this helpful guide to universal theme: Would the fictional characters respond in similar emotional or psychological ways if the situations in which they found themselves were set in a different time or place? If so, the story probably addresses universal themes. Here is a way to approach the topic:

- Begin the class period with a review of the last story read. Ask students to write a half page in which they summarize the story using the 5 Ws and H concept. This time, the H indicates how the author chose to tell the story— from what point of view.
- Add the definition of theme to the key terms you already posted on the board, overhead transparency, or projection screen. Displaying a word wall of the terms is another way to reinforce learning and remind students to use the terms in speaking and writing. Seeing the list grow throughout the school year shows them how much they are learning.
- You may find that beginning with abstract nouns will help. For example, is this a story about love, courage, loyalty, or regret? Then move on to writing complete sentence stating what the story portrays about this abstract concept. Of course, your students may not know the term "abstract" and saying "general" may be enough to get them started. You could then let them know that a more precise word to identify such nouns is "abstract."
- Some teachers generously post their resources online and you may find one that you can adopt as you introduce what can be a difficult literary device to teach and to learn. See sample theme presentations on the Internet. Visuals can heighten comprehension.
- Explain the significance of the plot for determining theme. Ask students to pay attention to incidents in the beginning, middle, and end of the plot, especially the conflicts the protagonist faces, the responses to the conflict, and attempts to overcome it.
- Mention that a theme should to be expressed in a complete sentence; otherwise, the idea is probably just a topic, not a real theme. Write this sentence with blanks left where there are parentheses, "*When* (indicate the situation the main character is in) *people* (indicate the response)." For example, "When little girls are hungry, they are tempted to steal" ("Goldilocks and the Three Bears").
- Ask the class to state possible sentence themes in previously read stories.
- Give them time to reflect on the stories, flip back through the textbook, and jot down their ideas.
- Remain open to new insights since some students might come up with themes that you had not considered—but require students to support their observations with text evidence from the stories taken from the beginning, middle, and end of the stories.

Figure 3.7. **Small group discussing themes.**

DRAFTING A SHORT STORY—USING WHAT THEY KNOW

As students learn the basic elements of narrative fiction, they are better prepared to write well-structured stories of their own. Now would be a great stop on the learning journey. Pause a few days, allotting time on the trip for students to utilize what they are learning to write a brief tale of their own. They can pattern or adapt the strategies of writers the students have come to know and appreciate. Some students are eager to begin regardless of whether they understand these elements. As they work through the process of prewriting, drafting, getting peer feedback, and revising for in-class publication, you should be able to determine what to review along the way. Whether pleasantly or unpleasantly surprised at what they know, encourage them to keep working.

Publishing Online Fan Fiction—Blog It!

Another way to encourage students to publish is to offer credit for students' contributions to online "fan fiction."[4] These "works in progress" are essentially readers' own writings designed either to extend novelists' printed prose or sometimes to comment upon novelists' works using "drabbles" (short,

100-words-or-less vignettes that rely on characters or settings from the original works). Fan fiction is like blogging (web "logging," or commenting on subjects and experiences) where fans write on special fan fiction websites.

CONCLUSION

The key to introducing narrative theory in middle school language arts is to use examples and illustrations from stories that engage the students and keep them reading, viewing, listening, and sharing stories. Use stories from the class text along with downloadable media files, especially short video clips. Keep in mind, this introduction or review of literary terms is designed to ensure that your students have the vocabulary with which to talk and write about the way fiction prose and poetry are shaped.

The short-term goal is to have a common word base, a foundation of academic concepts of the grammar of fiction, and a concrete understanding of these elements of literature. The longer-term goal is to prepare your middle school students with knowledge and skills that can serve them well when they reach high school, perhaps go on to college, and eventually to participate in neighborhood book discussion groups they decide to join as adults. Right?

SHORT STORY COLLECTIONS TO
RECOMMEND FOR SELF-SELECTED READING

The Friendship and the Gold Cadillac by Mildred D. Taylor
These two short stories by Mildred D. Taylor explore what it was like to grow up black in America during the 1900s. "The Friendship" is about the consequences that occur when a black man calls a white storekeeper by his first name.
The Gift of the Magi and Other Stories by O. Henry
These classic stories about life in the early 1900s are very accessible for middle school students. Well known for their surprise endings, O. Henry's stories are typically pleasant and entertaining.
Guys Write for Guys Read edited by Jon Scieszka
For this anthology, Jon Scieszka collected dozens of stories and illustrations from popular authors who write for boys. Scieszka's goal was to provide a wide variety of very short stories in order to help boys identify what types of things they like to read.
On the Fringe edited by Donald R. Gallo
On the Fringe is a serious and thoughtful collection of 11 stories about high school outcasts. Compiled in response to the Columbine shootings,

the stories include characters like Brian, who's considered a wimp; Jeannie, who's a tomboy; Renee, who decides to write about her school's outcasts; and Gene, who brings a gun to class.

Short and Shivery: Thirty Chilling Tales retold by Robert D. San Souci

This is a collection of 30 retold ghost stories from around the world. The tales are scary enough to hold middle school students' attention but not scary enough to concern parents.

A Wolf at the Door edited by Ellen Datlow and Terri Windling

Thirteen science fiction and fantasy writers contributed stories to this collection of retold fairy tales. The stories are meant to return to the older, more frightening, and complicated style of fairy tales.

The Wonderful Story of Henry Sugar and Six More by Roald Dahl

This collection of seven Roald Dahl's stories is funny, strange, and often irreverent.

Any collection of short stories by Edgar Allan Poe

Edgar Allan Poe's short stories are both fascinating and terrifying. Try using one of his stories as an introduction to a short story unit—students become more excited about participating in the unit when they experience how interesting short stories can be.

NOTES

Epigraph: Sybylla Y. Hendrix, from "Why our students study literature," *Gustavus Adolphus College.* http://gustavus.edu/academics/english/whystudyliterature.php (accessed April 3, 2012).

1. "English Language Arts Standards 'Anchor Standards' College and Career Readiness Anchor Standards for Language," *Common Core State Standards Initiative*, 2011. www.corestandards.org/the-standards/english-language-arts-standards/anchor-standards-6-12/college-and-career-readiness-anchor-standards-for-language/ (accessed March 15, 2012).

2. "English Language Arts Standards 'Anchor Standards' College and Career Readiness Anchor Standards for Speaking," *Common Core State Standards Initiative*, 2011. www.corestandards.org/the-standards/english-language-arts-standards/anchor-standards-6-12/college-and-career-readiness-anchor-standards-for-speaking-and-listening/ (accessed April 3, 2012).

3. "English Language Arts Standards 'Anchor Standards' College and Career Readiness Anchor Standards for Language," *Common Core State Standards Initiative*, 2011. www.corestandards.org/the-standards/english-language-arts-standards/anchor-standards (accessed July 12, 2012).

4. Fan fiction is still emerging as a valid educational activity and has not been addressed comprehensively in the educational literature, so be sure to check out the sites before recommending them to your students. See FanFiction.net as a sample.

Chapter Four

Crossing into Novel Territory

Reading Longer Texts

In Robert Peck's award-winning young adult novel *A Day No Pigs Would Die*, a young boy queries his father:

"Fences are funny, aren't they, Papa?"
"How so?"
"Well, you be friends with Mr. Tanner. Neighbors and all. But we keep this fence up like it was war. I guess that humans are the only things on earth that take everything they own and fence it off."
"I never looked at it that way."
"Time you did."[1]

In this narrative, father and son discuss how human beings create "fences," including physical and social walls between ethnic groups, generations, and individuals. It is likely that your middle school students are noticing such fences and are beginning to learn about those who live across the fences in their own lives. They are probably asking questions about gender, race, ethnicity, language, social class, disability, age, and religion.[2] Peck's moving novel offers a peek into the world of a 12-year-old boy who wonders about the real value of socially constructed fences, some of which he wants to tear down, others that he comes to understand, if not accept. This chapter offers ideas for teaching Peck's novel in ways that you can adapt to the modern texts you get to teach to your students.

For adolescents, peeking across the fence into the adult world can be like a trip into a new country where you can venture on and explore new territories. In Peck's novel, the boy's father, Vermont farmer Haven Peck, makes ends meet in the late 1920s by slaughtering pigs for others to eat. Why does the elder Peck earn a living that way? Do people really have to kill and eat pigs? Peck's son has to come to terms with adult reality.

Writings like Peck's help students discover other modern-day people and cultures. It can be frightening and confusing for adolescents to traverse childhood fences, but reading about life beyond one's fences can also be fun, engaging, and relevant to students' lives. So can imagining life beyond Earth's galaxy in novels like *Commander Chris and the Mystical Orb* by Mark Mattison. Students get to explore key ideas that can help meet school curriculum and Common Core State Standards for English Language Arts in areas like craft and structure as well as the ways authors of long works use some of the same literary devices as those who write short stories.[3]

As a middle school teacher, you have the honor and responsibility to guide students across fences into the stories about other persons and places, helping them to engage various literary forms and themes depicting what may be unfamiliar cultures. You can inspire students to learn how to interpret, understand, and respond critically to modern literature in the context of their own multimedia lives as they cross literary fences into novel territory.

This chapter explains how you can teach modern literature by delving with your students "into, through, and beyond"[4] a work of fiction. What follows also explains how to apply these strategies to any novel—classical as well as contemporary—in ways that are appropriate for your community. In fact, each subsequent chapter builds on the previous one and discusses different strategies that you can add to your traveling trunk of teaching options.

MOVING INTO, THROUGH AND BEYOND A BOOK

The California Literature Project recommends planning lessons to help student "into, through, and beyond" the literature.
Specifically:

Get into the book by
  • Encouraging students to make initial predictions
  • Providing background information
  • Identifying text-related vocabulary
Work through the book by
  • Reading aloud to the students
  • Having students read aloud and silently during class
  • Challenging students through active reading
  • Guiding students to write about the work
  • Connecting the book to students' lives
  • Fostering class discussion with student- and teacher-generated questions

Move beyond the book by
- Assessing student comprehension with performance and/or product options
- Assigning projects and essays
- Getting students involved in research about the book and its culture(s)
- Inspiring students to read more[5]

As you read further in this chapter, you can add to your suitcases, teaching ways that contemporary authors employ the essential elements of fiction. Here are concrete examples from Peck's novel to demonstrate how you can teach even reluctant readers the skills and literacies that they need in order to flourish in today's multicultural, multimedia societies.[6]

PREPLANNING THE UNIT

To ease your anxiety if you are teaching a book for the first time, estimate how much class time you need to spend on the book. Consider the following:

- Your school's homework guidelines and curricular goals
- The language arts standards of your course
- The interests, skills, and needs of your students, perhaps as reported by teachers who have had the students in English the previous year

Estimate how many pages of fiction your students can handle per day. Then plan a realistic reading schedule before launching the unit.

Depending on the book you are teaching, you may find it useful to bring in picture books to supplement your lessons. For example, to prepare for or expand the conversation about fences and society, bring in and talk about *Talking Walls* written by Margy Burns Knight and illustrated by Anne Sibley O'Brien. The book can be used to launch discussions about ways that figurative walls and fences may be used both to separate and/or protect. Picture books provide background information about people, places, and events that help student better understand the fictional worlds you may choose to explore with your students.

Deciding What Vocabulary

Vocabulary study is a topic to consider pedagogically before and during students' reading. For example, if you did not grow up on a farm, you may lack experience of the smells and sounds needed for teaching Peck's novel set in rural Vermont. The same may be true for your students. Be sure to introduce the students to the cultural language of the text; identify the specific vocabulary that students might not know, and determine how best to provide definitions or elicit definitions from them. It is perfectly fine for you to give students definitions of words unique to the book. Words that they need to add to their speaking and writing vocabulary can be handled differently. What words do students need to know during the next 40 days, the next 40 months, and the next 40 years?

Also consider having students create their own lists of new words as they read. Have them write in their journals and indicate the page number for each word or phrase. Then you can pull 20 or 25 words common to their lists, supply appropriate definitions, and discuss a few of them as they relate to the book. You can also ask the students to check any print or digital dictionaries and then write their own one-sentence definitions that fit the context of their reading. It is not useful to have students learn all the definitions of every vocabulary word on the list. Focus instead on the words that help them understand this particular piece of text.

Record It! Video Journaling

If students are already interested and motivated, you might want to allow groups of two or three students to make 45–60-second video recordings based on their written journals. You can ask them to write one journal entry as a group, collaborating on the content, but then delegating responsibilities for: (1) final drafting for reading on camera, (2) operating the camera, and (3) editing out any retakes. With most digital cameras, your young filmmakers can video in a compressed format and burn the video to a DVD or upload it to your school's computer server.

In some cases, you might allow them to post their video journals to a school server or public site like YouTube, but only after making sure that they will not identify themselves personally on the recordings or in the accompanying text captions. Remind them to hold the camera steady to avoid jerky movements, shoot images to capture the subject from mid-chest to top of the head, and, to create a more professional video journal, speak from an outline written on large cue cards. Students should include copies of the video script outlines in their journals.

For assessment, remind your budding video producers that video journals should display neatness, clear images, and good visual grammar, and be edited so the viewer-listener can follow along. On final drafts, hold them responsible for correct pronunciation and spelling in print journals.

COVERING IS NOT THE SAME AS TEACHING

Until students can understand and engage with a text, you are not ready to go to the next piece of literature, as moving too quickly leads to superficial student understandings. On the other hand, moving too slowly misses opportunities for greater textual engagement. So determine students' critical abilities, monitor their progress, and make appropriate scheduling and pedagogical adjustments as you go.

You can help them read more deeply, critically, and efficiently as you teach them a range of strategies to increase their reading comprehension. Your students may be familiar with some of these ideas but, because adolescents seem to have a more positive attitude toward more recently written literature, it often is better to teach and add to these approaches to reading literature while working with a modern book rather than with a more challenging classic novel or complex poetry. Reviewing what has been taught is an efficient use of time, especially if you present the same information in new ways.

GETTING INTO THE BOOK

A great way to begin a unit on the novel is to have students create a "novels" section in their written journals or a new folder on the digital one, and then to create subsections for the novels that you assign throughout the year. Their journal is a personal place for them to write their own reading summaries, responses, reflections, vocabulary study, diagrams, and drawings along with questions similar to the "Five Ws and H" mentioned in chapter 2 on teaching the short story.

Playing Online Audio and Video Files

If quality readings of the opening of the book are available online, you might want to play excerpts from them in class. YouTube and other video-posting websites sometimes include acceptable fan readings to be downloaded or played directly from the Internet. Avoid performance video clips that might frame the book visually for students before they have developed their own mental pictures of characters and settings. Chances are you have one or two tech-savvy students who can find recordings, download them, and bring them to you for previewing before playing them for their peers. Remember, what is done in your class reflects you.

Start lessons on journaling with open questions designed to get the students thinking and to familiarize them with this longer form of fiction. Questions might include: Do you recall a book that grabbed you from the first sentence? How would you define a "novel?" Other than length, how do you think a full-length book is different from a short story or a movie? Based on the title of this book, how do you think it relates to the essential question or themes we have been talking about so far this year? Try to create an open, exciting experience for students while avoiding any questions that would make your reluctant readers feel ill at ease. Resist commenting on their responses, even with facial expressions.

Your opening attitude sets the tone for the class. If they know that you enjoy fiction, they are more likely to read it expectantly. However, there is no reason to try to pretend false enthusiasm for a literary work you do not like. Even if you do not prefer reading fiction, you can share your enthusiasm for learning about something new. Of course, you want to allot time for them to read books they choose themselves. Several titles to consider appear at the end of this chapter.

Your young teens are not likely to take pleasure in a book if they do not understand the cultural context, time period, unusual references, and difficult vocabulary. Before you assign them to read too far in the book, spark their critical interest in the story and give them some helpful tools to begin enjoying and discussing the text right away.

Sparking Critical Interest in the Story

You can ignite interest in the book and elicit visual interpretation by having students do something as simple as examining the cover art of a paperback or the story illustrations in your class anthology. Give the students two or

Figure 4.1.   Illustration for Piggy Poem.

three minutes to examine that art and print individually or in small groups. Then ask them to predict and answer the following kinds of questions in their journals:

- Based on the graphic art, what do you imagine this book is about? (If there is a synopsis on the cover or first page, you might need to modify this question.)
- What have you already heard about this book—and does that word-of-mouth fit with your view of the artwork?
- What do you know about the topic/setting of the book? For example, for A *Day No Pigs Would Die*, "What do you know about raising pigs, the state of Vermont, or about the origins of baseball?"

No cover illustration? First check online bookstores or the publisher's website to see if you can find cover images for past paperback or hardcover editions. Even without a cover image, it's worth discussing the book design graphics. In this case, ask "Why do you think the publishers chose certain fonts, font sizes, colors, or word placements?" "What is the name of the font(s)?" "Why are there no graphics—photos, drawings, etc.?" Also talk about the publisher or reviewer comments—those promotions designed to convince the reader ahead of time what to think about a book. Where else do you hear or read comments about the arts (e.g., movie trailers and newspaper or Web ads for movies)?

These metatextual strategies—ways of talking about how texts communicate—create curiosity about the book. They also encourage students to own their own learning, since it is clear that they can learn from one another as well as from you. Students soon discover that it is educationally good to formulate and to express opinions (reasonable interpretations and evaluations) of texts. Finally, students who think only classical novels should be analyzed soon learn that modern texts can be examined as well as enjoyed—and that criticism can lead to greater enjoyment. In this case, criticism should not be limited to simple statements of opinions. Encourage students to expand their opinion statements with specific reasons. Remember, students do not have to like a literary work in order to appreciate it.

Locate and display images of the time period and/or part of the country to create intrigue. Picture books, encyclopedias, and the Internet are great sources for these images. Consider bringing in items to suggest characters or events and just setting them up in the classroom until needed. Sometimes a short poem on one of the topics in the books is just the spark to jump-start a book. These images and poems can be like travel posters advertising an adventure.

Using Student-Produced PowerPoint to Facilitate Early Discussion

As you begin discussion with students, write on the board one- or two-word summaries of their initial thoughts and feelings about the book. Then encourage interested students to compose simple PowerPoint slide(s) that contain one of these short summaries, selecting font and background colors designed to match the meaning of the summary. Students can add relevant highlighting or other features that help them explain their view of the book. Fonts and colors can "speak" to readers even though these visual images are not as literarily precise as "word language." This kind of assignment can teach media grammar—the psychology of color, size, and arrangement to influence messages. You can use online sites to familiarize yourself with media grammar if this is a new concept for you.

A student interested in drama might want to speak the word(s) interpretively as a looping soundtrack for each image. The student would try to say the word or phrase in a way that adds to the visual interpretation (combining oral and visual). For example, a student could contrast her or his oral interpretation with that of common text-reading software found today on most computers. Students rarely think about how computerized "reading" interprets language (such as computer-generated digital voice messages on GPS products and telephones).

Your tech-savvy teens may be interested in experimenting with a version of the PechaKucha format for this preliminary activity or as a final project. Simply put, this means creating 20 slides set to advance every 20 seconds as a speaker narrates.[7] You could create and model this format to introduce this modern novel using modern technology to supplement your instruction, then assign this PechaKucha format later in the school year.

Finally, students doing multislide presentations (one word or phrase per slide) can add a sound track that relates to the novel's subject or characters. Google the topic "pig lyrics." Students may wish to create one for Peck's novel. PowerPoint's player function creates a short "motion picture" that sets a prereading benchmark for later review. If students enjoy seeing the PowerPoint in class, consider showing it to them again at the end of the unit to discuss initial versus later impressions of the novel.

Taking a Random Walk through the Book

Ask students to write on a piece of paper any 10 numbers between the first and last page number of the book you are using. For example, 3, 7, 27, 59, 78, 87, 115, 143, 205, 212. Next, instruct them to turn to those pages, skim the paragraphs paying attention to names, dialogue, sentence structure, and anything that catches their attention. Copy into their journal a sentence from five different pages. Then, write a paragraph about what they think the sentences imply about characters, settings, and possible themes. Finally, meet in pairs and share the sentences and inferences. Return to these later to compare their early and later thoughts.

Applying Something Old to Something New

How about adapting one of those KWL charts that students probably used in elementary school? These kinds of graphic organizers that ask students what they *know*, *want* to learn, and have *learned* are useful resources to pull into the middle-level grades, too. Working with the familiar makes the unfamiliar less daunting. It's like seeing a McDonald's sign in the middle of the desert.

What do students know about Vermont (or the setting of your book), about the Shakers (or a particular group in your book), about the origins of baseball (or a cultural event in your book), or about this historical period? What do they hope to discover as they read? Save these charts for later in the unit. During the weeks that you are reading the book, an opening class activity could be to spend a few minutes filling in the L column or adding to the W column. If the book does not reveal answers to these questions, they could be the basis of a final project or performance for which students conduct brief research and then share in a written or artistic way what they have learned.

Organizing Quotations as an Appetizer

- Photocopy a randomized list of the quotations from the book you plan to teach. (Leave off the page numbers.)
- Ask the students to put the quotations in some kind of order that makes sense to them.
- Meet in pairs to compare the order. (Order is unimportant at this point. Thinking is.)
- Then talk briefly about what they think the book is about. What inferences can they make based simply on these quotations. (This is a good way to show the sentence structure the author uses, too.)

LETTING AUTHORS SPEAK FOR THEMSELVES

Although it is important to provide some background for the book, initially it is good to let the text speak for itself. Give the students only the information that they need to understand the beginning of the story. Then, as the story unfolds, supply additional information. Even if you have to do a lot of research yourself to prepare to teach an unfamiliar book, remember not to inundate the students with all of your newfound knowledge. TMI—too much information—can overshadow, even bury, the book. On a trip, it would be like touring five different museums on the same day—just too much to appreciate the craftsmanship of the works on display.

A host of textbooks, websites, academic books, and colleagues can help inform your own understanding of the text, but resist dumping all this newfound knowledge on the students. Focus on the basic aspects of the time and place that the students need to know in order to figure out the plot, setting, and characters in fiction. In carefully selected, age-appropriate texts, the authors can speak for themselves.

WORKING THROUGH THE BOOK

Adolescents, like many adults, enjoy hearing good readers. Think about how often you and your peers purchase or borrow audio books or attend events where authors read from their books. It is not surprising that one appealing way to begin teaching a book is to read portions aloud to your students. This gives struggling readers a chance to learn by listening and following along. It also helps English-language learners, partly because it connects the sound of the language to the printed words.

Since some international students' first language uses a non-English-style alphabet, they might need practice in associating sounds with the written English letters as they work to improve just their basic reading literacy. Hearing the words as they watch the text is another way to increase this association and expand their comprehension.

Try connecting early on with students' multiple intelligences by assigning different activities for them to do while listening in class. They might sketch in their journals, mold with clay, or jot notes in a chart about what is happening in the story. Since there is no "right" way to read, as long as students are keeping up and comprehending the text, engage nonaural learners with appropriate ways to formulate and express textual interpretations. Consider playing instrumental music during silent reading time. Music played in a rhythm that matches the beat of the heart at rest calms listeners and helps them to focus.

Fortunately, many books are now available in audio formats. People of all ages listen to voice recordings while computing, commuting, exercising, and even when patronizing libraries. The latter is rather ironic since until about the 4th century CE, all reading, even in libraries, was done out loud.[8] Recordings of some books are available online and from reading-for-the-blind programs.

Reading Silently

Although reading aloud to students is good pedagogy, students also need to be able to learn by reading silently. You can help students to stay on schedule by providing in-class reading periods. Doing so can eliminate the frustration for students unable to participate in class discussions simply because they are behind on reading. Consider having a prompt or question on the board before students arrive. Then ask them to use the first five to seven minutes of class to peruse their reading to find text evidence in the story to support their answer or just to catch up on the reading.

As they write, you can circulate among them, taking attendance, yes, but also stopping near individuals and adding to your own notes indications of student engagement in the task. Journaling in this simple writing activity focuses students on the day's topic while you complete record-keeping. Observing their responses and watching them read can help you identify students who may be experiencing difficulties. Pay attention to how long it takes individuals to complete a page of reading. If you have concerns and do not yet have the expertise to address them yourself, seek the assistance of a reading specialist or the advice of the department chair or a colleague.

Figure 4.2. Circulate and assist as needed.

Students Reading to the Class and in Pairs or Groups

Occasionally, give students the chance to read aloud with the whole class, in small groups, or to a partner. Students who especially dislike reading aloud may need to practice in a nonthreatening setting. You can invite such students to read aloud short passages of their choosing just to you; you can track their progress and encourage them personally. Remind students that public speaking skills are important for most careers and reading aloud can help them practice their articulation—clear pronunciation of words. Students work harder at it if they know that reading aloud is a significant step toward career success.

Of course you have the hams, too. Many of your young teens just love to play parts from the book, and the dialogue in the text often provides exceptional ways for students to gain insight into the personalities of the characters in the book. Some students even come to class begging to read a particular part. Encourage it, but also be sure to promote fairness by giving all interested students a turn reading aloud the most popular characters. Play the narrator if you want to ensure that the reading stays on track, but be wary of calling on students to read "cold."

READING TEXTS ACTIVELY

It is essential for students' future education that they become efficient readers. Students know that people read books for fun, but they might not realize that adults also read both fiction and nonfiction simply to enrich their lives. In short, middle school students can deepen their understanding of different cultures as well as the human condition. Students benefit when they learn that active reading requires careful attention to the text, regardless of the medium—print or electronic, aural or visual. In travel, it's like learning to read the road signs—those with words and those with universal symbols. It helps you get where you're going without getting lost . . . too many times.

One essential skill in active reading is recognizing how subparts of a larger text relate to one another. These text structures, sometimes called "rhetorical structures," include descriptive, sequential, enumerative, cause-effect, problem/solution, and compare/contrast relationships within a text.

Middle school students may recognize some of text features in expository nonfiction works and may need to be reminded of ways that text features work in fiction. In this case, they are paying attention to chapter titles, images that may be added to certain pages, diagrams, maps, charts, or unexpected spacing that sometimes appear in fiction. Chapter titles often are signals of what's to come. Authors of modern fiction sometimes choose to write from multiple points of view and the only clue to these changes may be an extra space between paragraphs or a flourish or line to indicate this shift in perspective. Students may be confused if they miss these subtle signals and cues.

Learning to Use Text Structure

If text structures are not defined or explained in your anthology, several websites include definitions and mini-lessons to help you get started. Most suggest that teachers

- Introduce the idea that expository texts have a text structure.
- Introduce common text structures.
- Show examples of paragraphs that correspond to each text structure.
- Examine topic sentences that clue the reader to a specific structure.
- Model the writing of a paragraph that uses a specific structure.
- Have students try writing paragraphs that follow a structure.

For students who are proficient with paragraph organization, do the last three steps (above) with longer chunks of text or entire chapters.[9]

Assuming Personae in Fiction and Biographical Writing

Once they have "met" the main characters, ask your students to sign up to keep a journal from one character's perspective and, as they continue reading the book, to write two- or three-sentence entries for each section of assigned reading. Allot in-class time for small-group meetings of those writing from the same character's point of view. Mix it up some days and construct groups with different characters meeting together and to talk for a few moments about the way their character is addressing the problems in the book:

- Is she or he making wise or foolish choices?
- Assisting or thwarting the protagonist?
- Alike or different from someone the student knows?

If your students have enjoyed this personae perspective, you could follow up their reading of the book with an assignment that asks them to connect their person with current events and answer questions like, "What would your chosen character have to say about something in the news today?" "What issues would interest them?" "What television shows or movies would she or he like?"

Students even make use of these techniques in their own "texting" and blogging without realizing it. You may be surprised by the number of students who employ such narrative skills by participating in online "fan" discussion groups or "fan fiction" websites where fans publish their own stories based on the characters and settings established by print authors or TV/movie producers. Yet students do not necessarily recognize the use of these techniques in fiction even if they watch many movies or voraciously read young adult stories. Most students do not see how these structures "work" in school-assigned reading. That is one of your jobs as their teacher.

When students read fiction, they enter into a story created by the author. They let the author transport them into a projected, imaginary world that shapes readers' views of the text's subject.[10] In order to accomplish this world-projecting storytelling, authors structure

- Relationships among characters
- Characters' motives
- Causal relationships between characters' thoughts and actions

Because of these author-created structures—along with readers' own real-life relationships—students quickly "learn to form expectations about a [fictional] text."[11] As they learn more about the structure of nonfiction, students' expectations rise in similar ways.

Tracking Character Development

Students wonder why characters think and act in particular ways. As they read, students speculate about why particular events lead to other events—like the age-old conundrums about why bad things happen to good people. Students begin mentally asking the same kinds of questions about fiction that they are starting to ask about life. Middle school language arts teachers can help them "to decide which strategies [or "techniques"] they should use to comprehend, interpret, and evaluate what they are reading."[12] As they learn to identify and examine the impact of intratext structures in their own reading, students engage the story or article as if conversing with the author and the characters.

Encourage students to write the questions in their journals as they arise in their reading. Then, when each question is answered, record that, too. Include the page number(s) so they can refer to them during classroom discussion and when writing about their experiences reading the book. This personal and sometimes communal dialogue in class discussion about the text is the nature of all literacies, regardless of the medium.

So how do students move from the book or article itself toward a more critical dialogue with it? The conversation has to start somewhere, but your students probably have not practiced taking notes when they see a movie, play a YouTube video, listen to an audio book, or read fiction. Therefore, a reader-response journal can effectively initiate their personal dialogue with a text. Here, they can make note of important passages, what they enjoy about the text, note important material for later study, and record questions.

Sticky notes can also be used in their textbooks, and some e-books have features for inserting annotations, too. Then they can copy those thoughts into their separate journal notebook, or save or copy into their digital journals while keeping the sticky notes or electronic notations for quick reference in their books. Suggest that students use different color techniques to code story elements or text structure and log their reactions, especially their questions. Propose that students use a specific color for specific characters or to note passages that strike them as potentially effective video or audio scenes for later recording.

Encourage students to visualize what is going on in the book based on the author's direct and indirect statements. Drawing maps and pictures in their journals helps some students hold on to those visualizations. Some students working online may find themselves doing searches to view items or places mentioned in their reading. Encourage such exploration; it expands understanding and enriches the overall reading experience.

Symbols for Marking Text or Making Journal Notes

Consider using text-marking symbols to remind students of the kinds of things that they should be noting and responding to in the text. Here are some basic text-engaging symbols:

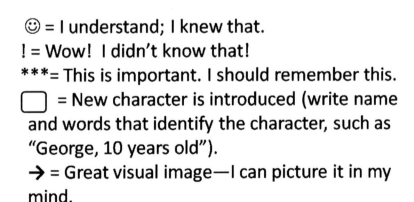

☺ = I understand; I knew that.

! = Wow! I didn't know that!

*** = This is important. I should remember this.

☐ = New character is introduced (write name and words that identify the character, such as "George, 10 years old").

→ = Great visual image—I can picture it in my mind.

? = I don't understand. Ask about this.

Figure 4.3. Symbols for marking tests.

HIGHLIGHTING ACADEMIC VOCABULARY

What about terms in the text that the students should be adding to their own speaking and writing vocabulary? What about words used in the book that also appear in the reading and conversations your students have in other classes? And what about general academic vocabulary used primarily in school? You can help students learn the meanings of and connections among words by identifying such academic words on their vocabulary list and asking students themselves to find the definitions in print or online dictionaries. Invite students to list the words with definitions alphabetically on a class website or to post comparative definitions on a class wiki. The wiki itself then serves as a kind of study sheet that students can print out or download to their own computers. The words that are specific to the text, though, are those for which you can provide definitions.

Like many veteran teachers, you may find it productive to maintain a word wall to which you add new words throughout the school year. Seeing is believing. As students view the wall daily, they catch on that it is important to learn and use the words. On a trip, it's like seeing the same advertisement on road signs. Soon you remember them and may even decide to visit the site or purchase the product. The same can happen with your students. What they see, they remember; what they remember, they are likely to use.

Reinforce the importance of students using new vocabulary words in their prose by offering small amounts of extra credit for incorporating the terms in writing for other classes. See chapter 1 for ways to organize such an assignment. Challenge your students to use their vocabulary regularly even if they are teased for their increased sophistication and even if they earn a maximum of 10 extra credit points per quarter!

Dividing the Labor Can Multiply the Results

Since many middle school students love to talk anyway, create small groups that will be responsible for showing the meaning of a few words on the list. For example, if your list is 20 words, have five groups responsible for four words each and do the following

"Calling on Cell Phones for Vocabulary Study—A Mini-Assignment":

1. Locate the assigned word in the literature being studied.
2. Determine how it is used (what part of speech) in the context of the literary work.
3. Look up the word in an online dictionary that includes more than synonyms.

4. Locate images to help classmates understand the meaning of each assigned word. The image should reflect the literal and/or figurative meaning—one that will serve as a mnemonic for the word. OR

5. Create original images, then photograph them using the camera feature on a cell phone or digital tablet. You can also stage a scene with toys, or have classmates pose for a scene.

6. Consider color, font, image, or music to portray the meaning of the word as used in the context of the literary work being studied.

7. Then, as a group, create a one- to two-minute PowerPoint, Prezi, or video presentation that reflects what the group has learned about the words, including original sentences using the words and synonyms, antonyms, and or appositives to help clarify the meaning.

This assignment utilizes the range of skills of a typical group of middle school students who represent multiple intelligences and has active and passive tasks that appeal to students of both genders.

The assignment is sure to be a success if you

- Design the lessons carefully to last three to five days.
- Have written instructions to supplement the oral ones.
- Demonstrate a sample product with the class helping you gather information on one vocabulary word.
- Allot group meeting time for 15–20 minutes of class during the half of class the first week that the piece of literature is being studied.
- Set a kitchen or digital timer each day to reserve the closing five minutes for clearing up and closing the lesson for the day.

It's worth the in-class time for such group work and language study, providing an opportunity to do no-stress formative assessments of your students that will help you adjust your instruction as you plan for further lessons. It gives students time to do what they do best—work together and learn from one another while exploring and applying skills that meet a range of Common Core State Standards.

Using Wiki Software to Create Student-Contributed Vocabulary Definitions

A "wiki" (like wikipedia.com) is a website for developing user-contributed content, especially encyclopedic definitions. Free wiki software enables anyone to start an online wiki on any topic, and even to limit access to users with necessary passwords. Best of all, language arts wikis provide a means for users to interact about words. Any approved user can add a new term, contribute a definition, edit or expand a definition, or even relate a definition to another word or text (such as a sentence or paragraph from the book). Wikis save records of all changes so you can see who is contributing, what they are contributing, and whether or not you need to resubmit an entry that was mistakenly removed or incorrectly edited.

Public wikis, like Wikipedia, generate disputes over differing interpretations of the meanings of words. Be sure to set down some rules for civil engagement among students—like posting only positive contributions, respecting classmates' opinions, and thanking others for their helpful postings before critiquing their contributions.

DEVELOPING PERSONAL
CONNECTIONS TO MODERN NOVELS

Relating through Common Circumstances

Textual literacy is the ability to critically relate fictional worlds to one's own life. These reader-to-self, reader-to-world, or reader-to-text relationships can work two ways—as a mirror and as a window. The novelist's or essayist's imaginative story is usually a mirror for some people even if it is not a mirror for others, such as your students. As a mirror, texts reflect familiar characters, settings, and situations. As a window, the same text could introduce students to unfamiliar people, places, and circumstances—including cultures, ethnicities, races, and geographies. Metaphorical windows can help students simultaneously understand themselves, their communities, other persons, and other communities.

As often as you can, select books that help expand your students' understanding of themselves and of others, to see across as through fences into novel territory. *Nerd Girls (The Rise of the Dorkasaurus)* and *The Downside of Being Up*, two recent novels by Alan Sitomer, though edgy, speak to issues on the minds of young teens. Include options to read nonfiction, like biographies and autobiographies, and see your reluctant readers bloom into eager ones.

Students soon discover that another person's mirror can serve as a window for getting to know those who are different from themselves. Reading then serves as a form of hospitality, like inviting neighborhood newcomers for dinner and conversation about mutual life stories.[13] Windows become venues for self-understanding as students begin to see similarities among those they read about and those with whom they live.

Reading about others enables students to see what all human beings have in common, across their cultural fences. Novels and essays express not only cultural particularities of time and place but also common aspects of the human condition, such as fear and loneliness, joy and delight, agreement and disagreement. For instance, each adolescent in every culture must eventually come of age; the process is universal even though it takes different cultural forms.

Relating through Personal Connections

Often students need encouragement and role modeling to learn how to connect personally with fictional and biographical texts. Please do not hesitate to identify appropriate personal connections that you notice between the text and your own life and encourage students to do the same. One way to do so is to ask them to write personal responses to the books and articles they read, and then to discuss those responses with their families, friends, or classmates.

Encourage conversation, but guide it so it does not become denigrating or disrespectful of what is different or simply unfamiliar. Choosing culturally relevant books and articles means selecting writing by and about the ethnicities represented in your school or classroom and also means featuring literature that introduces and expands your students' experience to those groups not represented there.

Although the Internet usually brings together like-minded people to communicate about things they already have in common (social networking, for instance, tends to be more "intra-culture" than cross-cultural), the Internet can

Figure 4.4. Students reading, writing, and thinking about texts.

also provide amazingly wide windows to cultures beyond students' existing life experience.[14]

HONORING STUDENT PRIVACY

Ask students to journal about their personal connections with the world of the book; such journaling promotes discussion because students articulate in writing thoughts they can then paraphrase out loud. Just remember, though, that some students are reticent about reading or discussing their reflections with the entire class. Respect their privacy and you can gain their trust and motivate them to read deeply and write honestly.

Consider giving students the option in class of folding down the page in their written journals if they do not want you to read their reflections. If you provide that option, keep your promise. But do inform them that if anything they write and leave open for you to read makes you believe they are a danger to themselves or others, you are bound by law to report it to authorities.

Also warn students about posting personal information online, since privacy is a major issue in the information age. One of the reasons that social networking websites such as Facebook are so popular is that students can regulate who they allow to access their postings by approving who their "friends" are—those who can access their website. But no public site is totally secure and what is posted today as a lark may be embarrassing or even dangerous tomorrow.

Privacy and tact are important literary issues; openness and honesty are essential to building trust in the classroom. So write in your own journal frequently, right along with your students. Doing so not only models this kind of writing but also reminds you of what it is like to reveal text-to-self connections with others. Share with your students some of the experiences you have had with your parents, siblings, and friends—and also admit that there are some experiences you would not, and they should not, write about online. If you respect students' privacy, they are more likely to share their journals with you—and they learn that responding to readings should be an ethical as well as an academic practice. In other words, invite rather than insist that they share or show what they write to others.

INSPIRING CLASS DISCUSSION

English teachers often approach the study of a book or article by giving students a list of discussion questions that can effectively ease students into the reading and demonstrate the types of questions and ideas that they should be considering. But you foster better, more engaging discussions when you encourage students come up with their own questions.

Regardless of how you settle on the questions, try a variety of discussion group formats—pairs, small groups, and the entire class. Some students are more inclined to read their journal entries and discuss personal responses to the text if they are in smaller groups. Still, middle school students like to push the envelope, test the boundaries, and interject topics that are on the edge—just for fun or attention—so it is important to circulate among them as they read and talk about their writing. If a student offers an inappropriate remark, a moment's eye contact, a subtle head shake, or a quiet admonition from you should be enough to refocus the discussion. As on a road trip when the sheriff is spotted, drivers adjust their driving behavior, and so do your students; when you are nearby, they are reminded of the rules of the road as they pertain to your class.

Interspersing Literature Circles

Think about setting up literature circles for a few chapters in the book your class is studying together. For this approach to reading and discussing literature, you create small groups of five or six students and assign or let them draw for roles to perform certain tasks. These responsibilities may include:

- Connecting what the class has read already and the book they currently are reading
- Pointing out ways words on the vocabulary list are being used
- Selecting a particularly interesting, humorous, or thought-provoking passage to read aloud to the members of the group
- Drawing a picture of a scene that is crucial to the plot or understanding of a particular character
- Bringing in an appropriate prop that illustrates an incident or symbolizes a character
- Keeping time to ensure that the group completes the tasks in the allotted time

The tasks can vary depending on the book you have chosen. See the Internet for numerous configurations of literature circles and roles based on the work of Harvey Daniels, and consider adapting this structure when reading a complex nonfiction article, too.

Adapting Think-Pair-Share Strategies

Having students work independently to think about a prompt, and then pair up and talk with a partner before one or both of them shares or reports to the whole class is an effective way to begin discussions about difficult passages or controversial topics, especially with shy students or those who tend to leap over into the driver's seat if not kept in their seat belts. Consider adding another layer to this familiar strategy and recommend that students find support for their responses in the text or article you are having them read that day.

As the students are writing their answers, you could circulate among them, looking over their shoulders, seeing who goes directly to a likely place in the text to find the answer. Don't be surprised if they go to an unexpected section and still come up with a valid response. When you notice that the majority of the students have something written, you can call on the students who have different but valid—maybe even opposing—answers. Then ask the class who agrees that Student A's answer seems logical and who thinks Student B's answer seems stronger, and then ask students to find additional evidence for either side.

Of course, modeling first and providing answer stems can help students get started. For example, in Gary Schmidt's *Wednesday Wars*, "I believe Mrs. Baker is . . . because . . . and this section on page . . . supports my observation." Or "Character A is a jerk . . . because . . . and when you look at page . . . you'll see that I'm right." Or "The passage on page . . . suggests the principal is prejudiced about . . . because of the way the author uses negative images." Or whatever.

Even though you may decide to conduct whole-class discussions, you still could incorporate some of the literature circle roles. If the majority of your students are reliable about completing homework, once you introduce the roles, invite students to sign up for the role they would like to play for the next lit circle discussion. And then assign for homework their gathering information to fill that role during the next class meeting.

On that day, you could have the students playing particular roles meet to compare answers during the first 10 minutes of class and then invite them as a panel to present their answers to the class. Or, after the small-group meeting, you could reconfigure the class so that each group includes at least one person fulfilling each role and have them "teach" that group what they learned. You may know this organizational pattern as jigsaw grouping. Each of these strategies increases students' confidence about speaking out loud among their peers and deepens their understanding of the text and ways others respond to it. Your English-language learners may flourish in these settings.

WRITING ABOUT A TEXT IN CLASS

Develop three questions about the recent reading, then ask students to answer one using specific references and selected quotations from a specified section, such as five of the seven chapters read so far, and incorporate the illustrative facts and words smoothly into the text of their essay writing. Encourage answering the question in their thesis statement as part to their introduction paragraph, then writing two or three body paragraphs that make a hearty P.I.E. with lots of rich, meaty filling, concluding with a summary or reflection on what they have written in the body paragraphs.

P = Point—state your point or position in response to the prompt.

I = Illustration—support your point with two or three direct references to the story. One of these can be a short quotation. "For example, . . ." (Give the page number in parenthesis following the reference or quotation.)

E = Explain the connection between your illustrations and your point: "This shows . . . ."

One of the themes in *A Day No Pigs Would Die*, for example, is often something must die in order for something else to live. When searching the novel, students find these examples: a cow nearly dies birthing the twin calves; a crow gobbles the frog; and the narrator's family eats animals they slaughter for food. Ultimately, Rob, the main character, suffers the death of his father and has to assist his mother with farm tasks, including killing his own pet pig so the family can have food to eat. A few students become so enamored of Rob's pet, Piggy, that they become vegans—at least while studying the novel. Of course, even as vegans they have to consume formerly living things. All life depends on other life.

Figure 4.5. Pie.

TESTING THOUGHTS ON THEME

While studying a book, students can examine further concepts of a theme—the overall message(s) of a text or what the text is trying to say about a topic. The concept of literature itself is sometimes defined by a work's universal themes about human nature and the human condition as well as by its aesthetic qualities. Themes, though, generally are statements about topics, not just the topics themselves; themes require a verb to indicate the author's viewpoint. "Life is grand" is a theme; "Life" is a subject but not a theme. "Fences make good neighbors" is a theme; "fences" is simply a topic.

Your students may have been introduced to this kind of thinking about literature in elementary school and used the SWBST approach. There they would fill in a graphic organizer in which they record what Somebody Wanted, But, So, and Then to reflect the main characters, the conflict, the attempts to solve it, and then the resolution. Using this SWBST chart may be a good place to start and then move on to the sentence statements about the book.

After you have explained to students the concept of a universal theme, let them try to discern what may or may not be a universal theme expressed through the text. Encourage students to experiment with theme statements in their own reading and journaling. What is the story saying to them? Also ask them to test or verify their ideas about themes with specific, supporting examples from the beginning, middle, and end of the novel. Students soon notice that most books have at least two or three overarching ideas that can be summarized in thematic statements that capture most individual responses to the text. In the biography or autobiography, what experiences are described that reflect what is true about people in general?

GRADING STUDENT RESPONSES TO A BOOK

Encourage formal and informal student responses to the book. Informal writing is more personal, so students should earn full credit just for demonstrating that they have read the selected material and responded responsibly to the prompt. Formal writing, on the other hand, calls for more precise literary analysis and is graded for form and accuracy as well as content. Consider the following samples from student journals:

Cressy's journal essay (Journal Entry #1) was a "Five Ws and H summary" (the journalistic who, what, where, why, when, and how) based on 7–10 verbs that describe the plot. She wrote this entry after two months of studying the elements of fiction and reading a number of short stories for which students were writing this kind of summary.

Robert cut school because he was made fun of. He found a cow who was in labor and having a calf. He is in Vermont, and 12 years old. He desperately tries to help the cow, because she is in pain and when the cow chokes, he reaches down her throat and pulls out the "goiter." She bites his arm and pulls him all around. His arm was gnawed and flesh was missing. He gets stitches and after being in bed for about a week, he goes to help his pa. Their neighbor that owns the cow thanks Robert for helping her, and gives him a pig! Robert is excited. His dad informs him of the care it takes to own a pig. Then they talk some more.

About a week after beginning a book, once students have closely read and discussed the exposition, your students should be ready to write personal responses, normally by answering "what" and "why" questions. Reading their personal responses helps you to learn which parts of the story interest students as well as whether students are missing important details that would then need to be addressed in class. You also learn more about the students as people—which can help with planning subsequent lessons to better meet learners' academic needs and accommodate their varied interests.

To prepare the students to write analytically, ask them to write journal entries in which they focus their attention on the elements of fiction or specific literary devices. For example, Kristen chose to write about symbols and similes, demonstrating an understanding of the former but not the latter device. Her incomplete Journal Entry #2 did not include an explanation of why each of her quotations is a symbol or a simile. Her entry revealed that she needed help identifying the ways that authors use symbols and similes; after she and others had pretest reviews in class, Kristen handled these kinds of questions well on the test.

Peck uses symbols as similes. On page number 104, it says, "And during fair week, I guest it's like a big brass band that can't stop playing." Another time he uses a symbol is still on page 104. It says, "Just like a mouth I know that's got blackberry all over it." These are both symbols in the book.

Warren rambled in Journal Entry #3, but his entry revealed which incidents caught his attention and which ones needed clarification. Sometimes students ask questions in class; other times, questions arise only in students' writing.

One of the things about this book is that it will start out with a conflict, then tell why that conflict arose. For instance, in the end of this section of the . . . [*sic*]. There is a man that goes and digs up his daughter from her grave. I didn't really understand the whole conflict of why he couldn't dig her up. Oh, also we now have proof that Robert is a Shaker because he goes to the meetings. I'm amazed that a pig would get to be as big as twelve year old boys. Because unless they get any bigger than that I probably wouldn't believe it was unless I saw it.

MOVING BEYOND THE TEXT:
ASSIGNING PROJECTS AND ESSAYS

As you do when planning each assignment, determine what you need to know about student understanding and design product or performance assessments through which students can demonstrate that knowledge.

Differentiating Assessments

Plan a wide variety of projects for assessing students via multiple intelligences. Identify projects that students enjoy, especially those that tie the book to their lives and include a written component that supplements their presentation. Design assessments to measure what you need to know and provide rubrics so students are certain to demonstrate that skill or knowledge. For example, let

- A musically inclined student write a song about the book or choose songs that appropriately reflect certain characters.
- An aspiring filmmaker produce a scene of a significant incident from the book.
- A photographer bring in photos of real places or staged scenes that reflect key settings or themes.
- A pair of drama buffs create and perform a short reading of a revealing scene and use simple props or wear simple costumes.

Each project or performance should include a brief writing or speaking component in which students refer to specific passages in the text that influence their decisions as they worked on this assessment project.

Below are some creative ideas adaptable to most classes and provide valid measurement for student records. The caution when assigning differentiated assessments is to monitor how much time each project is taking and to make adjustments so that students can complete your assignments without impinging on the homework time required for other courses. Your colleagues are sure to appreciate your thoughtful consideration of them and the work they are doing with the students you share.

Constructing Poems

Invite students to write a found poem based on the text you are studying. The literary equivalent of a collage, found poetry is often made from newspaper articles, street signs, graffiti, speeches, letters, or even other poems. "A pure found poem consists exclusively of outside texts: the words of the poem remain as they were found, with few additions or omissions. Decisions of form, such as where to break a line, are left to the poet."[15] For an assessment of your modern book, students could be required to use specific words and phrases they find in the beginning, middle, and end of the book and arrange these words and phrases into a found, but original, poem, or three short poems (one each for character, conflict, setting, or theme).

Students reading *A Day No Pigs Would Die* identify with the boy's physical and emotional growth and see that he is addressing the same kinds of social fences and same types of adult responsibilities that all adolescents must face. This may be the focus of their poems. When your students finish reading and begin discussing the entire book, ask them to capture these themes in a poem using exact words and phrases written by your author. Found poems can also be fun to record in audio and video format and played back to the class, using the principles discussed earlier for digitized presentations.

One poetic variation for this novel is a "Piggy Poem." Students write a 14–16-line poem about *A Day No Pigs Would Die* that portrays incidents, a memorable scene, or a favorite character. They may choose a specific poetic format and may enjoy writing

- An acrostic
- A lyric poem
- A limerick
- A sonnet
- A free or blank verse poem
- A shape poem

For these kinds of poems, evaluate the quality based on linguistic precision—vivid verbs and concrete nouns; fresh figurative language—hyperbole, metaphors, similes, symbols, and so forth; and, of course, factual accuracy with the novel. In her poem "Practice," seventh-grader Kristen seemed to be taken by the idea that although the boy, Rob, appears forced into becoming a man overnight, he really has been practicing for that role for much of the story.

> Tomorrow he is going to be a man.
> Yesterday he was a boy.
> It is hard for him, but he can.
> He can't play anymore with a toy.
>
> This man's name is Rob
> His father's name is Haven Peck
> The father taught him not to sob
> Haven did this slitting Pinky's neck.

Pinky is a hog.
But they found out she is a brood.
We will kill her in the winter fog.
Now she is going to be food.

It is Dad who died in May.
They were all sad.
Rob did the chores that day.
He couldn't just be a lad.

Another middle school student, writing about a different book (Jacqueline Woodson's novel *Locomotion*), reflects on a theme revealed through Lonnie, the main character, who is pondering the existence of God. Almina writes a pantoum-style poem, "Is It True?" in a voice that reflects that of a questioning young teen—maybe that of Lonnie or of herself.

Could there really be God?
So, is it true?
Lilli says so
I sorta-kinda believe it too

So, is it true?
They say he's everywhere
I sorta-kinda believe it too
But sometimes I don't see him no where

They say he's everywhere
I'm starting to believe
But sometimes I don't see him no where
I know he sees me

I'm starting to believe
So is it true
I know he sees me
Could there really be God?

LEARNING FROM TESTS

Test Analysis

Because students in middle school still are learning how to take tests and how to learn from the kinds of mistakes they make, schedule full-class meetings in your overall plans to prepare students to take those comprehensive assessments and then another class time to go over tests when you return them. On those posttest days, you could ask students to come with their self-selected reading books. If you finish your test analysis early, the students can begin or continue reading on their own in preparation for the next quarter's book report. This in-class independent reading time can be an opening to meet privately with the few students who may have done more poorly on the assessment than you or they expected. Often it is a minor issue that causes a major loss of points.

What topics should you cover during test analysis? First, ask the students to determine the kinds of errors they've made. Did they make errors because of

- Misreading the question or prompt
- Running out of time
- Misunderstanding a concept, term, or instruction
- Studying the wrong material
- Failing to respond to the question
- Missing clues to answers in the prompt or stem of a multiple choice question
- Other

Once the students determine the kinds of errors they have made, talk about ways to avoid them on the next test, and thus calm them down before the next assessment.

Analyzing Tests Can Lead to Student Confidence

You might choose to spend time talking about ways to develop the confidence that they are answering the questions correctly. One way is to have the students underline the verb that tells them what to do and put a rectangle around the direct object, the noun indicating what they should be looking for or working on. If they cannot write on the test/quiz, ask the students to write those key words on their answer sheet. Taking a few minutes to do something physical helps the test-takers focus on what is being asked of them.

If there has been vocabulary on the test or quiz, invite them to point out the clues in the sentences that could have helped the students know when they had chosen the correct response. For example, some sentences may have a synonym, an antonym, or a definition in the prompt question. As students learn to look for such clues, they are more likely to recognize the correct answers.

One of your additional tasks as a teacher is to help students develop better reading strategies and more efficient test-taking skills. Taking the time to do this immediately after administering the first few tests/quizzes is sure to reap positive benefits for both students and teacher. You are happier when students do well on your assessments, and you want to learn whether the assessments you plan actually reveal what you have taught. If, during your analyses with the students, you discover they are missing questions you were sure they would be able to handle easily, you may find it necessary to revise your questions or rework the layout of the tests/quizzes you administer.

It also is important to develop tests that ask the students to show what they know in a variety of formats—multiple choice, matching, true/false, paragraph writing, or short essay. This can be done incrementally. Early in the school year, design tests that include such a variety with questions requiring factual information in the first couple of sections, and then follow with prompts for short-answer responses. Those "fact questions" trigger the students' memories, and by the time they get to the sections that necessitate longer answers requiring them to show ability to interpret and connect the facts to other literature or life, the students usually feel confident they can handle this higher-level thinking. Depending on the skill development of the students in a particular year, you could reserve fact questions for interim quizzes, and focus on tests questions that require full sentence, paragraph, or essay responses.

CONCLUSION

As you prepare your reading list for the school year, check to make sure you have a variety of topics and genres that provide mirrors and windows to ensure that your students are learning more about themselves and about the world while they are meeting the Common Core State Standards for English Language Arts and/or the content standards set by your school. Modern books fit quite well into curriculum designed to be student friendly, culturally relevant to a broad range of students, and also academically rigorous.

For the most part, trust the power of the writing, read quickly, and then go back and discuss. You probably recall times in your education when a teacher or professor spent so much time analyzing the story, chewing it so much that it lost its flavor and you lost interest in ingesting the tasteless mush on your own. You, of course, want to avoid such blandness in your own teaching. Adapting ideas from this chapter and using the Internet to locate background information for your chosen book helps to enrich your instruction and capture their own hopes and fears in much the way Robert Peck does in his novel about Rob and his pet, Piggy.

With your careful attention, lessons utilizing and building on students' multimedia skills, and their multiple-intelligence learning styles, your student traveling companions will soon see that well-told stories and skillfully crafted essays can transcend the fences that people put up around themselves and between their communities. Your students discover that modern fiction, like *A Day No Pigs Would Die* and other novels such as those listed at the end of this chapter, can help all readers to erect humane gateways to shared understanding of the various experiences that separate and unify us as we seek to live harmoniously in what, at first, was novel territory.

MODERN NOVELS TO TEACH OR RECOMMEND TO STUDENTS

The City of Ember by Jeanne DuPrau: Twelve-year-old Lina and Doon live in the underground City of Ember and are instrumental in helping to prevent permanent darkness from overcoming the town. Movie version leads to an interesting compare-and-contrast activity.

Commander Chris and the Mystical Orb by Mark Mattison: Zoom off into outer space with skateboarder Chris and experience new people, new places, but old problems that require ethical decisions about friendships. This sci-fi adventure will expand minds and vocabularies of students intrigued by science and interested in sports.

Ella Minnow Pea by Mark Dunn: Written entirely as correspondence and set on the fictional island of Nollop (named after Nevil Nollop, author of the phrase "The quick brown fox jumps over the lazy dog," a sentence containing every letter of the alphabet), this novel demonstrates what happens when a town is forbidden to use certain letters in word or speech.

Holes by Louis Sachar: Louis Sachar's Newbery-winning book tells the story of Stanley Yelnats, who is wrongly accused of stealing and ends up at a boys' detention center called Camp Green Lake.

Hoot by Carl Hiaasen: Today's kids are bombarded with ideas about "green" living and how important it is to save the environment. Studying *Hoot* is a way to launch discussion and generate concrete solutions.

Joey Pigza Swallowed the Key (and sequels) by Jack Gantos: Jack Gantos's award-winning novels follow off-the-wall Joey Pigza as his zany behavior lands him in one laugh-out-loud predicament after another. The audio books are read by the author and are very entertaining.

The Last Book in the Universe by Rodman Philbrick: Spaz lives in a future where the Earth has been devastated by the "Big Shake," geographical regions are harshly governed by "latch bosses," and people are entertained by mini-probe needles shooting information right into their brains. The book prompts big questions about the future and whether one person can make a difference.

Time Stops for No Mouse by Michael Hoeye: Watchmaker mouse Hermux Tantamoq's slow-paced, hardworking existence gets turned upside-down when extraordinary aviatrix Linka Perflinger comes into his shop.

Uglies (and sequels) by Scott Westerfeld: Tally Youngblood lives in a future world where, at 16, all people are given an operation to make them beautiful. This book is perfect for older reluctant readers.

NOTES

1. Robert Newton Peck, *A Day No Pigs Would Die* (New York: Alfred A. Knopf, 1972), 18–19.

2. Fran Claggett, Louann Reid, and Ruth Vinz with Cammie Lin, *Daybook of Critical Reading and Writing: World Literature* (Wilmington, DE: Great Source Education Group, 2008), 105.

3. "English Language Arts Standards 'Anchor Standards' College and Career Readiness Anchor Standards for Language," *Common Core State Standards Initiative,* 2011. www.corestandards.org/the-standards/english-language-arts-standards/anchor-standards.

4. California Reading and Literature Project (CRLP) participants, *Literature for All Students: A Sourcebook for Teachers* (Sacramento: California Department of Education, 1985).

5. Adapted from CLRP participants, *Literature for All Students.*

6. Random House offers a free guide to "reaching reluctant readers" at www.randomhouse.com/highschool/RHI_magazine/pdf/scales.pdf. For example, millions of dollars are spent by school districts each year to purchase computerized reading programs; these programs test students on the novels they have read and reward them with points that ultimately lead to prizes and other incentives. Often, however, there is very little personal attention offered to readers in schools that use such programs. www.randomhouse.com/highschool/RHI_magazine/reluctant_readers/scales.html.

7. PechaKucha is an event where participants present 20 slides, each slide taking 20 seconds, so each presenter has a total of 6 minutes 40 seconds for his or her presentation. Macmillan Open Dictionary at www.macmillandictionary.com/open-dictionary/entries/Pecha-Kucha.htm (accessed May 13, 2013).

8. Alberto Manguel, *A History of Reading* (New York: Alfred A. Knopf, 1996), 42–53.

9. Adapted from "Using Text Structure" (Washington, DC: National Education Association, 2008)

10. National Council of Teachers of English, *Standards for the English Language Arts* (Urbana, IL: National Council of Teachers of English, 1996), 31.

11. For background on vocabulary squares, see Karen D'Angelo Bromley, Karen Bromley, and Judy Lynch, *Stretching Students' Vocabulary: Best Practices for Building Rich Vocabulary Students Need to Achieve in Reading, Writing and the Content Areas* (New York: Scholastic, 2002), 85.

12. National Council of Teachers of English, *Standards.*

13. See David I. Smith and Barbara Carvill, *The Gift of the Stranger: Faith, Hospitality, and Foreign Language Learning* (Grand Rapids, MI: Eerdmans, 2000).

14. Smith and Carvill, *The Gift of the Stranger.*

15. "Poetic Form: Found Poem." *Poets.Org: The Academy of American Poets,* 1997. www.poets.org/viewmedia.php/prmMID/5780 (accessed March 12, 2012).

Chapter Five

Teaching Classical Fiction

Where the Ghosts of the Past Speak Today

"Are you the spirit, sir, whose coming was foretold to me?"

"I am!"

"Who and what are you?"

"I am the Ghost of Christmas Past."

"Long past?"

"No. Your past. The things that you will see with me are shadows of the things that have been; they will have no consciousness of us."

Scrooge then made bold to inquire what business brought him there.

"Your welfare. Rise and walk with me."[1]

A ghost. Prophecy. Time travel—long before *Back to the Future*. Spooky! But Dickens's *A Christmas Carol* is also interesting, engaging, and moving—just the kind of offbeat adventure that middle school students enjoy. Then again, middle school students are adults in-the-making. They have the capacity to dig deeper than the surface narrative. Like adults, young teens have experienced regret, guilt, and hope. How appropriate that these students should read the works of authors who molded their deepest fears and wonderings into timeless works of fiction. This chapter can help you get started looking back at the classics and help your students see what these authors have to say to readers today as they look more closely at the craft and structure of literary writing, thus expanding their knowledge as they travel along this journey into more complex literary works.

Unfortunately, your students probably do not immediately see the value in the classics. Middle school students sometimes think, "If it's a classic, it must be old!" And, in adolescent logic, if it's old, how can it be good? It is your privilege as their language arts teacher to prepare your students to enjoy what may be the most challenging and rewarding reading experience of their school year. Charles Dickens's *A Christmas Carol* is a marvelous story to begin a classroom expedition into the classics, give students an opportunity to grapple with a work of exceptional craft and thought, and extend their learning experience across genres, cultures, and centuries, as recommended in the anchor standards of the Common Core State Standards.[2] Teaching the classics helps students learn about the past, aids in their understanding of the present, and prepares them for the future.

During their excursion back in time and into another place, your students will learn that authors of classical fiction use several of the same literary devices you have taught your young readers to pay attention to in works you already have read together. Of course, no classic is culture-neutral. Consider using *A Christmas Carol* by Charles Dickens because of its universal themes, mindful of the distinctly religious symbols and overtones. Even if you choose other novels that have remained relevant over time, such as those by Alcott, Golding, L'Engle, Lowry, Orwell, and Twain, the instructional and pacing ideas here will be useful to you.

The different level of attention to content and style of classical writing usually requires students to slow down and put into practice reading strategies that can be transferred to demanding reading in other content areas. The classics not only provide opportunities to study language and sentence structure in ways that some of the contemporary young adult books do not but also help students recognize and understand allusions to these older works that arise in contemporary art, music, and literature. Mainly, many of the classics simply are a joy to teach and read!

So, when you have a choice, carefully choose an appropriate balance of classical and contemporary texts that work in tandem to teach the students assigned to you, and select literary works that are fun to teach.

Even the most challenged readers develop a sense of confidence as learners when they can talk knowledgeably about the classical works that their older friends or siblings may have read in the honors and Advanced Placement courses. There is no good reason to deny them the pleasure of the classics. Carol Jago, author of the foreword to this book, has written compellingly about keeping the classics in the curriculum in her book *With Rigor for All: Teaching the Classics to Contemporary Students*. In some situations, just knowing the story will suffice. Depending on the school setting, you may find some of the well-written/drawn graphic novels of the classics will be more accessible to your students. Publishers are providing excellent support materials in graphic novel form for classics like *Great Expectations* by Charles Dickens.[3]

Perhaps the one important reason for studying a classic is to show students that, although times change, people don't. Still, it takes a different kind of preparation to allay apprehensions and ease students into understanding and appreciating the classic novel. For one thing, the classic novel is usually set in a time and place completely unfamiliar to contemporary middle school students. And a second, it likely was written for an audience with entirely different expectations of its writers.

MAKING THE CLASSIC ACCESSIBLE

Right away, make it easy for middle school students to get into the novel. Timing makes a difference. With *A Christmas Carol*, you could plan to begin the novel in December. Many television, movie, and theatrical performances of this well-known story run during the holiday period and numerous commercials allude to it. So, why not capitalize on the time of year? The season provides a milieu for reading the text, especially for students whose family may not observe this particular holiday; reading this particular classic may help them understand some of what they see and hear about Christmas. Another attraction for this book is that the students are surprised that the real story is not "all that long" and that they can comfortably finish it in the three and a half weeks between the traditional Thanksgiving and Christmas vacations.

You could use other bridges to the literature you decide to teach. You may find the classic you choose works better if you correlate it with the course work the students are studying in history or science. For example, you may decide to teach the classical thriller *Dr. Jekyll and Mr. Hyde* when students are studying an aspect of genetics in science, or *Call of the Wild*, *The Red Pony*, *Johnny Tremain*, or *Across Five Aprils* when they study American history.

Another way to ease student concerns about studying a classic novel is to prepare a study packet. When students complete the packet on their own, they experience a sense of accomplishment; the packet also provides a sense of security. The study packet does not need to be collected or graded for anything other than completeness. It simply supplements your teaching and supports student learning. In addition to (or in lieu of) a journal, the packet becomes a repository for information to study for the quarter or semester exam. Some of the individual class activities that follow are the kinds that students can do in a packet—vocabulary work or text-to-world connections, and the recording of current news that relates to issues raised in the classic novel you choose to teach.

Figure 5.1.   Scrooge.

GETTING INTO THE NOVEL—PROVIDING A CONTEXT

On the first day of the unit—after the students have made a classics section in their written or digital journals—lay out the context for the novel. In the case of *A Christmas Carol*, it is helpful to explain that, in 19th-century London, families with leisure time depended on literature for entertainment. They didn't have the technology of today and so relaxed after a long day of school or work through reading, not expecting the story to end quickly in order to get on to something else.

  Those readers enjoyed imagining what the people and places in the books look and act like; consequently, the authors wrote numerous pages to describe characters' physical appearances and relationships and to establish the setting in terms of time and place. Often these early novels would be read aloud by a family member sitting near a candle, lantern, or oil lamp while the rest of the family sat nearby and may have even closed their eyes and let the words of the author paint pictures in their minds. Clearly this was a different time. If you are teaching a fantasy novel, remind students of the different world the author may create. Resist the temptation to show pictures too soon.

Overview before Reading

After distributing the books, give the students a few moments to peruse them. Ask the students to examine any included graphics. As they begin reading, students may express disagreement with the choices the editors have made to depict characters or places. Their opinions are worth a discussion, so let it happen. It means they are paying attention. To raise interest in verifying suppositions, ask the students to take a random walk through their book as described in chapter 3. Young teens enjoy guessing and rejoicing when they are right!

As the students flip through the pages, invite them to point out what they see that is familiar to them. In *A Christmas Carol*, some recognize the names of Scrooge, Marley, and Tiny Tim. Many have seen television versions of this story with humans, Muppets, or cartoon characters playing the parts. This probably gives students a false sense of security—they know the story. On the other hand, the fact that the story is familiar might entice students to read the "real" one for themselves.

Is there anything unusual about the structure of the novel you have chosen? *A Christmas Carol* is divided into staves, not chapters. Staves are similar to the stanzas in traditional hymns or poems. Be sure to clarify formatting features in the book you are teaching, remaining aware of considerably longer descriptive passages than students are accustomed to, or a complete lack of chapter divisions at all!

Creating the Mood to Get Students into the Mood

From the first paragraph, build excitement about the book. Be creative. To help evoke the mood when you begin reading aloud, you may dim the classroom lights and ask the students to imagine they are sitting in a room lit by an oil lamp and heated by a fireplace. If your classroom accommodates such an arrangement, pull your chair into a place where the students can sit on the floor around you. Read slowly and dramatically. Ask them to visualize the story—to let the author's words "paint a picture" on the canvas of their minds. Yes, they are likely to be wiggly; that's okay. Just pause, give them the "eye," smile, and continue reading. For some of them, it may have been years since they last sat and listened to a story.

When you finish a particularly vivid passage, ask the students to draw what they "saw." Some students may recognize this as a "Sketch to Stretch" visualization strategy they learned in elementary school, and it is a way of stretching their imagination. Sharing these quick sketches with partners expands the comprehension of both those drawing and those viewing. It is worth taking the time to get the students involved on the first day. If you can hook them at this point, they are likely to continue reading with understanding and pleasure.

Of course, to prepare for this dramatic reading, you must practice ahead of time reading the section aloud. Select and read just enough to give the students a good sense of the story and yet raise curiosity enough to want to continue reading on their own. Although there are professional recordings of many of the classic novels and you may decide to use excerpts from them another time, it is better for the students to hear you read well. It will be your voice they hear in their minds when they begin to read on their own, reminding them that you care enough about them to prepare and read so impressively the book the class studies together.

Classical texts like *A Christmas Carol* are generally available in dramatic audio readings. In fact, some classic film clips are available free online and can be played in class just as audio clips without using the video. Complete dramatic readings typically are available through online audio distributors such as iTunes. So, go ahead and plan lessons during which you play a few audio clips for the students so they will be more intrigued about the story. Audio versus video requires the students to imagine what the characters and settings look like without preset, preconceived visual images and can also open up initial discussion about the text's setting as reflected in the linguistic codes such as grammar and dialect.

Figure 5.2. Reading and listening enrich the experience.

Deciding on Vocabulary Lists That Include Academic Words

The vocabulary in classic novels is often difficult and merits direct study. To begin, select 8–10 words from the first section of the novel. Initially, do not get hung up on teaching the words—you are better served by getting into the story right away. For now, quickly give the definitions and move on. The point, of course, is for students to understand enough words to be drawn into the story.

Include a list of suggested vocabulary words and page numbers in the study packet and encourage the students to refer to lists during various lessons. Draw attention to the words students should be adding to their speaking and writing vocabulary during upcoming lessons by posting them in the room. Reading the words, copying them, seeing them daily, and being encouraged to use them in conversation and writing all are ways to reinforce learning. Some publications of classic novels may have vocabulary already pulled out for you, but you know your students and may need to tailor and personalize the list.

On subsequent days, as you progress through the novel, you could have pairs of students look up and copy into their notebooks words and the definition that best fits word usage in the novel. For this type of vocabulary study, there is no need to focus on other meanings of the word. Have volunteers read the definitions of the assigned words and urge students to make necessary corrections in their own notebooks. Students working on handheld computers may resist this writing assignment, thinking they have only to hyperlink the words. Please insist that they write because the physical act of writing in and of itself is a heuristic—a way of learning that has long-term retention benefits.

While reading a classic novel, you may wish to point out vocabulary words that are important for students to use in their own writing. As a guideline, check the Internet for lists of vocabulary that students need to know for academic reading. You also can find graphic organizers showing a variety of ways to have students study these new words. Ask students to pair words for different reasons: near synonyms, antonyms, same part of speech, etymology, reminds them of something, and so on. What color does this word sound like? Be patient and persistent. Learning vocabulary takes time. Make it fun and imaginative, but not silly.

Encourage the students to keep a list of words that challenge them and then assemble a class list to work on together. Later in this chapter is a writing assignment requiring students to incorporate some vocabulary words from the novel into a story the students write themselves. When students are encouraged to use the words in speaking and writing in school and out of school, they are more likely to remember them. Consider planning a class meeting during which students use the vocabulary words as they discuss the story. Yes, there will be giggling; there also will be learning. You may recall the maxim that if you use a new word 10 times in a day, it is yours for life. Challenge the students to test the adage.

WORKING THROUGH THE NOVEL

One way to ensure that your students are engaged in the novel right from the beginning is to help them grasp firmly the main characters, the setting, and the conflict, or problem to be solved. Then you are ready to dig into serious discussion about character motivation, writing style, use of literary devices, and development of theme. You want to spark thoughtful talking and insightful writing. In this section are examples of ways to increase interest and maintain momentum while studying classic literature.

Accepting Admit Slips

This activity frees students to acknowledge that reading this classic novel is a challenge and that the language and sentence structure are stumbling blocks for them. At the beginning of the next class period, ask each student to use his or her books and to write three questions he or she has about the first section of the novel you have assigned. Notice who is up to date on the reading by seeing how quickly or slowly students can find passages, as this will show if the passage is familiar or new to them. You may need to adjust your day and give time for students to catch up on the reading.

Once the students write their questions, collect them and assign a short vocabulary exercise. This assignment could be a set of 10 words you have chosen from the next reading assignment. As the students are working in pairs to complete the vocabulary assignment, you can read and organize the admit slips. These questions then form the basis for the discussion of this section and help the students clarify details of the story so they can follow what they read.

Sampling Study Questions for Classic Novels

You could adapt study questions that fit your novel similar to those that follow for *A Christmas Carol* and can be used as homework or in-class assignment with students working alone or in pairs. For example, you could say, "As you read the story, mark or record answers to the following questions. Then, in your own words, summarize in your reading journal what you've learned from this reading." And then project the following questions or print and distribute them as part of a study packet.

Stave One—"Marley's Ghost"

1. How has Dickens used direct and indirect characterization to reveal the personality of Ebenezer Scrooge? (Students indicate page numbers to support their answers.)
2. Who is Marley? What part does he play in setting up the conflict of this story?
3. What is the weather like in this stave? How does it affect the setting and mood?
4. List 7–10 verbs to summarize the events of the plot in this stave.
5. What questions do you have about this stave? Ask them at the next class meeting.

Stave Two—"The First of the Three Spirits"

1. At what time does Scrooge awaken?
2. List the places Scrooge is taken by this ghost. What do we learn about Scrooge?
3. Who uses a candle extinguisher in this stave? What does this character do with it?
4. What does the candle extinguisher symbolize in this stave?
5. What questions do you have about this stave? Ask them at the next class meeting.

Conducting P.I.E. Discussions

Using the questions the students write on the admit slips, conduct a discussion starting with the more frequently asked questions first, and direct students to consult their texts to find answers to the questions. To keep the discussion focused on the author's words, remind them of P.I.E. responses, where the student states the point, illustrates with a reference to a specific incident or sentence from the text, and then explains how that information in the text answers the question. Or you could distribute the admit slips, set your timer for five to seven minutes, and have pairs or triads of students search the text and be prepared to share answers with the class when the buzzer rings.

Do not be surprised if discussion on the first section takes two or three full class periods; the language and style may be more difficult for the students. It is worth a little extra time to clarify the basic elements of character, setting, conflict, and point of view presented in the exposition. However, be alert to the fact that spending too much time dilutes the power of the story. Students lose interest and resist reading any more. It is always a balance for teachers. The more vigilant you are to what the students know and are able to do with this novel, the more likely you are to pace it just right.

Assign students to read section two. The number of pages you assign should be based on complexity of the novel you choose and the pace of reading you know your students can handle. Be prepared for grumbling but do not be discouraged if it takes the students a few days to get into the rhythm of classic writing. Instead sustain your enthusiasm; you know the richness of the novel you have chosen to teach them. Need a boost? Now may be a good time to play an audio portion of the novel or again read another passage aloud. Hearing passages read aloud gives your reluctant students a voice in their minds as they read silently to themselves.

Drawing to Interpret Descriptive Language

Here is an example of how a descriptive writing assignment from *A Christmas Carol* is used, but you can adjust the details based on the book you and your students are reading. You need white paper, colored pencils, pens, or crayons to draw in the packet or journals.

Direct the students' attention to the visual images Dickens creates with his language—vivid verbs, concrete nouns, and humorous details. Ask the students to reread the description of the Spirit of Christmas Past, and then as accurately as they can, draw what they visualize. Circulate among and encourage students as they draw but resist the temptation to comment or evaluate. Pay attention to those who go back and reread to find the details and to those who seem to retain the image and quickly begin to draw. Neither is cause for concern. Some students may be confident about what they remember; others may not. Some may not have read and are trying to catch up right then and there. Either is fine. More will be ready for the next step.

Once most of the students have completed the drawings, invite two or three of them to draw their pictures on the board or on large pieces of butcher paper. Because Dickens's descriptions are so detailed, the students notice lots of similarities in their drawings. To focus attention on the language and pattern of the writing, invite students to read aloud passages that appeal to them to stoke their interest and create more attentive readers once they see how well they can interpret Dickens's descriptive writing. This version of the "Sketch to Stretch" activity expands and extends student comprehension of what they are reading, while their drawings also help you see what they see when they read.

Enhancing Understanding with Summary Writing

To deepen their understanding and create a record of key points from the book, teach your students to write brief summaries. You may choose to teach formal summary writing or simply have students track a sequence of events. Ask the students to list the places that the Spirit of Christmas Past takes Scrooge or, in other classic novels, where the action moves from place to place. After students record the locations, they can summarize in a couple of sentences what the locations infer about the character and what they learn about the character's life at each of these places. This unfolding information about the character's personality and attempts to solve problems naturally leads to conversations about some of the themes in the book.

TEMPTING STUDENTS TO CHEW FOR THEMSELVES

A narrative text is more powerful when it is not dragged out for too long. So when you sense that the students are relatively comfortable with the structure and style of the text, assign them to continue reading for homework or allot in-class time for reading. Read quickly and then come back and discuss elements of style and the author's use of literary devices. Remember, you are working from a complete reading of the text. You can "see" things they do not notice until they have finished and can reflect on the book as a whole.

Sheridan Blau suggests that teachers enjoy tackling difficult texts for their students.[4] He compares teachers' predigesting of literature for students to mothers chewing food for babies rather than letting children chew for themselves. His point? Don't do that. You may recall on your own travels to different areas of the country or over to another continent that though the cuisine usually is different, it often is the fresh meats and vegetables seasoned with exotic spices that make the dining experience both delightful and unforgettable. As you teach your students to analyze the literature on their own, they begin to experience the flavor of language, the joy of reading, and the thrill of discovery you may have been hoarding for yourself. Let your students masticate for meaning and savor the flavor of the classical novel.

Setting Pace for Reading

As you continue escorting your students along this journey, encourage them to draw an important scene or new character, summarize the events, and discuss the section. Then introduce new vocabulary. Continue assigning reading for homework or for 15 or 20 minutes during class time. There is no need to hesitate permitting such in-class reading. You instruct partly by the way you allocate time for classroom activities and skill building. If it is important for students to learn to read independently, you must allot some class time to model and to help them develop that skill.

In addition to modeling silent reading, you can carefully observe the students as they read, noticing their reading pace, who marks the texts, uses sticky notes, or writes notes in their journal, practicing the skills that you have been teaching. Observe which students read by moving their lips or using their finger to stay focused. Neither is wrong if it helps the student stay focused and read efficiently.

The use of fingers to guide reading is a skill often taught to those who experience dyslexia or who learn speed-reading. It is not necessary to stop students from using such reading aids. Just determine who uses them so you can adapt your teaching to accommodate student needs and reading speeds. Not sure what to do? Ask for assistance from a reading specialist. If there is no specialist on staff in your building, ask your department chair, a more experienced colleague, or go online to learn what resources are available in your area or elsewhere on the Internet.

Posing Intelligent Questions

Continue to ask thought-provoking questions—those that require more than superficial reading to answer. It is at this stage of the story, about halfway through the book, that you can ask students to predict the outcome. By now the protagonist recognizes that he or she cannot solve the problem alone and may be seeking the assistance of someone or something else. Soon, the protagonist may be challenged to make moral or ethical choices to solve the problem of the conflict. You could ask questions about point of view and how that author's word choices color or flavor the story.

Encouraging students to consider options and to make predictions are other ways to refocus their attention on the characterization and motivation. Do the choices the characters make seem logical to the way the author has developed the personalities of these characters? If not, why not? How does this disconnect affect your students' appreciation of the story? In the same situation, what choices would your students make to solve the problem? Why? Why not? What has happened that is unexpected? Does it make sense?

Using Video Adaptations

Video, picture books, animated cartoons, and graphic and comic book adaptations can promote student interest, increase comprehension, and lead to worthwhile discussions. Borrow a DVD from the school collection or local library to show portions of the story or look for appropriate clips online. View the video ahead of time to choose appropriate scenes to show and to time the length so you can plan effective use in class. Look at a variety of adaptations until you find one that you like and serves your purpose for showing it. Characterization? Setting? Pacing? Filmmaking? There is no need to hold off introducing media grammar—the ways that visual messages are structured as in advertisements, websites, and film—just do not spend so much time on the media terms that students are distracted from the novel. This viewing experience can be one to which you refer when you present a more in-depth lesson on media literacy.

Before showing the video clip, tell the viewers the questions you plan to ask at the end. This helps the students focus on some of the aspect of media grammar—film shots, use of color, timing, screen shots, cuts, and so forth. Allow time at the end of the period for students to discuss the director's or artist's choices for depicting character, setting, and action. Ask students how the viewing is different from the reading. Are they surprised, pleased, disappointed? Why? Why not?

Showing visual versions of the novel can help avoid wounding fragile young egos, too. This activity gives students an opportunity to assess and even confirm the assumptions they have been making as they read. And, in a nonembarrassing way, viewing clarifies scenes or passages for those who may have misunderstood something. You know that classic novels can be challenging reads for today's middle school students, so arrange various ways for them to figure out the plots and the characters. If you are teaching a novel that does not have a DVD or other visual format that you can locate, you may use something set in a similar time or place. You can be confident that visual aids can supplement and expand student understanding and increase their appreciation for this older, classic work of literature.

Recognizing Dynamic and Static Characters

About two-thirds of the way through the novel is a good time to reflect on and examine the static and dynamic characters in the story. Although a dynamic character changes as the story unfolds, the static characters usually do not. Instead, they serve as foils for the dynamic characters. Use this academic terminology as you ask questions to point out the different types of characters. Here are a few examples of questions about character development based on *A Christmas Carol*:

1. What specific evidence is there of changes in Scrooge?
2. What is most different about the interaction of this Spirit with Scrooge and that of the other two Spirits?

3. What do you learn about Scrooge based on his interaction with other characters?
4. Through what means do you learn most about Scrooge? Direct or indirect characterization? From what he says or what he does? What others say about him? How others respond to him?
5. Which characters do not change even though they appear in several episodes?

The best literature has clear examples of how and why the characters have changed. Before calling on students to verbalize their answers, remind them to support their observations with specific passages from the text, explaining why those passages prove their point.

Rereading these passages helps to clarify concepts and reinforce vocabulary. Hearing the language reminds students of ways authors structure sentences to create certain impressions on their readers. No matter what novel you are reading together, there is plenty to talk about on this topic of character motivation and development, use of structure, and choice of vocabulary.

REFLECTING ON THE WHOLE BOOK— SUMMARIZING AND MORE

Dedicate a class period to a summary activity. This may be a time to use the same or a different video version of the book to show the concluding scenes and to ask the students to discuss their responses to the directors' choices. This critical thinking about what they see versus what they read raises their awareness of the power of visual and graphic images to create different responses. You may ask students to compare what they anticipated in the beginning or predicted in the middle with what they now know at the end of the reading. What caused the change in their understanding?

MOVING BEYOND THE NOVEL

You are not truly finished teaching a novel until you have given students opportunities to connect what they have learned with their own life and with other fiction or nonfiction works. Making connections is not just a higher level of thinking; seeing connections demonstrates why we study rather than merely read and put away the text. One creative way to accomplish this is to have students use their own experience and creativity to write an additional section for the book, an epilogue set sometime in the future and maybe even modeling the style of the author.

For whatever novel you decide to teach, the following is a set of guidelines to which you can hold the students accountable when they write epilogues:

- Include at least three characters from the original book.
- Retain their personalities and build on details that have been presented.
- Incorporate seamlessly at least seven words from the vocabulary list.

Tie up your novel study with a class presentation of these writings of episodes set in the future. Students enjoy hearing what their classmates come up with and talking about what a classic novel means to them personally.

Grading Stories the Students Write

You can give a holistic grade for the students' stories, evaluating them based on their adherence to the prompt, especially if you do not allot time for multiple revisions. Ask yourself the following questions:

- Have they created a logical epilogue, including three characters who have grown from the descriptions presented in the original work?
- Are the incidents in keeping with the situations introduced by the author?
- Does the vocabulary flow seamlessly (or relatively anyway) into the text of the story? It may or may not, depending on the style and the vocabulary

Figure 5.3.   Students reviewing drafts of stories.

words the students choose to use. If the words are used correctly, go ahead and give full credit. If they all stand out like a palm trees in the desert, lower the grade somewhat.

Student Responses to Creative Writing Assignment on *A Christmas Carol*

The following are two seventh-grade student responses to that assignment; Cressy wrote the first and Amanda the second. The italicized words are words from the vocabulary list Cressy used. Notice the difference in reading for vocabulary when one of the students italicized the words and the other did not. Are the vocabulary words Amanda used still noticeable?

Stave six of *A Christmas Carol* by Cressy (with italicized word from the class vocabulary list):

Years later, Scrooge forgot all about the *spectral* creatures that he had seen. It was Christmas Eve, actually, when he remembered a *vestige* of what had happened to him years ago. He was having Christmas dinner with his nephew and family at his nephew's house when he remembered. He *pondered* if he should tell his nephew, or if that would cause *tumult*. With a *persevere* attitude, he determinedly decided to tell his nephew.

Scrooge waited and *loitered* in the kitchen while dessert was being made, and decided to break his news to his nephew after their sweet dessert. Just about when he was ready to tell, he got a strange feeling. Should he tell, or not? He decided to wait a while until the others finished, so he and he nephew could be alone. Then he would tell. While Scrooge was waiting, he decided to try the dessert, which tasted *odious* to him, or maybe he just wasn't in the mood to eat, for he had something important to tell his nephew. His now *genial*, bouncy attitude gave him the feeling that now was the time to make his move, or else he may never come to telling his nephew, and if he didn't tell, it was possible that nephew could get confused about why his uncle likes Christmas now, when he used to hate it, and his nephew's confusion could possibly take Scrooge's genial attitude away.

"Nephew, do you remember how I used to be *caustic* about Christmas, how I thought it was *odious*?"

"Yes, I do."

"Well, have you ever stopped for a moment to think, 'Why did my *covetous* uncle change?'"

"Actually, yes, I have!" replied the nephew, whose cheeks turned a *ruddy* red.

"I used to think Christmas was one of the most horrible things! Now I like it because three ghosts taught me about Christmas and my life. The ghosts of Christmas Past, Present, and Yet to Come. They all took me places, and I learned that on Christmas people are happy and jolly, and I should be happy and jolly, too! Christmas is a time to love, not *ruddy*. I know that now, because through the ghosts, I learned!"

"Wait, do you mean . . . real ghosts? How is that possible?"

"I'm not sure, but you have to believe me, Nephew! How else could I have changed from hating Christmas so much to loving it so much?"

"I don't know, but . . ."

"I urge you to believe that I am telling the truth!"

"You expect me to believe that ghosts came and toured you around and taught you about Christmas?"

"It may sound odd, but ghosts toured me around to many different places. I even went to your house! I saw the family playing giving, and having fun! I saw it, I know it Nephew, I was in your house!"

"How did you get in my house?"

"I'm telling you, the ghost brought me!"

"I still don't believe you!"

"Fine! I'll get proof! I'll prove to you that the ghosts are real, and they changed me!"

Scrooge slumped back, wishing he could take back what he just said. How was he supposed to get proof? "Maybe," he thought to himself, "I can talk about what happened to me the day I was changed—my whole adventure told in detail. Then he ought to believe me!"

Scrooge poured out his whole story.

I, for one, would feel compelled, for Scrooge told his story with such drama and compassion. I don't believe in ghosts, but Scrooge had a pretty convincing story.

Scrooge stopped to catch his breath when his nephew started trembling violently. The nephew's face turned paler than porcelain, for behind Scrooge, there stood three ghosts.

The next stave six was written by Amanda. Called "10 Years Later," and it reflects how she was learning to integrate sophisticated reading vocabulary into her own writing.

Scrooge sat in his nephew Fred's house listening happily to the tumult around him. Fred's five, ruddy faced children playing and running around gave Scrooge such joy that he nearly hopped up and joined them. But if Scrooge had been an old man a decade before, it was nothing compared to what he was now. And although he was no longer the covetous man he had been and gave his money generously to all who needed it, he was now feeble and cane-ridden. This, however, did not dampen his genial personality and was often told he and his nephew had identical dispositions. He sold his house nine years back quite cheaply to a poor family with over a dozen children for they could fill that old house much better than Scrooge or Marley ever could. I wish I could have been there while they were moving in, for they filled the house with such love, joy, noise and bodies. I'm sure the house nearly fainted from surprise for it had been a stranger to all of that which this blessed family brought to it for most of its life. Scrooge had then moved into, well, not exactly a small house, more, an average sized house in the suburbs of the city, retired from his counting business, and gave it to his former clerk, Bob Cratchit to make up for his cruelty and underpayment of him.

Scrooge shifted to a recumbent position and scooped up his youngest great-nephew, Dean, and began reading him a book, which Scrooge had bought the boy the day before. Dean greatly resembled Tiny Tim who was now growing into a handsome young man. But not only on the outside did Tim and Dean resemble each other but also in spirit, for both were always optimistic. Scrooge finished reading to Dean and stood up to take his leave. He said good-bye to Freddy, the eldest great-nephew, gave Ann, the second eldest, a hug, and patted Jill and Mill, the twins, on the head, who were currently having a glorious tea party with their two favorite dolls. He then kissed Caroline, his niece, on the cheek, clapped Fred merrily on the shoulder, and thanked them both for having him with which they both responded it had been a great joy to have him. He let himself out of the house into the street and started hobbling home, waving cheerfully to every man, woman, and child that came into his sight.

While Amanda obviously needed work on pronoun agreement, she clearly captures the style of Dickens with the complex sentence structure and second person point of view—speaking directly to the reader as though the two of them were seated together as Dickens shared his now classic tale of transformation. She used vocabulary words: tumult, ruddy, covetous, genial, and recumbent.

CONNECTING ASSIGNED BOOKS
WITH SELF-SELECTED READING BOOKS

Here is an interesting assignment to encourage additional reading. Have the students read a collection of short stories and write an essay recommending three of the stories to three characters from class readings. (See Teacher Resource D in the appendix.)

Reporting on *The New Oxford Book of Ghost Stories* by Dennis Pepper, seventh-grader Warren recommended a story for Scrooge. Here is an excerpt from his essay:

Another story from *The New Oxford Book of Ghost Stories* is called Snookered. Snookered would be good for Scrooge from a book called *A Christmas Carol* by Charles Dickens. I would recommend that Scrooge read this story because then he would know that it's not just him that are visited by people that they know that have been dead. In Snookered by Catherine Graham, the story is about a man who is playing a game of pool and finds that his friend, that had just died, was helping him win. In *A Christmas Carol*, Scrooge is confronted by his old friend Marley who had died a couple of years ago. In both, they again get to meet their old friends.

Warren identified the stories and characters from our class text. He explained why a character from our text might enjoy reading a story about a character from a book that Warren had read independently. The assignment gave him an opportunity to reflect on our course text and to demonstrate how well he understood the short story he read on his own, both effective and efficient ways to practice and show proficiency in the Common Core State Standards of English Language Arts anchors for reading, writing, speaking, listening, and language.

CONCLUSION

Middle school students appreciate classical literature, especially if the related pedagogy aids in accessing texts that address the kinds of universal themes that young adults are already pondering. Offer students a variety of options for entrée into what may be a more challenging piece of literature, provide support with vocabulary study, read-alouds—yours or that of professional readers—encourage sketching and drawing, show visual versions, and invite students to connect what they read to their own lives, to what they see around them, and to other literature they have read.

While a book like *A Christmas Carol* can be especially challenging to teach in a multicultural community in which many families are not very familiar with Christmas traditions, it also may prove to be a wonderful window for those who just enjoy the writing of a talented storyteller. As you guide your young readers into, through, and beyond classical literature, you also are helping them move closer to reaching the Common Core State Standards for English Language Arts in reading, which says: "Through wide and deep reading of literature and literary nonfiction of steadily increasing sophistication, students gain a reservoir of literary and cultural knowledge, references, and images; the ability to evaluate intricate arguments; and the capacity to surmount the challenges posed by complex texts."[5]

Whatever classic text you select, be sensitive to the cultural nuances as you explore with students the universal themes reflected so well in novels revered so long as the classics.

CLASSIC NOVELS TO CONSIDER TEACHING OR RECOMMENDING TO STUDENTS

Animal Farm by George Orwell: *Animal Farm* is a simple but powerful allegory about the corruption of a socialist society. When the animals of Manor

Farm oust their drunken master, they at first establish a fair and seemingly perfect society.

The Giver by Lois Lowry: The utopia of 12-year-old Jonas's society seems perfect. There is no poverty, crime, sickness, or unemployment. Everyone is given an appropriate job and mate. It isn't until Jonas begins his training as the new Receiver of Memories that he questions his model existence.

The Lion, the Witch, and the Wardrobe by C. S. Lewis: When air raids during World War II drive children out of London, four siblings end up staying with an old professor in his country house and pass through a wardrobe to find themselves in the land of Narnia. It's a great choice to entice reluctant readers to read the classics.

Lord of the Flies by William Golding: What happens when a group of boys crash lands on an island and they are left to govern themselves? The stranded boys' initial attempts to establish a fair government quickly turn to chaos and violence. Raises lots of concerns for discussion and for writing.

The Phantom Tollbooth by Norton Juster: In this fantasy story, Norton Juster uses literary concepts to create characters, settings, and even a primary plot. Milo is bored with everything until a tollbooth magically appears in his room.

A Wrinkle in Time by Madeleine L'Engle: Madeleine L'Engle, a wonderful, "intelligent" children's author, employs science and philosophy in the fantastic adventure story of Meg Murry—a young woman who feels different from other kids her age. A necessary caution: if students do not understand the science, they will probably not enjoy the book unless extra research is included before using the book with a class.

NOTES

1. Charles Dickens, *A Christmas Carol* (New York: Viking, 2000), 36–37.
2. "English Language Arts Standards' Anchor Standards' College and Career Readiness Anchor Standards for Language," *Common Core State Standards Initiative*, 2011. www.corestandards.org/the-standards/english-language-arts-standards/anchor-standards-6-12/college-and-career-readiness-anchor-standards-for-language/ (accessed March 15, 2012).
3. National Geographic–Hammond and Heinle distributes an extensive list of classics as part of their ELT Graphic Novels series designed primarily for English-language learners and may be appropriate for middle school readers of any ability.
4. Sheridan D. Blau, *The Literature Workshop: Teaching Texts and Their Readers* (Portsmouth, NH: Heinemann, 2003).
5. Notes in *Great Expectations*, adapted by Brigit Viney and script by Jen Green (U.K.: Heinle, Cengage Learning EMEA, 2010).

Chapter Six

Teaching Historical Fiction

Opening the Past Imaginatively

I will always be grateful to her for one thing. She taught me my letters. My mistress, I realize now, like many women of her class, had very little education. She read slowly and laboriously, and it always took her several tearful afternoons to compose a letter to her family in Portugal, or to her nephew in Madrid, a young man who was a painter. Yet Mistress had a great deal of practical wisdom, and she knew many things because she trusted her judgment and cultivated her memory.[1]

Three sentences. A mistress, a slave, a painter. Tearful afternoons, practical wisdom, and judgment. From Spain to Italy, and beyond—all brought alive through the magic of one work of historical fiction that transports 21st-century teens to 17th-century Renaissance Europe: *I, Juan de Pareja* by Elizabeth Borton de Treviño. Three sentences and thousands of miles spanning hundreds of years. There is an entirely engaging education in one novel of historical fiction thanks to a splendid writer like Borton de Treviño and others on the list that ends this chapter. With the ideas here and this or another accessible work of fiction, you can have a great time exploring the past and meeting the academic needs of your students as well as the curriculum and Common Core Standards for English Language Arts for reading works that "offer profound insights into the human condition and serve as models for students' own thinking and writing."[2]

Not only is teaching historical fiction fun, but it also is an excellent way to integrate the English/language arts with other subjects like social studies, science, and the arts. Like tour companies that include visits to museums or ancient towns as part of their travel packages, you can do the same with your curriculum. Consider collaborating with colleagues in other departments, choosing a literary work that introduces or reinforces a historical period or explores some scientific concept your common students are learning in one of those content areas. You can create together a course of study that meets the requirements of both content area state and national standards and presents integrated lessons critical to a successful program for adolescents, helping them see and make connections across the disciplines. It also makes for an enriching experience for you.

WONDERING WHY THIS HISTORICAL NOVEL?

I, Juan de Pareja, by Elizabeth Borton de Treviño, is written as an autobiography from the point of view of Juan, an African slave inherited by Diego de Velázquez, the court painter for King Philip IV of Spain who reigned in the 17th century. Juan became the assistant and a friend to Velázquez and later an accomplished painter in his own right. One of Juan de Pareja's paintings now hangs in the Prado Museum in Madrid, Spain, and Velázquez's painting of Juan is in the New York Metropolitan Museum of Art. See images of both paintings at art sites on the Internet.

If you are looking for an engaging book to expand your reading list to include works from and about other cultures, this one works. It may become an immediate favorite to teach if you are inspired by a colleague like my friend Suzanne, who was "a closet art historian." She pointed out that Velázquez's work reflects four schools of European art. Descriptions in the book introduce readers to specific 15th- and 16th-century painters' artwork and the distinctive characteristics of chiaroscuro, baroque, realism, and idealism. Borton de Treviño, like many other historical fiction authors, writes so clearly students hardly realize how much they are learning. But you can ensure that they do so from the very beginning by letting them help build the foundation as they conduct simple research on the historical period.

The novel *I, Juan de Pareja* is set during the Renaissance, an epoch of people, places, and incidents that influenced art, science, and exploration then and now. In the novel, Rubens (1577–1640), the famous Flemish painter, visits the Spanish Court, and Velázquez travels to Italy to purchase art for King Philip. Imagine the budget! This novel also talks about friendships—a topic that middle school students love to talk about. The characters are faced with ethical dilemmas that can elicit lively student conversations about issues of right and wrong. Studying historical fiction gives students an opportunity to meet standards as well as see interdisciplinary connections to what they study in other classes.

The premise of the story is the fact that the painting *Las Meniñas*, in which Velázquez includes a portrait of himself, has the Cross of Santiago painted

Figure 6.1. Boy looking up from book.

onto his garment in a style quite different from his own. Borton de Treviño's tale attempts to explain who painted this cross and why anyone would do so. That is a good reason to display a copy of *Las Meniñas* in your classroom while you and your students study this particular historical novel. Images of famous artwork like this are readily available on a range of websites and in books with Renaissance art found in most libraries.

GETTING INTO HISTORICAL FICTION NOVELS

Begin explaining to students the features of historical fiction and the fact that they are going to be reading one. Share with them that historical fiction may include real people, real places, and real events. Following Louise Rosenblatt's reader-response approach, encourage the students to look for the familiar, even in a piece of fiction set in a time hundreds of years before they were born. Susan Zimmerman and Chryse Hutchins use different terminology but also urge teachers to have students make connections when reading literature.[3] These educators advocate such relationships as

- Text to self (between the novel and their own lives)
- Text to text (among the people, places, and incidents in the novel)

- Text to text (between this and other literature students have read)
- Text to world (between this book and historical or current events)

When you teach a work of historical fiction, it is important to set the scene. For *I, Juan de Pareja*, give a brief overview of the Renaissance period, an era whose style in art history began in Rome, Italy, and spread through Europe from 1450 to 1600. Following the medieval era, this was a period of intense revival in all areas of math, science, arts, and humanities.

The Renaissance is often referred to as the rebirth of the classics, as the participants looked to the texts and monuments of the Greco-Roman civilizations for inspiration and direction.[4] This could be a good time to do a quick word study on the prefix and root of Renaissance! Teaching vocabulary in context makes it easier to remember.

Presenting Oral Presentations Gives Overview of People and Events

To help set the stage for students to acquire a richer sense of the historical period and to practice their research skills, you can let them look for information about the real people, places, and events of the period in which the novel is set and report to the class what they learn.

Consider assigning them to research the people of the golden age that Borton de Treviño mentions in her foreword, such as Galileo, Rembrandt, and Sir Walter Raleigh. Most of the names on this list are so well known that students have little difficulty locating facts for a brief two- to three-minute informative speech. The same is likely to be true for the novel you choose since historical novels tend to be written about famous events, well-known places, or legendary people.

Depending on your students' access to resources, you may decide to spend a week on this assignment, allowing in-class time for research, writing, and practice. To reduce innocent plagiarism, you may wish to include mini-lessons on note-taking, summarizing, documentation, and making citations. It is a good idea to assign students to use time at home to practice their delivery, perhaps in front of two adults who sign a form confirming that they have heard the speech. This also is a way to let families and friends know what their child or friend is learning.

This mini-assignment you are giving your young adolescents has a real purpose for conducting simple research, collaborating with a peer, practicing speech writing, and giving oral reports. If it is not realistic to expect your students to complete this assignment at home, allot in-class time for

pairs of students to give their speeches to each other or recruit faculty and
staff at your school to be listeners. You may be surprised how many school
support staff members are delighted to play a part in the academic education
of the students they serve as secretaries, janitors, bus drivers, and cafeteria
workers.

Including Women of the Renaissance

As you prep for teaching this novel, notice in the foreword of the novel
I, Juan de Pareja that many of the names—such as Galileo, Rubens, and
Shakespeare—are familiar, but none are women. Your students may find it
difficult to locate information about women of the Renaissance, other than
Joan of Arc.[5] Nevertheless, students should be able to locate online informa-
tion about:

- Elisabetta Sirani—the lightning-quick painter who opened an all-female art
  school and became an international sensation
- Artemisia Gentileschi—a colleague of Elisabetta Sirani, was the first woman
  to paint large-scale historical and religious pictures. She was known for her
  inventive use of techniques developed by the Italian artist Caravaggio, who
  once worked with Raphael in Rome.[6] Susan Vreeland's *The Passion of Artemisia* is told from the point of view of Artemisia Gentileschi.
- Grace O'Malley—the mother of three who ruled the high seas as Ireland's
  pirate queen and freedom fighter.
- Christina of Sweden—the eccentric Swedish monarch who awakened her
  country to the wonders of Renaissance art, science, and literature.
- Gracia Mendes Nasi—the Spanish humanitarian and philanthropist whose
  "underground railroad" during the 16th century saved the lives of countless
  persecuted Jews.[7]

If you choose another book and decide to do this assignment, carefully
check for and include women of renown from that historical period.

For ease in assigning topics, simply have the students pull for numbers
based on the number of names on your list of historical figures. Students
with the same number can work together to decide how to best make their
presentation, which should include the following information based on the
five Ws and an H: who, what, when, where, why, and how. Whatever list of
people you offer your students should reflect both genders, as well as cultural,
social, economic, and political incidents, representative of the historical setting of your book.

Sample Assignment Sheet for Oral Presentation Based on Historical Personages

1. Use a print or online encyclopedia to find the answers to the following questions about the person you are assigned to give an oral report:
   - Who is the person?
   - What is he or she famous for doing?
   - When was he or she born?
   - Where was he or she born? Locate the country on a world map.
   - Why is his or her work (invention, discovery, etc.) important in contemporary society?
   - How was his or her work (invention, discovery, etc.) viewed during his or her lifetime?
2. Record the information that tells where you get your facts. Include:
   - Author (if one is listed)
   - Title of article or encyclopedia entry
   - Title of encyclopedia or website and its URL
   - Number of volumes (if applicable)
   - City where published
   - Publisher
   - Year the book was published, article posted, or website updated
3. Highlighting what you learned, write a one-page summary to make an engaging informative speech. Include a picture, if one is available. (A written summary of 250 words takes about two minutes to speak.)

If your students are tech savvy and have access to resources, consider challenging them to prepare slides for PechaKucha presentations. These are based on a Japanese concept of 20 slides paced to advance every 20 seconds during which someone narrates, making a 6 minute 40 second presentation. This could mean subdividing the task among four or five groups. Each would be responsible for five or four slides each. Depending on the book you choose, this subdividing could be into categories. For example, for the *Juan* book, the subdivisions could be art, science, math, and religion. Let students decide. Save the slides and show them again before the test or exam.

Validating Student Research

To expand their knowledge, extend their recall, and validate the significance of their classmates' research, assign students to keep notes as their peers speak and include questions based on these reports; this is also an opportunity to demonstrate on an exam what they have learned during their study of the historical novel. While the students are researching and once they have presented their oral reports, keep the list of researched names visible (written on the board, on a poster, or projected on a screen) when students enter the classroom. Assignments in this unit support many interdisciplinary curricula, as students are likely to encounter these names as they study history, science, and art. Keeping such a word wall with these names is just another effective way to reinforce the valuable new information they're learning!

Symbols and images help students remember details. In the students' journal sections set aside for notes about this historical novel, ask them to create a chart on which they list the names of the historical personages with space to include five Ws and H facts as well as a column in which to draw in symbols or images. During the presentation by classmates, have your students take notes in their journals. At the end of the presentations, as you review this information, invite students to recommend appropriate symbols or images to serve as memory aids.

For example, for astronomer Galileo, someone may suggest a telescope; for dramatist Molière, the happy- and sad-face drama masks. Deciding appropriate symbols is another way to teach to the multiple intelligences your students have, those who learn best by drawing and those who learn best by viewing. Consider asking one of the more artistic youngsters to draw the symbols for the class to copy. This can be a fine time for you to stand aside and let them shine.

REINFORCING LEARNING

During the first couple of weeks that the class reads and discusses the novel, schedule a four- or five-minute review of the historical personages at the beginning of each period. One day, you could project or show the symbol(s) for 10 or more of the historical figures and have students name the person(s) and something for which each is famous; another day, read the names and ask the students to draw the symbol or write a fact about the person. To avoid having to collect and grade these quickie quizzes, you could conduct "honor" checks. While the students are writing their responses, pick up your grade book and have it ready to record how they did right away.

Immediately following the quiz, go over the answers and ask the students to indicate to you how many they missed, using their fingers held close to their chests so that only you can see them. Then, just record a check-plus, check, or check-minus instead of a letter grade. If someone misses more than five, enter a minus sign. Commend them all for their work, and move to the next activity for the day. Your daily checks encourage them to study their notes and by the second week most of the students are able to identify these famous figures and recall a pertinent fact about each one. They also will be better able to understand the novel you are studying, too.

Occasionally, some of your students extend the assignment on their own and bring in articles or ads from the newspapers or magazines that allude to or mention the people on your list or show some symbol of the times. You could ask the students to search through the telephone book, the local newspaper, or online websites to see how many products and companies carry these Renaissance names, or names of people or places in the book you are studying.

Set aside a space in the classroom, hang up a blank posterboard, and encourage students to bring in examples. They can add these examples to a poster that all can view during your study of the historical fiction novel. For, *I, Juan de Pareja*, you could label the poster "Renaissance Today" and watch as a collage of student contributions emerges. Or you could have students add their findings to a gallery you set up in a class wiki just for this purpose; just another way to have students paying attention to the world around them, thinking about what they are reading, and contributing to the learning environment they share with you. Or, in the image of a school year being an extended tour, keeping a travel album of people you meet and places you visit.

OFFERING EXTRA CREDIT—YES AND NO

Yes, it is fine to offer extra credit when students find the names of the people mentioned in your text in their history or science texts or in the newspaper. Yes, you want to ensure that the students are making connections, not simply finding the names and earning unwarranted extra credit. To help control dependence on the extra-credit option, limit the percentage of extra points students may earn each marking period to about 5 percent. These extra points can help a student who has had a slow start to make up for homework points missed earlier in the marking period, or to make up for a poor test or quiz score taken when the student has had been tired, ill, or distracted by some personal issue. With young adolescents, it doesn't take much for them to have an off day!

Extra points should never be so weighty that they make it unnecessary for students to earn passing grades on required curriculum content. Most important, extra-credit points should not require extra work for you, the teacher. All extra-credit work should be submitted and recorded at least a week before the marking period ends. This early cut-off date reduces the temptation for students to misdirect their attention from learning and showing knowledge of required course content and skill acquisition just to raise their quarter grade.

And enforcing this early cut-off date preserves time for you to grade those assignments needed to determine the student grades for that marking period.

WORKING THROUGH THE NOVEL

If possible, teach the historical novel in the spring. By this time, your students already have studied the structure of fiction and several short stories that illustrate the elements of fiction, and they know the literary devices authors use to enhance the storytelling. Your maturing young teens know to set up a section in their journals for this new kind of novel and to write notes as you present facts about the period in which this particular historical novel is set. When you begin your unit, just remind them that historical novels are fiction, with plotlines followed in much the same way as short stories.

By spring, your students know to pay attention to facts revealed in the exposition, but you may need to review ways to mark their texts or to take notes in their journals. For example, you could have them use a pencil to circle the name of each character the first time each is encountered in the reading. Then, underline the words or phrases that identify that character. If they are using an electronic version, they can highlight and annotate as you have taught for reading digital texts.

If students are not allowed to write in their books, they can list the names of new characters in their reading journals, including the page numbers and a few words or phrases the author uses to identify those characters. Then, ask them to remain alert, as they continue reading, to see if or how the author rounds out the characters through direct and indirect characterization. By this time in the school year, your students know that the protagonist is a dynamic character, so they are watching to see what encounters bring about the change in this character from the beginning through the challenge of the conflict and on to the falling action and resolution.

The students can identify the setting by putting a rectangle around words and/or phrases that indicate time and places; or students can record this information in their journals. This kind of marking or writing forces students to slow down a bit while helping them get to know the people and places in the book, so they're less likely to become confused as the action intensifies and conflict complicates. Because *Juan* is written as an autobiography, the students quickly notice that the point of view is first person and can predict that the major problem to be solved is that of growing up and surviving the challenges that Juan encounters during his lifetime. From which point of view has the author of your book written?

As with all direct instruction of reading, according to Carol Jago, past president of the National Council of Teachers of English, your ongoing challenge is "to help students refine how they examine a piece of literature without destroying their confidence as readers."[8] Teaching students to be active readers increases their self-reliance on their own ability to understand whatever they read, whenever they read, and for whatever purpose they read. Paying attention to the craft and structure of the writing leads students toward the curriculum standard goals you are charged to help them reach.

Stimulating Interest in Styles of Painting

As art often reflects the social, economic, and political milieu of the times in which the artists live, it is worthwhile to bring in photos, artwork, artifacts, or articles. They all can give a richer sense of the historical period in which your novel is set. The school media center likely has many resources your librarian will be delighted to have you check out and use in your classroom. The Library of Congress (loc.gov) maintains an extensive collection of photographs readily accessible on the Internet to you and to your students. Encourage your students to explore and bring in artwork and photos relating to the content of your work of historical fiction.

You could adapt your presentation of art terms by preparing a handout for the students with information such as that below. Use PowerPoint to present visual examples of each style. During the slide presentation, read some of the narration that defines and illustrates key terms: *chiaroscuro, baroque, realism,* and *idealism.* In the Language Arts Resources section of the companion website for this book is the *I, Juan de Pareja* PowerPoint presentation prepared for this section of the unit. (See http://teachingenglishlanguagearts .com/.)

- *Chiaroscuro*—"treatment of light and shade in a picture."[9] Caravaggio, an Italian artist, is known to have used this style.
- *Baroque*—a "style of art and architecture that prevailed in Europe from about 1550 to the late 1700s, characterized by the use of curved forms and lavish ornamentation."[10] Rubens is a key baroque painter; be careful about showing paintings of his nude (not "naked") models.
- *Realism*—(in art and literature) "the picturing of life as it actually is."[11]
- *Idealism*—(in art and literature) "the representation of imagined types rather than of exact likeness of people, instances, or situations."[12] The students may be disappointed when they learn that Velázquez seemed to stray from his philosophy to paint what is "truth."

Showing the works of such artists as Murillo, Michelangelo, Titian, and Raphael helps students understand references about the art that Velázquez and Juan saw during their trip to Rome.

If you and your students are enjoying this adventure with art, consider letting them demonstrate their new knowledge of art. Create a scavenger hunt during which students find examples of various paintings and styles in the library books with collections of Renaissance art. You can do the same with historical novels set in other times and places. The National Archives has valuable resources on American artists. Artcylopedia.com has searchable pages that make the hunt less daunting for you. Let students post what they find on the class wiki or create a Prezi or PowerPoint presentation that they show one day in class. If you are teaching a different historical novel and would like to incorporate a visual arts component, do so. Many of the art terms apply to painting styles of other historical periods. Among the historical novels that work well for this kind of study are

- *Across Five Aprils* by Irene Hunt
- *Bud, Not Buddy* by Christopher Paul Curtis
- *Esperanza Rising* by Pam Muñoz Ryan
- *Code Talker: A Novel about the Navajo Marines of World War Two* by Joseph Bruchac
- *Girl with the Pearl Earring* by Susan Vreeland

The Library of Congress website and numerous open access websites provide historical photographs to enhance the study of each of these titles. The LOC site also has sound recordings of real people from American history. Including auditory resources supports students who learn best by listening, and hearing real people talk about their lives and times can make these historical personages come alive for all your students.

Connecting Geography and Map Study

Velázquez and Juan make two trips from Spain to Italy; this story gives their itinerary, as do many historical novels. Ask students to locate the places on a map and follow the journey by marking the places they visit. You could print out copies of a blank map that includes outlines of Europe with France, Spain, and Italy, or of the places mentioned in your book.

For those reading *Juan*, this map work gives the students a sense of the distance between towns and the kind of topography the two characters had to cross to get to the Mediterranean Sea, and then on to their destinations in Italy. Since map reading is a skill most adolescents are expected to acquire, asking them to refer to and use maps while studying in your class provides opportunities to practice that skill as they expand their understanding about what is going on in the novel they are reading with you.

Using Google Mapping for Historical Literature—Search It!

If you have access in the classroom or a media center to the Google Mapping website, you can view the following with students:

- Current street-view images of historical sites
- Traditional, satellite-image, and topographical maps of locales
- Website previews of sites about historical buildings, events, and people

Using the GPS satellite feature, students may be able "see" the places they are learning about in the novel you study together.

EXPLORING FRIENDSHIP: A MULTILAYERED THEME

Elizabeth Borton de Treviño artfully describes friendships between King Phillip and his court painter, the court painter and his slave, the apprentices and a slave, a dwarf and a slave, and a male and a female slave. These relationships are ready-made springboards for discussions about the nature of friendship. You could get the discussion off the ground by writing the word *friend* in the center of the whiteboard, on a poster, or on something you can project for all to see as you write, and then asking the students to brainstorm for words to describe a friend. Without commenting, list their answers around the word "friend" forming a weblike cluster.

Next, ask them to open their journals to the section on this novel and do a quick write on friends or friendship. Set your timer and write along with them. Having them write nonstop for three or four minutes to describe their concept or experience with friends usually elicits a level of honesty that may be missing in more prepared writing. They may write about a friendship that went well, one that dissolved, or one they wish existed. Then invite a few students to read aloud what they have written, respecting their privacy if they choose to decline, as unedited writing sometimes reveals emotions too raw to share in public. So, again, honor the choice to pass. While they are writing, you could create a word cloud of the terms they used and project it to sum up your discussion. See Wordle.com.

Round out the lesson by asking the students to write about the friendships they notice are developing in your novel. Which surprised them? Which do they think will develop, continue, or end? Why? Why not? To help the students to go beyond a simple listing of facts in their speaking and writing, encourage them to continue using P.I.E. paragraph format—where they answer the questions by stating their point, using specific incidents from the text to illustrate that point, then explaining the reasons they believe the incidents show that the friendship identified begins, continues, or ends.

Because the P.I.E. writings are more objective than their quick-writes, the students often are more willing to share them. In fact, students might disagree and even debate their differences about friendship. Challenge your students to take an opposing stance that they can support with evidence from the book. Doing so, they experience what it is like to give serious consideration to a different point of view—which is good practice for developing open minds about others.

WRITING ABOUT AND DISCUSSING ETHICAL ISSUES

The Association for Middle Level Education (AMLE) recommends that teachers address ethical issues while developing curricula. One of their publications even argues that any "curriculum design that does not provide opportunities and support for student to do 'right things' along with the significant adults in their lives is sadly incomplete."[13] The word "ethics" normally refers to defining, analyzing, and using standards of right and wrong, moral and immoral conduct—making right, but often tough, decisions.

Several of the characters in this autobiographical novel are faced with just such choices. As your students read about them, they may identify with these situations even if they disagree with the characters' choices having to do with selling humans as slaves or using mentally and physically challenged persons to entertain the royal children.

Very likely equally evocative topics arise in the book you choose to teach. Some raging debates may arise among students when you challenge them to consider the actions and attitudes expressed in the stories they read. Do what you can to monitor but not squelch heated but respectful exchanges of ideas, and let students know that it is perfectly all right to agree to disagree.

RESPONDING HOLISTICALLY TO LITERATURE

Fran Claggett says that teachers often dissect literature so minutely that students lose sight of the work as a whole, and she recommends using art and graphics to give readers an opportunity to "make it whole" again.[14] Here is another opening to assign art, music, or poetry writing for that purpose: to help students reassemble the parts of the story, to see the novel as a whole work of literature.

One assignment asks the students to compose a narrative poem, similar to a ballad, in which they tell the whole story in quatrains. In this case, have the students include at least five four-line stanzas to account for the exposition, rising action, climax, falling, action, and resolution of the story. If you choose to teach historical fiction at the end of the school year, your students already have had an in-depth poetry unit during which they learned that writing can be a poem—even if it does not have a set rhyme or rhythm pattern—as long as the writing "convey[s] a vivid and imaginative sense of experience, especially by the use of condensed language."[15]

Amanda's six-stanza narrative about *I, Juan de Pareja* follows:

> I am Juan de Pareja
> A black man living in Spain in the seventeenth century
> I once was a slave
> To Mistress Emilia and Master Diego Velázquez
>
> Mistress Emilia died of a plague
> It nearly took my life too
> But a caring friar saved me
> Who I called Brother Isidro
>
> I was taken to Master Diego
> By Don Carmelo, a terrible gypsy man
> He made me beg and steal for my food
> And then in turn stole things from me
>
> I finally got to Master Diego
> A very talented painter
> I made his paints and was
> His one and only helper
>
> I was his slave for many years
> Until he saw my painting
> And then he freed Lolis and me
> And we married
>
> My dear wife and I
> Live now in Seville
> Master is long gone
> But he is still alive in my hand and my heart.

Amanda captured some of the elements of the exposition, plot events, and even minor conflicts between Juan and Don Carmelo that may have arisen because Juan was a slave. However, when she concluded with a subtle hint on the theme of the unlikely but friendly relationship that grew between master and slave, Amanda reflects the essence of poetry with "But he is still alive in my hand and my heart." One would expect "my heart," but the "my hand" suggests an artistic, poetic bent reflected in Amanda's other work. She found a simple image to embody the love and talent that grew during Juan's years with Diego de Velázquez.

ASSIGNING ALTERNATIVE
END-OF-NOVEL ASSIGNMENTS

The following are other kinds of creative, open assignments to offer at the end of a unit to show what students have learned in ways that may not have been revealed in earlier assignments. The students are free to choose their idea and structure to demonstrate what they know. Possibilities include:

- Create a melody for each of three or four of the main characters (à la the Darth Vader theme from *Star Wars*).
- Bring in samples of music that reflect key scenes (like mood music).
- Bring in three or four different published songs that have lyrics that could have been sung by three or four different characters. Which song would each character sing and why?
- Create original music for any of the three previously mentioned situations.

You may choose the "Entering Art" assignment in the textbox as a whole-class assignment or allow students to adapt it for an end-of-the-book project. For each, make a portion of the grade a written page or two in which the students explain the reasons for their choices and indicate the page(s) of the text that support their choices.

One parent complained that I was "dumbing down" the curriculum when I allowed students to use artistic projects to show their understanding about the characters and their relationships and roles in the literature. However, after visiting my classroom to see the students' artwork, he noticed and acknowledged the sophisticated levels of comprehension they reflected. He was so impressed with the depth, breadth, and creativity of the work that he asked if he could sit in the class for the remainder of that unit!

You can be sure your alternative assignments are well designed and serve as successful alternative assessments if you

- Determine in advance what you want to learn about the students
- Tell students the knowledge on which they are being evaluated
- Give students options to show that knowledge in their dominant intelligence

ENTERING ART

1. Step inside the artwork. Let its space become your space. What does it feel like as you journey into the painting? Where are you? What do you hear? Smell? What do you notice under your feet? Imagine you can touch something in the painting. What would that be? How would it feel?
2. Write about the artwork as if it were a dream. Bring the scene to life and leave us in that moment. Use "In a dream, I . . ." or "Last night I had the strangest dream . . ." or simply, "I dreamed . . . ."
3. Write about the scene as if it is happening now, using present tense and active verbs. Begin with "I am . . . ." Move around inside the work and make things happen. Begin a line with "Suddenly . . ." in order to create surprise, moving into something unexpected.
4. Write about the work as if it is a memory. List short, separate memories or one long memory. Both invent and remember as you write.
5. Imagine the art as something you see outside a window. Begin with "From my window, I see . . ."

Art illuminates
lessons we teach our students
and they understand.

—Anna J. Small Roseboro

CONCLUSION

Historical fiction as a genre offers a rich source of multidisciplinary material for teaching in middle school. It provides a luxury side trip on this school-year journey, the kind one would experience visiting an archeological dig while on a trip to the modern high-rise city of Kuala Lumpur. You could teach the novel simply as another fictional text. Or you can treat it as a way to have students look at the past to see the present and perhaps at ways to change the future. Assignments accompanying this particular genre not only give your students opportunities to refine their research skills; hone their speaking abilities; discover new people, places, and events; view art by renowned painters; and write about and discuss issues of friendship and ethics, but also to meet many of the Common Core State Standards outlined in English Language Arts and Literacy in History/Social Studies, Science, and Technical Subjects[17] or those set by your course curriculum.

Like the mistress described in *I, Juan de Pareja*, your students may at first find that they read historical fiction slowly and laboriously and that they have to spend tearful afternoons writing. But once they have the pleasure of getting to know about people and places, delving into another time period through reading, writing, viewing, and discussing ideas to which they can relate today, they feel more confident and competent in demonstrating their refined common core skills and the personal challenges they face in the 21st century.

NOVELS TO CONSIDER FOR
TEACHING HISTORICAL FICTION

Al Capone Does My Shirts by Gennifer Choldenko: It's 1935 and Moose Flanagan has just moved to Alcatraz Island with his family so that his father can work as an electrician. Moose has to help with his autistic sister, Natalie, who has been rejected from a special school. Great book for lessons on character development, voice, and setting.

Catherine, Called Birdy by Karen Cushman: This hilarious novel is written as the diary entries of 14-year-old Birdy, daughter of an English nobleman in the 12th century. Impeccably researched, the book includes wonderful (and often disgusting) details of life in the Middle Ages. Great book to study characterization, setting, and dialect.

Crispin: The Cross of Lead by Avi: *Crispin: The Cross of Lead* is a great book to accompany a study of medieval England. After his mother dies and he is accused of murder, 13-year-old Crispin flees from his home. Armed with only a lead cross as a clue to his father's identity, Crispin seeks to uncover the truth of his past. Students are caught up in the story and do not even realize how much they're learning about the Middle Ages or the art of good storytelling.

Eagle of the Ninth by Rosemary Sutcliff: What an adventure! Marcus Flavius Aquila seeks to discover what may have happened to the Ninth Legion of the Roman army stationed in Britain during the reign of Emperor Hadrian, the legion in which his father served and that disappeared. Middle school students are intrigued by the unusual friendships that emerge between the Roman soldiers from the south and the blue tattooed people in the north. Viewing excerpts from the 2011 movie *The Eagle* can be a part of an assignment for students to compare what they read with what they see on the screen.

Nectar in a Sieve by Kamala Markandaya: Set in rural India and told from the perspective of a woman who at 12 years old had to marry a man she had never met, this tale of growing up and raising a family of her own engages middle school students who may never have considered the challenges faced by the narrator whose story begins when she is their age. Twenty-first-century students may be able to find similar themes in contemporary news stories about the environment and global warming.

Nightjohn by Gary Paulsen: In the 1850s, slaves in America are beaten or dismembered if they attempt to learn to read. Why then would a man who had managed to escape from slavery return in order to secretly teach other slaves how to read? *Nightjohn* is a wonderful but gritty story that gives an accurate portrayal of slave life in the 1800s.

Number the Stars by Lois Lowry: In the mostly troubling genre of Holocaust fiction, Lois Lowry chooses to tell an uplifting, true story focusing on the bravery of the Danish people who helped more than 7,000 Jews escape to Sweden from the perspective of 10-year-old Annemarie Johannesen whose best friend is among the Jews hoping to escape. Pair with *Night* by Elie Wiesel to show that even in the worst of times there is hope.

Island of the Blue Dolphins by Scott O'Dell: Based on a true story, *Island of the Blue Dolphins* tells the remarkable tale of a 12-year-old Native American girl, Karana, whose home island of Ghalas-at, located off the coast of California, is evacuated, and she jumps the boat to stay with her little brother who has been left behind. After her brother dies, Karana must survive on her own for 18 years.

The Ruby in the Smoke by Philip Pullman: Sally Lockhart has none of the "important" skills that young women of her Victorian English home are expected to have. This baffling mystery is part satire of the "penny dreadfuls" of Victorian England and would serve well as part of a study of literary genres.

NOTES

1. Elizabeth Borton de Treviño, *I, Juan de Pareja* (Canada: HarperCollins, 1993), 6.
2. *Core Standards*, 2011. www.corestandards.org/assets/CCSSI_ELA%20Standards.pdf (accessed May 17, 2012).
3. Susan Zimmermann and Chryse Hutchins, *Seven Keys to Comprehension: How to Help Your Kids Read It and Get It* (New York: Three Rivers Press, 2003), 50–51.
4. "Renaissance," *WordNetWeb*, http://wordnetweb.princeton.edu/perl/webwn?s=renaissance (accessed April 3, 2012).
5. "Outrageous women of the Renaissance: Warriors, artists, rulers, and thieves," *Education World*, www.educationworld.com/a_books/books126.shtml (accessed April 3, 2012).
6. "Artemisia Gentileschi and Elisabetta Sirani—Two women of the Italian Baroque," http://newexpressionist.blogspot.com/2009/03/artemisia-gentileschiand-elisabetta.html (accessed April 3, 2012).
7. "Outrageous women of the Renaissance," Wiley, December 31, 2003, www.wiley.com/WileyCDA/WileyTitle/productCd-0471235091.html

8. Carol Jago, *With Rigor for All: Teaching the Classics to Contemporary Students* (Portland, ME: Calendar Islands, 2000), 55.

9. *Advanced Dictionary* (Sunnyvale, CA: Scott, Foresman, Thorndike-Barnhart Series 1988), s.v. "chiaroscuro."

10. *Advanced Dictionary*, s.v. "baroque."

11. *Advanced Dictionary*, s.v. "realism."

12. *Advanced Dictionary*, s.v. "idealism."

13. Chris Stevenson, "Curriculum that is challenging, integrative, and exploratory," *This We Believe . . . and Now We Must Act I*, ed. Thomas O. Erb (Westerville, OH: National Middle School Association, 2001), 63.

14. Fran Claggett with Joan Brown, *Drawing Your Own Conclusions: Graphic Strategies for Reading, Writing, and Thinking* (Portsmouth, NH: Heinemann. 1992), 5–6.

15. *Houghton-Mifflin College Dictionary*, 1986, s.v. "poetry."

16. Terry Williams and J. Williams, "Image, word, poem: Visual literacy and the writing process," National Council of Teachers of English annual convention, Detroit Institute of Art, 1997.

17. *Core Standards*, 2011, www.corestandards.org/assets/CCSSI_ELA%20Standards.pdf (accessed May 17, 2012).

Chapter Seven

Taking T.I.M.E. to Teach Poetry

Words, Words, Words
Words stir me
When I hear them,
When I read them,
When I write them,
When I speak them.

Words urge me
To keep listening
To keep reading
To keep writing
To keep speaking.

Let me hear you,
so I can know you.
Let me speak,
so you can know me.

Prodigiously stirring words
help me know you.
And viscerally urging words
help me know me.

—Anna J. Small Roseboro, "Words, Words, Words"

Young teens can be apprehensive about studying poetry. Some believe there is a key or secret code to understanding poetry and only teachers have the key to decipher that code. Experienced readers know that is not the case; it is a matter of understanding the genre and approaching poetry in a different

Figure 7.1.   Artist, Linda Hargrove.

way—paying special attention to poets' careful selection and arrangement of words. The lessons in this chapter are designed to provide you and your students with a set of strategies that can help them approach, read, understand, analyze, write in the style of, and write about classical, contemporary, structured, and free-verse poetry. Students will be reading closely and developing those Common Core State Standards for English Language Arts[1] anchor skills relating to reading, writing, speaking, listening, and viewing, as well as using technology for learning, publishing, and showing what they know.

PREPARING TO TEACH POETRY

Scrounge as many books of poetry as you can from the school or neighborhood library and your department library, and borrow from your colleagues. If several of you are teaching poetry at the same time, consider borrowing a library cart so you can merge your poetry collections and move the cart easily among your rooms. To make this a really rich experience for your students, have a ready trove of poems for students to mine during their study. If your students have access to technology at home or at school, assemble a list of age-appropriate websites to post as a hyperlinked list on your webpage so students can access them quickly. At the end of the chapter, there is a list of collections and links to inspect and select as resources you can make available for students to peruse and use. Even if you are in a high-tech setting, lots of print books should still be on hand. The visuals in them will spark interest and increase understanding.

Using a Poem to Introduce Poetry Analysis

Begin with a poem to explain the process. Consider the poem "Unfolding Bud" by Naoshi Koriyama, as it provides a useful metaphor for the experience the students have when they read poetry. This poem seems to allay some of their anxiety about understanding poetry. You may have the poem posted or projected or distribute printed copies but, at first, do not read the poem aloud. Instead, without saying anything more, let the students look at it for a couple of minutes. Sometimes silence gives space for student learning.

"Unfolding Bud"

One is amazed
by a water-lily bud
Unfolding
With each passing day,
Taking on a richer color
And new dimensions.
One is not amazed

At first glance,
By a poem,
Which is as tight-closed
As a tiny bud.

Yet one is surprised
To see the poem
Gradually unfolding,
Revealing its rich inner self,
As one reads it
Again
And over again.[2]

Now, use a multiple readings format. Here is how it works. Ask the students to read the poem silently, paying attention to the punctuation and marking words or phrases that catch their attention. Next, read the poem aloud yourself. Then, ask them do a "jump in" oral reading. One student begins reading and stops at the first mark of punctuation (comma, semicolon, period, question mark, etc.). Another student, without raising his or her hand, continues reading until the next punctuation mark.

Students are likely to giggle when more than one student begins reading aloud at the same time, but just start over and encourage students who jump in at the same time to listen to each other and to read together as one voice. It usually takes three or four false starts before the students get the idea and are comfortable reading aloud this way. Other students can continue jumping in to read until the end of the poem.[3] Relax and allow the pauses between readers to be moments of resonation and reflection. False starts encourage students to pay attention to the words, lines, and punctuation, and thus expand their understanding of the poem.

This first day is a good time to talk about the value of multiple readings and why it often is necessary for this condensed form of literature. The "Unfolding Bud" poem by Naoshi Koriyama is a great conversation starter for this topic. In the poem, Koriyama compares reading a poem to watching a water lily bud unfold. It takes time but is worth the wait.

When teaching poetry, resist the temptation to ask students what the poem "means." This phrase incorrectly suggests there is only one meaning for a poem. The phrase "what it says" encourages the students to look at the individual words and respond with a literal meaning, which can be the first step to analyzing poetry. The subsequent steps include determining whether the poem is saying something about a bigger issue or idea and whether the poem is speaking metaphorically.

Some poets may not have begun writing their poem about big universal issues; they may have written simply to re-create a very personal observation or experience. Yet, when read by others, their poem speaks to the readers about issues quite different from the literal ideas intended originally. Often these bigger ideas do not emerge or manifest themselves on the first or second readings. "Unfolding Bud" closes with the lines "over and over again," which suggests that poetry is somewhat different from some prose and drama in that, more often than not, multiple readings are required to understand poetry.

Some poets, like Quincy Troupe, are very aware of the fact that poems can be seen to mean lots more than the words on the page. Share with your students these excerpted stanzas from his poem, "My Poems Have Holes Sewn into Them." Have fun with the unusual way the words are laid out on the page. Note particularly the last words in each line, the punning, and the use of the ampersand sign instead of the word "and." How do these features affect the reading? (Won't "ampersand" be fun to teach your middle school students?) What about Troupe's use of only lowercase letters?

my poems have holes sewn into them
& they run, searching for light
at the end of tunnels, they become trains
or at the bottom of pits, they become blackness
or in the broad, winging daylight
they are words that fly

. . .

my poems have holes sewn into them
& their voices are like different keyholes
through which dumb men search for speech, blind
men search for sight
words, like drills, penetrating sleep
keys unlocking keyholes of language
words giving sight to blind peoples eyes

. . .

my poems have holes sewn into them
& they are spaces between worlds
are worlds themselves
words falling off into one another
colliding, like people gone mad, they space out
fall, into bottomless pits, which are black
holes of letters that become words
& worlds, like silent space
between chords of a piano
—Quincy Troupe[4]

Reading Poems in Alternative Ways

If you would rather not use "jump-in" reading to introduce the unit, slowly read the poem aloud yourself, allowing time for the words to make their impact. Ask a single student to read the poem according to the punctuation, rather than just stopping at the end of each line. This second reading helps the students focus on the fact that poems sometimes include punctuation, and that the punctuation serves the same functions as that used in prose, clarifying the meanings of words organized in a particular order. It still is beneficial to have a third reading of the poem by another student who, by this time, may have an idea of what the poet may be trying to express, and this student may choose to emphasize different words or to read at a different pace and thus offer a third level of understanding. Either approach—jump-in reading or multiple readings—demonstrates the value of repetition to allow a poem to reveal itself to the readers and listeners.

DEFINING POETRY: A FOUNDATION FOR DISCUSSION

The first day of the unit is a prime time to provide the students with a definition of poetry, a distinctive genre of literature that sometimes baffles and sometimes thrills readers with its versatility. Use the definition in your anthology or the one that follows. In either case, dictate the definition and then have the students write in the poetry section they have set up in their reading journals.

> Poetry is literature designed to *convey* a vivid and imaginative sense of experience, especially by the use of *condensed* language *chosen* for its sound and *suggestive* power as well as for its meaning and by the use of such literary devices as *structured* meter, *natural cadences*, rhyme and metaphor.[5]

You may want to read the definition a couple of times, letting your voice emphasize the italicized words. Then, slowly dictate the definition so students can write the definition in their journals. Finally, project the definition so they can verify their writing. Why this laborious start? Hearing, listening, writing, and viewing are ways to reinforce the concept. This definition will form the basis of subsequent reflections on the form and function of poetry studied throughout the unit. Having a definition of a specific kind of writing aids close reading and deeper understanding of the genre and helps students to make sense of it as they experiment with writing it.

Take a few moments more and ask the students what they think the italicized words mean in the context of poetry. If no one offers definitions, direct the students to find the words in a print or digital dictionary and to share the definitions with the class. It is good to have stored dictionaries under students' desks or on shelves around the room so students can reach them quietly and easily. It should not be unusual to see one or more of them reaching for a dictionary during any class meeting. Those students who use computers regularly can be encouraged to leave a dictionary link right on their desktops.

Now return to the poem "Unfolding Bud" or "My Poems Have Holes Sewn into Them" and again ask the students what they imagine either poem is saying to them about reading poetry. What elements of the definition have Koriyama and/or Troupe used in their poems?

To solidify student understanding, end the lesson by having the students read aloud, in unison, the definition of poetry they have written in their notebooks, and then, like a Greek chorus, read one of the opening poems. The left side of the class can read stanza one, the right side stanza two, and in unison, the whole class can read stanza three.

SWIMMING AROUND IN POEMS

For homework, you can assign the students to peruse their literature anthology or other poetry collections they have, can borrow, and find in the library or online. Ask them to read four or five poems, and then handwrite into their notebook at least one poem they particularly like. If such an assignment is not a realistic expectation for the students you have, allot some in-class time for them to look through their available poetry collections. Just ask the students to select and copy into their own notebooks one or two poems that attract their attention. For those using computers, encourage them to type the poem rather than simply copying and pasting. The physical act of handwriting or typing the poem slows them down a bit so they can pay attention to individual words, line structure, and pattern in poetry, three of the distinguishing features of this genre of literature.

Your students then have a self-selected poem to refer to and share with the class later on during the unit. The value of this assignment is that it gives the students an opportunity to read a variety of poems for which they are not required to do anything more than choose one they like. And the bonus? They are likely to read twice as many poems this way than if you were to assign them a specific one to read for class. The next class meeting simply record in the grade book whether or not each student has the poem. The goal here is to get them reading poetry and to become more at ease with this literary form.

USING POPULAR SONG LYRICS
TO INTRODUCE POETRY—PLAY IT!

Encourage students to bring in song lyrics that are appropriate for sharing in class. Until you point it out, probably few young adolescents recognize that song lyrics often are poems. Having your students bring in song lyrics and poems of their choice also is a way for you to become more familiar with what your students enjoy. They also feel as though they are a part of the learning process because they're the ones helping to shape the lessons. Depending on the students you teach, you may wish to collect and read the lyrics first, and then use them for a lesson later in the unit. If you have time, ask students to bring in 10–15-second musical samples of the choruses for their selected song lyrics. Play a few of these as examples of poetic repetition.

SHARING POETRY T.I.M.E—
A STRATEGY FOR POETRY ANALYSIS

Poetry T.I.M.E has been around for decades and has been passed along from teacher to teacher across the nation.[6] You, too, may have been taught this way and find this clever acronym just what you need to organize your instruction and entice student learning. If you choose to use this idea, you are likely to have former students return to express their appreciation for having a mnemonic that serves them well on standardized and placement tests as well as

Figure 7.2.   Poetry: Understanding poetry takes T.I.M.E. Artist, Linda Hargrove.

on final exams in other courses. In relation to poetry, T.I.M.E. stands for *title*, *imagery*, *music*, and *emotion*.

Knowing this acronym can help students unlock meaning in poetry. Since poems often require multiple readings, the T.I.M.E. really is a pun and refers not only to the fact that it often takes more time to read and write poetry but also to elements of a poem that, when considered independently, can lead to a deeper understanding of the poem in its entirety. Taking T.I.M.E. for poetry will help them recognize the holes poets like Quincy Troupe may have conscientiously or unconsciously sewn into their poems.

The Letter "T"

Begin with T, for the title of a poem. If a poet has chosen a title, it often serves as a hint to what the poem is about, the emotion or opinion the poet has about the experience related, and may be a peephole into the interior the reader will explore once inside the poem. The T also could stand for the Thought or Theme of the poem. This is a flexible acronym and you can decide the best one, two, or three of these word(s) to use with the students you have.

Just for fun, project a copy of the poem "Finalists" by Nancy Genevieve. Do not show the students the title when you ask them what the poem is about. Then, show them the title and ask how their understanding of the poem changes. Ask them to look at the poem they have written in their journals. How might the meaning be changed if there were no title?

"Finalists"

Seven turkey vultures

on the uppermost gable
of the cow barn

Preening.[7]

Next, draw the students' attention to concepts about the speaker and audience. Published poetry is meant to be understood. You may choose to clarify this idea and specify "published poetry" because many people write poetry just for themselves and may not care whether anyone else even reads it, let alone understands it. Generally, though, a poet is someone saying something to someone.

That first someone is "the speaker," who may or may not be the poet. For example, you may have a poet, an elderly woman, who writes a poem in the persona of an adolescent boy. In this situation, the poet is a woman, but the speaker in the poem is a boy. Looking at the kinds of pronouns used, the vocabulary and images can help the reader imagine the audience. One visual

Figure 7.3.   Poetry is someone saying something to someone. Artist, Linda Hargrove.

way that helps students think of poetry as a piece of writing with a message is to use a graphic design with three spaces, such as that depicted in figure 7.3

After they make this full-page chart in the poetry section of their journals, ask your students to draw a picture of a possible speaker on the left; on the right, draw a possible audience: one person, a special person, or a group of people. Then, in the rectangle in the center, they could write a summary of what the poem could be saying and quote a couple of lines from the poem to support their opinion.

Demonstrate how this could work by referring first to "My Poems Have Holes Sewn into Them" by Quincy Troupe and then to "Unfolding Bud" by Naoshi Koriyama. Draw the graphic organizer on the board and then ask students, "Who could be the speaker?" "Who could be the audience?" For the Koriyama poem, typical answers include a parent talking to a student who is doing his or her homework and who persuades the young person to hang in there and not give up just because the poem is difficult to understand after one or two readings. Some students may respond that it is a teacher speaking to an individual student or to the class as a whole.

To reinforce the ideas of speaker and audience, distribute a copy of Emily Dickinson's poem, "I'm Nobody." Ask the students to read it and think of as many different speaker and audience sets as they can. You could ask them to imagine this poem is to be spoken by a character in a play or in a movie. What could be the setting? Who could be the speaker? Who the audience? The only limitation is that the sets must be supported by the words of the poem. Your middle school students may come up with combinations or settings such as

- A student new to the school talking to another student at lunch time
- A prisoner talking to another prisoner
- A new teacher at the first department meeting
- A boy at the playground during a pickup soccer, football, or basketball game
- A rock singer waiting to perform on a TV program
- An actress trying out for a part in a play to another actress
- A parent talking to another parent during the school open house

If you are in the mood, act a little silly, ham it up, and reread the poem in the voices and persona of the pairs the students suggest. Or have students do so! Great fun! Makes the point, too, of multiple possibilities but common messages.

The Letter "I"

"I" stands for the imagery of poetry. Poets use words to help create pictures, emotions, or memories of incidents in the minds of the readers and listeners. Poets may use sensory or figurative imagery or a combination of the two. Sensory imagery appeals to one or more of the five senses through which we experience the world: sight, hearing, taste, touch, and smell. Many poets appeal to these senses as they recreate their own experiences in poetic form.

Rather than presenting this portion of the lesson as lecture, simply draw or project an eye, an ear, a mouth, a hand, and a nose on the board. Then,

Figure 7.4.   Poetry: T = title, thought, theme. Artist, Linda Hargrove.

ask the students to label the drawings and give examples of words or phrases that appeal to the senses. Prepare for the lesson by looking at a variety of poems, compiling sample lines from poems that illustrate appeals to the various senses. Better yet, invite students to offer lines they recall from lyrics of songs familiar to them—but be prepared with your examples to prime the pump . . . to get them thinking.

This would be a good time to ask students to look back at the poems they copied into their journals at the beginning of the unit. Set your timer for five minutes and have students look at their poems and mark images. Then, reset for ten minutes, invite the students to pull their desks together or turn to a table partner and share these poems, pointing out examples of sensory images from their chosen poems. Working with the poems they have chosen validates the assignment to choose and copy them into their notebooks. Invite volunteers to read aloud to the class lines that illustrate the sensory images they find. Variety spices the lessons and increases interest.

Next, direct their attention to figurative imagery. Most of your middle school students learned about similes and metaphors in earlier grades and are able to define them for the class. Some know "personification"; fewer know "hyperbole," "symbol," and "allusion." Be prepared to introduce these devices and give students definitions and examples. Here are some simple definitions of these types of figurative imagery:

- *Simile*: a comparison between two things using "like" or "as." Example: The thunder roared like a bear.

Figure 7.5. Poetry: I = imagery. Artist, Linda Hargrove.

- *Metaphor*: an implied comparison between two things without using the words "like" or "as." Example: Adolescent trees bow in obeisance, ancient trees resist in vain.
- *Hyperbole*: exaggeration to create an effect. Example: That goldfish is as big as my leg!
- *Personification*: giving something nonhuman the characteristics of a person. Example: The dog smirked and snatched up my sandwich.

Occasionally a poet uses a *symbol*—something concrete that stands for something else: an abstract concept, another thing, idea, or event—for example, a "flag" is a cloth on a stick. But a certain configuration of colors and shapes such as stars on a blue rectangular field in the upper left corner of a red and white striped cloth suggests the American flag, which stands for the nation, for freedom, and patriotism. Symbols can be a great opening to talk about cultural contexts, too. For example, a snake or serpent symbolizes different ideas depending on the culture, the religion, or the nation. Red in some cultures is a sad color representing blood or anger; in other cultures, it is a happy color representing marriage or royalty.

An *allusion* is the reference to another body of literature, a movie, or an incident the writer believes the readers know. Allusions can help the writer create an image with just a few words because the writer believes the allusion automatically triggers memories, ideas, or emotions from its reference in the poem. Your students may enjoy playing with this poetic device in much the same way Nancy Genevieve has in these few lines from her poem "A Kiss":

Enchanted innocent kissed the frog
and heard only a croak in reply.

Will you, child, kiss it again
and give him another try?
Or will you release him
and then begin to cry?

Or worse will you never ever
give another frog a chance?[8]

In Western literature, allusions are frequently made to the Bible, with its Hebrew and Christian Scriptures, and to Roman and Greek mythology, Shakespeare's writings, and fairy tales. Sometimes a reference may be made to familiar movie, like *Star Wars*, or to a historical incident, like the Civil War or the Gold Rush. If your students represent a range of cultures and national origins, select samples from the literature and historical events that are more familiar to them. Consider stories, myths, and sacred texts your students may know from literature and life in Central and South America, Asia, India, Africa, and Australia.

You could spend the remainder of the period looking at examples of poems that have strong imagery. Project copies of the two poems already discussed as a class. Then, ask students to find examples of various kinds of imagery to share and compare with a partner, and encourage them to copy favorite lines into their journals. Remember, in finding their own examples, the students read much more poetry than if you provide all the examples. Equally important is the fact that each year you teach the unit you should be learning and can be discovering the kinds of poems that interest students in each different class.

Students may enjoy pointing out the figurative language in "Evening Cicadas" and "The Pond" by Nancy Genevieve:[9]

Evening cicadas

tune up for night
practicing their

lull-a-bye for summer.

This short poem illustrates so well the personification that can brings such a personal appeal to a poem. What images do your students notice in this next one?

Bubbles frozen in ice
pearls of silence
waiting for spring.

Crystals etched in glaze
petals of illusion,
blooming by night.

Twilight bathed in mist
flames of fading,
seeping into no more.

Patterning Poetry

An assignment that always evokes positive responses and pretty good poetry is one on patterning poems.[10] Ask the students to select one or two of the poems that they particularly like. Next, ask them to think of a memorable experience of their own. Finally, invite them to pattern the structure and imagery of one of their chosen poems to recreate the experience of that particular incident. Of course, if you are writing poems along with them (and you should), you experience what it feels like to write on demand as you are asking them to do. Then you, too, have something newly written to read during sharing time.

For example, you could ask your students to write a lyric poem patterned after Robert Frost's "Acquainted with the Night" or a folk ballad like "Barbara Allen," based on a personal experience:

"The Ballad of William and Anna"

Oh, it was around Christmas time
When the marriage, it was planned.
The family and friends all came to see
Sir William wed Lady Ann.

The musicians were seated, all playing their songs
Awaiting the groom to appear.
And seated among the guests that day
Sat his former love, Lady Mear.

The minister signaled the groom to come out
To stand with best man at the right.
The minister motioned the guests to stand
As the bride marched in dressed in white.

Lady Mear, she stood with hankie in hand
Weeping for the man she had lost.
She'd been too proud to accept the ring
Sir William had gotten at cost.

The bride advanced at a stately pace
By her handsome groom to stand
Lady Mear, near the aisle, could be heard for a mile,
Shouting, "Hey Lady Ann, that's my man!"

Sir William's response to the lady's outburst,
"You had my heart in your hand.
You cast me aside. Yes, I did love you first,
But today, I'll wed Lady Ann."

So that day long ago about Christmas time,
The guests got more than was planned.
An old love turned mean in quite a wild scene
When Sir William wed Lady Ann.

—Anna J. Small Roseboro,
patterned after "Barbara Allen," by an anonymous poet

The Letter "M"

"M" stands for music or the sounds found in poetry. According to the definition used earlier, poets chose words "for their sound and suggestive power." Look at three aspects of music and poetry: rhythm, rhyme, and the sound of words. Some poets arrange their words to create a pattern of beats or *rhythm*. If your students are ready, teach the ITADS, an acronym for five common poetic rhythm patterns—*iambic, trochaic, anapestic, dactylic,* and *spondee*. These words identify the patterns of stressed and unstressed syllables that students surely are expected to know and use in high school.

During this lesson on music, mention to the students that ITADS patterns are called the "feet" of poetry with only one stressed syllable in each foot. Explain that a poem's rhythm, or the "meter," is named for the number of feet or beats per line and the kind of foot that is in each line. For example, a line of poetry with four feet or four beats is tetrameter (*tetra* is Greek for four). If the feet are iambic—one unstressed syllable followed by a stressed one—the line is identified as iambic tetrameter. Have fun by asking students to identify the rhythm patterns of their own names. Anna is trochaic. Jamar is iambic. Roseboro is dactylic. What are the patterns of your name?

Moving to the Music of Poetry

Because many students are kinesthetic learners and can remember what they feel physically, you should demonstrate the rhythms of poetry that

RHYME

MUSIC

RHYTHM

SOUND

Figure 7.6. Poetry: M = music. Artist, Linda Hargrove.

way, too. Read a poem with a strong beat while the students are standing up and marching in place. How about inviting students to clap their hands, tap one foot, or snap their fingers to the beat?

To use that abundance of adolescent energy, have the students march around the room when you read William Wordsworth's poem about daffodils, "I Wander'd Lonely as a Cloud." Rather than wandering quietly, stomp loudly. Use your arms to sway broadly from side to side to show the rhythm of the waves in John Masefield's "Sea Fever:" "I *must* go down to the seas again, to the *lonely* sea and the sky." Of course, the students see right away the rhythm of song lyrics, but you could save this until later. For now, acknowledge that "Just as some poetry has a specific rhythm pattern, so do the lyrics or words of some songs you know." Students can mark their poems using a "u" above unstressed syllables and a "/" above stressed syllables. They soon can see the patterns, count the stressed syllables, and determine the number of feet per line.

A second way to look at the music of poetry is to consider the *rhyme*, which occurs when words with similar sounds are used in an observable pattern. The rhyme may occur at the end of a line or within a line. Students can discover the pattern of rhyme by using letters of the alphabet to indicate repeated sounds. For example, begin writing with the letter "a" at the end of the first line of poetry. If the second line ends with the same sound, write "a" again. If it ends with a different sound, change to "b." Continue throughout the poem to determine if there is a pattern and what the pattern is.

I wandered lonely as a *cloud*	A
That floats on high o'er vales and hills	B
When all at once I saw a *crowd*	A

What's the pattern of the "Ballad of William and Ann"? How about the narrative poem "The Cremation of Sam McGee," in which poet Robert W. Service uses both internal and end rhyme? The macabre story is intriguing, too. Check out the online versions with recorded renditions by both Robert Service and Johnny Cash. Your students may enjoy the photos, too.

Now for the kicker! Point out that free and blank verse poetry have no systematic rhyme pattern. You probably plan to discuss this kind of poetry later in your unit but should mention it now, particularly if students bring in examples of free verse poetry or notice it in their class anthology. This is why it is good to begin the unit with the definition of poetry that mentions structured meter or natural cadences. Your discussion of the music of poetry gives space to talk about blank and free verse without having to provide another definition or having to backpedal when students point out that some poetry is unstructured in terms of rhythm and rhyme.

Seeing Song Lyrics as Poetry

Now is an optimal time to ask selected students to read aloud the lyrics of their favorite songs. Most of them have a steady beat and many of them rhyme, making more concrete the connection between poetry of music and poetry in books much easier to comprehend. Be prepared for students to show more interest in what they bring to the class. Show your enthusiasm as you look at and listen to what they bring. They are providing you a window into their world and what you learn reveals what they know and indicates what you may need to teach or reteach as you continue planning learning experiences for your poetry unit. Combine the familiar with the new by encouraging your students to use the vocabulary of poetry as they talk about poems they choose themselves.

If you have the nerve of most middle school teachers, you can "prove" the link between poetry and music by singing the "I'm Nobody" poem to either "Yellow Rose of Texas" or "America, the Beautiful"! Even if you are a very good singer, the students probably are going to laugh at you, but they will also remember the lesson. Is that not the goal of teaching?

A third way to talk about the music or sound of poetry is to point out *onomatopoeia*, words that are spelled to imitate the sound they describe. Middle school students love making peculiar, sometimes shocking and vulgar noises. One way to exploit that particular pleasure is to have the students write poems that capture the sounds of everyday experiences. Warren, a seventh grader, wrote "The Kitchen" about the sounds in his home. Like Shakespeare, Warren enjoys making up words, too.

With a cling clang
Not a bang or dang
a swish and a wish
all the dishes are in the sink
screech creach
open
close
scuffles ruffles
a sea of bubbles and water
a crounging rounging
with a turn of the knob
all the dishes are clean
then click click click
whoosh.
Are you hungry for lunch yet?

Another way to address sound as you discuss the music of poetry is to consider repetition of vowels (*assonance*) or consonants (*consonance* or *alliteration*). Most middle school students recognize tongue twisters as examples of alliteration.

Students are intrigued to learn that the sound of words suggests certain emotions, too. For example, a poet who wishes to convey the emotion or sense of experience in a calm, peaceful way is likely to select soft-sounding consonants like *l*, *m*, *n*, and *s*. If the memory is unpleasant or bitter, the poet is likely to pick hard consonants that must be forced through the lips and teeth to be formed, like *p*, *t*, and *f*, or guttural sounds like *k*, *g*, and *j*. A graphic way to illustrate this can be pointing out that most obscene words in English include these harsh, guttural, and dental sounds.

Of course, you need not to say them aloud or write them down. Students know the words if you refer to "the F word" or "the S word." Students smile and smirk, and your point is made. If many of your students speak other languages, and if you can maintain control of the class, you may ask these students if profane words in their language follow this pattern of harsh sounds. Again, let them think, but not speak, the words. The point is made.

The Letter "E"

The "E" stands for the *emotion* of the poem, both expressed by the poet and experienced by the reader. How do students discover these emotions? By paying attention to the kinds of images (comparisons to positive or negative things), and the music, rhyme, rhythm, and sounds of the words the poet chooses to use to convey the experience of the poem. The students may find examples of emotions expressed such as pride, love, grief/distress, fear, joy, jealousy, or shame/embarrassment. They may experience similar feelings as they read or hear the poems, but the emotions expressed and experienced often are not the same. Have them try their new analyzing skills reading and talking about "The Boy in the Window" by Richard Wilbur.

If the students are ready, go ahead teach them that the "tone" of a poem refers to the author's attitude or feeling about the topic or experience related in the poem. On the other hand, "mood" refers to the way the poem makes the reader feel when he or she reads or hears a poem. To help make the link more personal, you can draw their attention to the M in mood and say, "Mood means the way the poem makes ME, the reader, feel." That usually is sufficient instruction at this time. As you teach these poetry terms, continue to encourage students to use them regularly when talking and writing about poetry. Such use raises the level of their conversation and expands their working vocabulary—and makes them feel oh so sophisticated.

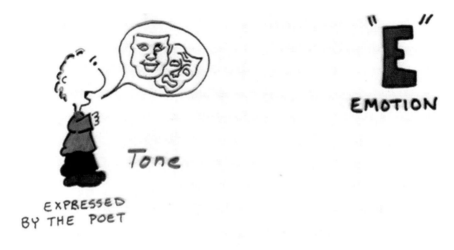

Figure 7.7. Poetry: E = emotion. Artist, Linda Hargrove.

SPENDING T.I.M.E. READING POEMS INDEPENDENTLY

One way for students to practice reading on their own without feeling undue pressure is to ask them to continue bringing in poems and to point out the ways their self-selected poems reflect the various elements already studied. This subtly entices them to read more widely. They are likely to return to the books skimmed before and come across poems that speak to them differently this time. Giving this assignment again also reveals to you how students' choice of poetry is being modified by the series of lessons you are teaching. Invite them to post their choices on your class wiki, remembering to include the title, author, and source. Or they can print out copies and staple those on a bulletin board set aside for this purpose in your classroom and labeled "Poems We Like."

As they seek out poems, encourage your students to interview their family members to learn about their favorite poems. It's surprising how amazed middle school students are to learn that their moms, dads, aunts, uncles, and even grandparents had to memorize and recite poetry as regular part of their literature course work! If your students speak languages other than English at home, invite them to bring in poems by favorite poets in those languages and read them aloud to the class. This affirms their heritage and expands the cultural experience for you and their classmates, while demonstrating the universality of poetry!

Allow plenty of class time for students to immerse themselves in the poetry you have assembled in the classroom, their anthology, and the websites such as those listed at the end of this chapter. Those students who have not done so before may now choose to bring in lyrics from their favorite songs. Appropriate ones, of course!

You know to alert your students to the fact that poems address an array of topics in a variety of ways. And remind your eager young teens to use their judgment on which poems would be appropriate to share in class. Thankfully, by this time in the school year, you have established a classroom milieu for sensitive reading and sensible selections. However, reminding them at this time is still a good idea.

Notice in "Questions to Ask about Poetry" the use of "a message or theme" is to keep the poem open for the students to draw from it what the poem says to them. As soon as you suggest the "meaning," your students begin guessing and hoping they come up with the "right" answer. With self-control, you can let the poems speak for themselves.

As you plan to teach poetry in a more formal way, schedule time for students to complete an extensive poetry project such as those described in the "Language Arts Resources" section on the companion website for this book. There are two outlines for poetry units in which students collect and share poems they find and ones they write. See Teacher Resources C, D, and E in the appendix and on this book's companion website, http://teachingenglishlanguagearts.com. Both poetry units require students to write original poems as a way to practice the various poetic devices you study. Most students choose to include a metaphor poem similar to the one Kristen writes about looking at photographs in a family album, "Memories."

> Pictures are memories
> They evoke emotions unexplainable
> Remind you of your past,
> Giving clues for your future.
> They make some people remember

QUESTIONS TO ASK ABOUT POETRY

1. What does the title suggest about the poem?
2. Who could be the speaker? Indicate clues in the text to support this supposition.
3. Who could be the audience? Indicate clues in the text to support this supposition.
4. What literary devices/techniques has the poet used?
5. How do these elements work to create the total impact on me? (mood)
6. What do you think the poet feels about the topic of this poem? (tone)
7. What do I imagine is a message or theme of the poem?
8. What clues in the text support this claim?

> Long Forgotten Friends
> Or
> Never Forgotten Enemies
> For others they are
> Excellent Parties
> Or
> Horrible fights
> Either way
> Pictures are still Memories.

CONCLUSION

Few readers deny either that poets tend to write cryptically or that it takes more effort to discover what poets have to say to their listeners and readers. When you teach your students to tell the T.I.M.E. of a poem, you give your adolescent readers a golden key they can use for life. Using this key, they know to look systematically for different aspects of the poem on each reread. They experience delight of discovery and enthusiasm of empowerment when you give them T.I.M.E. to study this genre of literature. As when traveling in a new country and sampling new and different foods, the students may even develop gustatory joy from sampling this form of literary expression. Through the guided practice you offer, your squirmy adolescents slow down and pay attention to the words, the form, the sounds, and eventually the messages in poetry. They may even astonish you when their careful reading leads to interpretations similar to those that published critics write about the poems!

Your middle school traveling companions are ready to demonstrate how close they are coming to the Common Core State Standards for English

Figure 7.8. Poetry: Manageable key. Artist, Linda Hargrove.

Language Arts anchor standards for reading that recommend students know how to "interpret words and phrases as they are used in a text, including determining technical, connotative, and figurative meanings, and analyze how specific word choices shape meaning or tone."[11]

By the end of your formal instruction along this school-year journey, your students will feel far more confident about studying this challenging literary genre. They may not have the ease of Huck Finn's friend Emmeline Grangerford and be able to "slap down a line . . . just scratch it out and slap down another one,"[12] but they now are able to read, write, and talk more confidently about poetry in their own way. Your young teens can respond to those "prodigiously stirring words" and feel comfortable putting pen to paper to capture the "viscerally urging words" that become poems of their own.

BOOKS AND WEBSITES TO
SUPPLEMENT THE TEACHING OF POETRY

Books

Joshua Blum, Bob Holman, and Mark Pellington, *The United States of Poetry* (New York: Henry Holt, 1996).

Catherine Clinton, ed., *A Poem of Her Own: Voices of American Women Yesterday and Today* (New York: Harry N. Abrams, 2003).

Sharon Creech, *Love That Dog* (New York: HarperCollins, 2001).

Stephen Dunning, *Reflections on a Gift of Watermelon Pickle* (Glenview, IL: Scott-Foresman, 1995).

Bobbye Goldstein, ed., *Inner Chimes: Poems on Poetry* (Honesdale, PA: Boyds Mills Press, 1992).

Sara Holbrook, *By Definition: Poems of Feelings* (Honesdale, PA: Boyd Mills Press, 2003).

John Hollander, ed., *Committed to Memory* (New York: Academy of American Poets, 1996).

Paul B. Janeczko, ed., *Seeing the Blue Between: Advice and Inspiration for Young Poets* (Cambridge, MA: Candlewick Press, 2002).

Gail Carson Levine, *Forgive Me, I Meant to Do It* (New York: HarperCollins, 2012).

Molly Peacock, Elise Paschen, and Neil Neches, eds., *Poetry in Motion: 100 Poems from Subways and Buses* (New York: W. W. Norton, 1996).

Belinda Rochelle, ed., *Words with Wings: A Treasury of African American Poetry and Art* (New York: Amistad/HarperCollins, 2000).

Michael Strickland, ed., *Poems That Sing to You* (Honesdale, PA: Boyds Mills Press, 1993).

Patrice Vecchione, ed., *Revenge and Forgiveness: An Anthology of Poems* (New York: Henry Holt, 2004).

Patrice Vecchione, ed., *Truth and Lies: An Anthology of Poems* (New York: Henry Holt, 2001).

Voices: Poetry and Art from Around the World, selected by Barbara Brenner (Washington, D.C.: National Geographic Society, 2000).

Websites

The Academy of American Poets
American Poems
Favorite Poem Project by Robert Pinsky
Poems Daily
Poetry 180: A Poem a Day for American High Schools
ReadWriteThink

NOTES

1. "English Language Arts Standards 'Anchor Standards' College and Career Readiness Anchor Standards for Language," *Common Core State Standards Initiative*, 2011. www.corestandards.org/the-standards/english-language-arts-standards/anchor-standards-6-12/college-and-career-readiness-anchor-standards-for-reading/ (accessed April 6, 2012).

2. Naoshi Koriyama, "Unfolding Bud," *Christian Science Monitor*, July 13, 1957. Reprinted with permission.

3. This "jump-in" reading was demonstrated in the San Diego Area Writing Project and in workshops presented by Sheridan Blau, former president of NCTE and director of the South Coast Writing Project in California.

4. Quincy Troupe, "My Poems Have Holes Sewn into Them," *Transcircularities: New and Selected Poems* (Minneapolis, MN: Coffee House Press, 2002), 98–99.

5. *Houghton-Mifflin College Dictionary*, 1986, s.v. "poetry."

6. Poetry T.I.M.E. is not original to me. It's an acronym I picked up along the way, and because it stuck, I've used it with success for more than 30 years introducing students to poetry analysis.

7. Nancy Genevieve, "Finalists," *American Religion and Literature Society Newsletter*, ed. Deshae Lott (Spring 2007).

8. Nancy Genevieve. "A Kiss," *NYX: Mother of Light* (Tampa, FL: NOX Press, 2001) and *ELM* 5, no. 2 (Spring 1997).

9. Nancy Genevieve, "The Pond" and "Evening Cicadas," *NYX: Daughter of Chaos* (Tampa, FL: NOX Press, 2002).

10. Louann Reid and Fran Claggett, *Daybook for Critical Reading and Writing* (New York: Great Source Education Group, June 1998).

11. "English Language Arts Standards 'Anchor Standards' College and Career Readiness Anchor Standards for Language."

12. "If Emmeline Grangerford could make poetry like that before she was fourteen, there ain't no telling what she could a done by-and-by. Buck said she could rattle off poetry like nothing. She didn't ever have to stop to think. He said she would slap down a line, and if she couldn't find anything to rhyme with it she would just scratch it out and slap down another one, and go ahead." Mark Twain, *The Adventures of Huckleberry Finn*, chap. 17.

Chapter Eight

Reading, Writing, and Performing Drama

Playing It Right

I order you to be silent! And I issue a collective challenge! Come, I'll write down your names. Step forward, young heroes! You'll all have a turn; I'll give each of you a number. Now, who wants to be at the top of the list? You, sir? No? You? No? [Silence] No names? No hands. . . . Then I'll get on with my business.

—Cyrano, in *Cyrano de Bergerac* by Edmond Rostand

Cyrano's rousing speech may not have been as successful as he would have liked, but he certainly delivered it with enthusiasm and passion. You need the same passion to draw your students into reading and performing drama. In this chapter are techniques that can elicit a far better response than poor Cyrano received.

Drama permeates teachers' and students' lives via TV, movies, school productions, YouTube, and many other venues. This pervasiveness makes it a challenge to teach dramatic literature simply by reading it or writing drama without reading it—but that is just the way some drama is handled in middle school English classes. That need not be the case with you.

Middle school students need to stretch their dramatic creativity, imagining what words could sound like spoken aloud and what characters and scenes could look like on stage. Teaching a work of drama is a superb opportunity to broaden your students' experience with literature and to expand their understanding of the unique features of this literary genre. This chapter describes ways to help your young teens further develop their own expressive, oral reading and their creative writing skills, as well as practice those Common Core State Standards anchor skills that help students "analyze how two or more texts address similar themes or topics in order to build knowledge or to compare the approaches the authors take."[1]

Here are ideas from lessons on *Cyrano de Bergerac* for seventh graders and *Romeo and Juliet* for eighth or ninth graders. Even if you select other plays traditionally taught in middle school like *The Diary of Anne Frank* by Frances Goodrich and Albert Hackett, *A Raisin in the Sun* by Lorraine Hansberry, or *A Midsummer Night's Dream* by Shakespeare, you can adapt these ideas for your setting. The list at the end of the chapter gives you other ideas of plays to consider.

Drama, like other narrative literature, is written to tell a story of characters facing conflict. In this genre, dramatists create their narratives to be performed by actors who assume the roles of characters in the story. The setting—the time and place—is revealed primarily through sets, lights, props, and costumes, and readers must rely heavily on the dialogue, which reveals character and advances plot. Unfortunately, middle school students are tempted to skip those important stage directions; inexperienced readers tend to jump directly to the dialogue, causing confusion and frustration when they do not understand what is really happening. Consequently, the aspects of drama to teach first are its unique features, beginning the unit by pointing out those distinctive elements as you remind your maturing readers that characters and conflict are common to fiction in general.

PLANNING AHEAD

Plan your assignments so students can read aloud each day, ensuring that all who want to do so have an opportunity to read one major role at least once. If students can be depended upon to study the scenes ahead of time at home, assign parts as homework so students can practice reading aloud. Otherwise, allow class time for silent reading so your students can be familiar with the lines and are able to read them expressively in character. Few things dampen enthusiasm for studying drama more than poor oral reading. To interpret the roles effectively, your young actors need to know what is going on and what the lines portend.

Keep in mind, too, that plays are written to be viewed in a single theatrical sitting (perhaps with intermissions). Therefore, if you stretch out the initial reading over too many days or weeks, you lose the essence of the drama. Keep the action alive. Once the class has read the exposition of the play and the students are familiar with the main characters and the problem(s) to be solved, move as quickly through the play as possible. Then after you have read the entire play, go back and talk about the effectiveness of the literary devices the dramatist has used to create the play.

This doubling back reinforces and clarifies what may have been missed on the original reading. Even if you are a skillful reader, you are not likely to have come to the level of understanding you have on just a single read of the play. To enhance the conversations and enrich the discussion, assume a complete first reading is needed and allot time for rereading and time for small groups to perform selected scenes. Eventually, the students will write their own original scenes, so allot time for reading aloud their drafts to help ensure their final scripts sound more like real dialogue.

As students begin working in groups to make decisions on how to act out the play, anticipate the four natural stages of development: forming, storming, norming, and performing. Be prepared for students to grumble that their part is too large or too small; encourage them to decide on staging that includes simple costumes and/or props; consider naming as the director "whoever is creating the biggest stink!" Most of all, keep in mind during this time of middle school students preparing to present scenes that the best-laid plans often are better modified than forced.

The keys for success are to have and explain a goal, and then let the students plan how to implement it. However, they still need you there. Be observant; step in firmly so students use more of the class time practicing than bickering. Setting your timer to ring 10 minutes before the period ends helps. Then, use those final 10 minutes to rearrange the room, to reflect on what went well, and to remind the students of the next day's assignment. The sooner they begin planning and practicing, the more likely your young thespians will learn and enjoy drama. Oh yes, this is a noisy activity!

Attending Live Performances

Check to see if a local theater company is scheduled to perform the play your students are to study. If so, try to attend it. Preparing to go see the performance provides another occasion to talk about the difference between reading a play and seeing it performed. Even if it is not convenient to take the whole class to a play, you may be able to invite members of the cast to visit your school. If a different but appropriate play for young adults is being staged, still consider taking your students to see it. Experiencing a good live-theater performance enhances your teaching and extends their learning.

Many community theater groups have educational outreach programs established to introduce students to live theater. You may have local actors who would count it a privilege to come to your school and talk about their profession with students. You may even find a live performance in another version for students to see, such as a ballet or an operatic staging of *Romeo and Juliet*.

Figure 8.1.   Seeing live drama enriches written drama.

If you begin planning early enough, you should be able to coordinate your lesson planning with one such scheduled local production.

What if performance prices are high or your school is not near a college or civic theater program that may offer lower rates? Ask around. Consider local community theater groups. Put out the word that you are looking for someone in the area with stage experience; you might find a terrific and inexpensive guest speaker thrilled to come. Also, investigate organizations that might help underwrite the cost of bringing in a touring group, such as service organizations like the Kiwanis, Rotary, Lions, and Optimist Clubs; local philanthropic foundations and arts associations are possibilities, too.

Planning the Field Trip

If you are new to your school or district and you decide to plan an outing to the theater, consult with your administrator and seek advice from other teachers who have experience with field trips. Trips can take weeks of planning: coming up with the finances; raising the funds for those who cannot afford tickets; transportation; chaperones; and permission slips. Do not be dissuaded by naysayers. Attending a live performance can be an eye-opening experience well worth the effort you expend. Careful planning can make it a pleasure.

Young students enjoy being known as a respectful audience. You can help them become one. Ushers at local theaters know which schools and which teachers have well-mannered students. You can inspire commendable behavior even in rowdy young teenagers. Believe it or not, what they wear makes a difference, but no need to tell them how important it may be to you. Instead, urge students to dress for the occasion with special attire appropriate for your community. When teenagers are dressed well, they seem to behave better.

The public talks. Do what you can to prepare your students to confirm your school's good reputation or to surprise others that your particular class is better behaved than expected. For some students, this may be their first experience with live theater. It is exciting for them. Some will be awed by the ambience. You can allay their anxiety and reduce their squirrelly behavior if you can show them pictures of the interior and a layout of the facility. This will increase their curiosity and prepare them for what to expect. Encourage them to talk about the experience before, during the ride to, and from the theater and afterward in the classroom—but not during the performance. They are not watching a movie! For young teens, this entire process may be a highlight of the school year. They may even decide to write a play about their going to see one!

LITERARY DEVICES AND VOCABULARY IN DRAMA

Studying a play is an excellent venue for expanding or reinforcing the list of literary terms taught about in fiction and in poetry. For example, as you study *Cyrano de Bergerac*, this list could include those elements that Rostand used so brilliantly, such as:

- Allusion
- Ballad
- Dramatic irony
- Mood
- Verbal irony

If the play is in your anthology, you may rely on the literary terms and vocabulary featured in the text. The editorial staff usually does a fine job of selecting words middle school students need to know to understand the play, along with some that would be good for them to add to their speaking and writing vocabularies. Of course, take time for students to look up and talk about any other words that interest them or trip them up when they are reading or discussing the play you have chosen. I suggest teaching drama during the second semester, when the students are comfortable with each other, with you, and with literary vocabulary; are open to acknowledging gaps in their understanding; and are accustomed to looking up words they do not know.

GETTING INTO READING THE PLAY

The best preparation to attending an off-site performance is a good in-class experience with a play. Start right with the list of characters, the author's description of setting, and the stage directions. Encourage students to predict. For example, if there are family members, ask the students what conflicts they anticipate among those persons considering their age and gender. Think about the setting. What is likely to occur in the time and place the author has chosen? Based on the stage directions, where should the characters be positioned when the curtain opens?

If the students previously have studied the elements of fiction, they anticipate from these opening observations and can even predict that the play will follow the now familiar plot line with exposition, rising action, climax, falling action, and resolution.

Establishing Visual Historical Context for a Play—Project It!

Dramatic scripts tell the readers as well as the director when and where the action takes place. If the time and place are unfamiliar to students, show them photos or video clips to help them visualize the setting as they read the dialogue. Websites like YouTube and Vimeo, along with video archive sites, provide tens of thousands of short clips that were shot in historical locations or recreate historical settings and locations, and illustrate both costuming and dialogue for historical periods. These sites are not always easily searchable by keyword, so it's best to search concretely by the names of films that you have already linked to a period. Preview everything.

Staging Tableaux

To help students get a feel for drama, ask them to read the opening scene silently. Then, with no explanation from you of what they have read, invite one student to come silently to the front of the class and stand where a specific character would stand if he or she were on stage. Then, one at a time, beckon other students individually to assume the persona of particular characters and to take their places in relation to those already positioned there in the front. Ask the rest of the class to observe silently until all of the scene's characters are positioned. At that time, call for students to "Freeze"—stand in place without moving—to create a tableau, montage, or representation of that scene.

Now, ask the class its opinions of the character placement. Before those in the tableau lose their concentration and begin squirming or melting, unfreeze them so they can return to their seats to join the discussion. Invite participants from the tableau to identify lines from the play that support their own choice of position. Other students can look at the text of the play to determine the passages that justify the tableau just presented or to propose an arrangement more accurate to the text. Of course, those who disagree should be asked to quote from the text to show why an alternate placement seems more accurate. Taking time to consider placement on the stage will help your students visualize this play as they read and to write more realistic drama when they begin their own scripts.

Journaling Sets the Stage for Understanding

Your well-taught students know to pay attention to what happens in the opening sections of any work of fiction, whether short story, narrative poetry, or novel. As they continue reading the play on their own, they are able to follow the plotline and to answer in their journals the five Ws and H questions (who, what, when, where, why, and how) regarding information about the play.

Assigning this writing activity about the opening act focuses students' attention on the main characters as they are being introduced, as well as on the conflicts, which playwrights reveal early in the exposition of their works, usually by the end of Act I. Yes, the script lists the names in the cast of characters; some dramatists even mention the relationship among the characters, but the reader/viewer usually does not know the personality or motivations of these characters until the play begins. Since you want your students to be able to follow the play without having to go back too often to figure out who's who and what's what, assign this five Ws and H journal entry right away.

Getting a firm handle on these relationships initially can make the rest of the reading go more smoothly. Then you can spend your time inviting students to read aloud, in character, and to discuss their understanding of the plot while paying attention to character development, plot advancement, and theme revelation. Don't get bogged down in analytical mud for the first read. The students do not have enough insight yet to hold insightful discussions about structure. They still are trying to figure out what happens next. Save those conversations for the reread.

Now, after closely reading Act I, trust the author to show what is going on among the characters so the members of the audience can understand the personalities and conflicts themselves. This approach to quick reading is in keeping with the idea that plays are written to be viewed in one sitting or at least a single theater visit.

As when beginning other works of fiction, during the first few days of reading a play, remind students to mark their texts, use their sticky notes, or to record in their journals the words or phrases that reveal specific facts about characters, especially motivation. By this time, most of your students already are active readers, so there is no need to plod through the entire play, stopping to identify this basic information, but do answer questions as they arise.

Taking Notes while Reading

Although a quick read is usually best for overall narrative comprehension, many film-oriented students may have difficulty tracking characters because they cannot see them. These students may benefit from a simple graphic organizer. If your students are not permitted to write in their books, ask the students to keep character-related notes in their reading journal. They can make three columns:

Column One: Character Name
Column Two: Character Traits
Column Three: Page Number

You may find that some students visualize better when they draw a diagram of the set or create charts with arrows, boxes, and circles. Periodically, invite your young students to share with their classmates the strategies they devise themselves to help them make sense of the text. Shared peer perceptions increase peer comprehension.

These notes and drawings can prepare students to participate actively in discussions about ways the playwrights unveil the personalities and motivations of the characters. Writing and graphically representing these facts and impressions lead to deeper reading; students pay attention to the crucial information the dramatist reveals in the opening scenes, thus reducing confusion and frustration later. Once these details are firm in their minds, students can read more confidently. Nevertheless, you probably have to remind your students that reading a play is different from watching one. As readers, they must use all the clues the playwright gives in the dialogue and in the stage directions to imagine what the characters look like and what movements they may be making on stage.

GETTING THROUGH THE PLAY—ART, ACTING, AND VIDEO

Young people are more inclined to assume a persona when they have something to hold or wear so they feel disguised. Begin with a brief talk about which props or items of clothing would be appropriate for each character. You may have students bring props from home, ask to borrow some from the drama teacher, or provide them yourself, keeping props simple and avoiding realistic looking weapons—just much too tempting for shenanigans from mischievous adolescents.

Mask Making

To get the students to reflect more imaginatively on the personalities of the characters, have them make character masks using inexpensive paper plates and colored markers or crayons. Once you assemble the materials, students can complete the assignment in a single period, choosing colors and symbols that reflect the specific traits of their assigned characters. This creative artistic assignment reinforces learning and appeals to those who show what they know by drawing and those who learn by seeing.

This assignment also sends students back to the text. When they show their masks to the class, each student should quote the lines that substantiate their choice of color, symbol, pattern, or arrangement of images on their mask. These lines can be written neatly on the back of the mask, making them visible to mask makers as they describe their artistic depictions to the class. Students often are surprised when peers choose the same color to symbolize different personality traits. With textual support, those choices are validated.

For example, with the play *Romeo and Juliet*, one student may choose red to reflect the love between Romeo and Rosalind, his lady love before Juliet. Another may use red to show the fiery temperament of Mercutio. A student may use black to represent Juliet's despair while another uses black to represent the stubborn stance the Montagues and Capulets take on keeping their children apart.

The same holds true for symbols. When students support their choices with the text, most results make sense. One student may decorate her mask with birds to represent literally the swan and crow mentioned in the script and also to represent figuratively the flightiness of the characters. Another may use dog food bones to reflect Mercutio's speech about "a dog" and the "house of Montague." The colors and symbols selected are not as important as the reasoning students offer based on the text. Much is revealed to them, their peers, and to you.

Drawing and Playing with Childhood Toys

Other ideas to enhance and reveal comprehension include:

- Drawing or bringing in pictures to represent the play's characters
- Picking movie actors and actresses to be cast for certain parts
- Designing a playbill
- Selecting a musical style for the play
- Bringing in childhood toys and dolls to represent characters and scenes
- Making sock puppets to use when reading a scene
- Using children's building blocks to recreate sets

These assignments call upon students' imagination and help students to connect and to contribute to the discussion inspired by their own creative ideas and artistic skills. Of course, the students should be asked to find evidence from the text of the play to support their choices.

Such activities reinforce learning by seeing, hearing, and doing. Because students have written in their journals the words from the text and discussions, have experienced reading and hearing parts read, and have seen the visuals (photos or drawings in their text), they are more likely to remember the particulars of the plot and theme and to make connections between the actions in the plays and their own lives. These visual depictions also provide memory aids students may recall during written assessments and when they begin drafting their own plays.

Deciding to Show or Not to Show

To supplement the study of a play, you may decide to show video clips. You could use clips of the same scenes from different productions—such as different versions of Hansberry's *A Raisin in the Sun*, or an English production and French version of *Cyrano de Bergerac*.[2] In addition to using clips to give more insight into the setting, show a video clip of a conflict similar to one dealt with in the play you are reading. Afterward, ask the students to compare the way each set of characters responds to the conflict. Showing a video of the play you are studying may be a good time for an in-context talk about the grammar of film. See online websites for more extensive suggestions for incorporating media grammar in language arts instruction.

Comparing and Contrasting Film Versions of Plays

When you study *Cyrano de Bergerac*, for example, you could show video clips both from an English version of the play and also the French version of the play starring Gérard Depardieu. The French version can be advantageous even if students don't speak that language; students can pay attention to the action that is implied by the dialogue they've been reading. The fact that this version is performed "in the field" and "on location" and not on stage provides an opportunity to discuss how stage and screen communicate differently—especially with camera angles, close-ups, scene transitions, and audio/sound. This lesson may give students ideas about lighting and sound instructions to include when they flesh out the scripts of their own plays.

Then ask students to discuss or write about the differences they note between the two media. Some students are disappointed because they have imagined the people, places, and scenes to be different from what is shown in the video. This gives an opening to talk about the power of language to create images in our minds and the pleasure of reading widely and independently.

The key for you is to decide why the video clips are being shown and to determine whether they help or hurt students to reach the standards for reading, viewing, and critical thinking laid out for the course. Sometimes more is just too much.

KEEPING THE PEACE WHILE ENJOYING THE PLAY

As the students get further into the play, they are eager to read aloud and act out the scenes. And, because they are adolescents who have a strong sense of fairness, it is important for you to be perceived as such. To be fair, arrange it so each one who wishes to read a "good" part has the opportunity to do so; keep a chart of who reads which part each day. At the end of each class period, during those closing 10 minutes, you can write on the board or project a list of characters they are to meet in the next day's scene(s) and then ask for volunteers to prepare for the reading.

Those who have had small parts should have first choice of the character they would like to read the next day. Those who are scheduled to read ought to understand that they are expected to practice reading their lines aloud at home so they can read in character during class, without stumbling over unfamiliar words. Holding this casting session at the end of each class period is a subtle way of tantalizing them all to keep reading to find out what happens next and anticipating how well their classmates are going to interpret the upcoming scenes.

If practice at home is not realistic in your school setting, invite the readers to come before or after school and practice in your room. Young teens abhor embarrassment, so they take seriously their responsibility of bringing alive the characters in front of their peers. And meetings like this can be a great opportunity for you to have one-on-one time or get to work with a smaller group of students.

Acting Scenes and Creating More Tableaux

Allotting time to act out the scenes is particularly important to ensure that your teaching appeals to multiple intelligences—especially your visual, auditory, and kinesthetic learners—and to make play reading a more authentic way to experience this genre. To demonstrate the ways that dialogue demands certain action and activity, you could give the same scene to multiple groups and ask them to do a dramatic reading that includes some staging and movement. If your class tends to be noisy, with talkative young teens, how about assigning them to present scenes silently, with pantomime only! Then, after they present the scene, ask the group members to justify their choices for acting or reacting.

Creating tableaux again, of the later scenes in the play, further reinforces student understanding of the relationships of characters one to another. This time, raise the level of reflection and observation and ask students to pay attention to posture as well as position in relation to another character. One may have a dominant character standing, a neutral one sitting, and a subservient one kneeling. Students may decide to have one character standing farther away from the audience and another nearer, depending on the mood of the scene. In a quiet scene, ask the students to decide what gestures would be appropriate during a particular speech. What would the nonspeaking characters be doing during that speech? Why?

You can maintain more consistent control in the classroom during acting scenes by planning backwards—clarify for yourself what you expect to accomplish when you schedule lessons for the students to act out scenes. First, consider the dynamics of each class: How have the students interacted in prior situations? Next, give clear directions before "letting them loose," and then circulate among them as they work. Finally, set your timer to signal about five minutes before the end of the period. That way, you can call the students back to order and conduct a short oral reflection on what they learned by acting out the scene. When students know what is expected, what is allowed or not allowed, and know that you are nearby to help them behave themselves, they usually live up to your expectations. You can achieve your goals and retain your sense of humor.

Deepening Understanding of Literary Devices

By the second semester, your middle school students are at ease identifying, discussing, and writing about most of the literary devices, with the exceptions of theme and irony. So, when you plan lessons for drama study, design activities to help them develop greater confidence with these features of literature. You could quiz them with quotations from the play and ask students to identify the speaker, the situation, and the importance of that speech to characterization, plot advancement, or setting. These informal assessments measure their retention of this knowledge.

Middle school students grasp the concept of dramatic irony fairly quickly when you use examples from movies. Dramatic irony creates suspense when the audience knows something a character does not know, and the audience waits with anticipation to learn who will tell, when the information will be revealed, and how the character will react when she learns—for example, in a murder mystery when the audience knows the killer before the detective learns, or in a love story when the audience knows that character A is dating character B, but character B also is dating character C, the best friend of character A!

To understand and identify literary themes in plays, students must understand the plot line so students may find it useful first to refer to their one-paragraph summaries of the five Ws and H questions. Just as you taught during the short story unit, ask the students to write thematic statements in which they identify the universal situation based on the conflict, and the relatively common response to the situation, based on the character's response to the conflict. Your students may bring up the fact that people in their culture may respond in subtly different ways. Honor these cultures as students themselves explain those differences.

It may help your students write these theme statements if you remind them of what they learned in the short story unit. For those who need it, provide a sample formatted sentence with missing words:

When people _____ (the students fill in the situation), they _____ (the students fill in the response to the situation).

For one homework assignment, ask students to try writing some of these sentences in their reading journals or digital notebooks. After students write the theme statements, they can later convert the SWBST phrases (Somebody Wanted But So Then) into simple sentences that generalize the concept captured in their preliminary drafts. Students, like Kristen, soon recognize the universal quality of plays in much the way they saw them in other literary works studied this school year.

Kristin's statements about theme in *Cyrano de Bergerac*:

- When people have a crush on someone, they show off for their crush. (In some neighborhoods, "crush" is also slang for the object of one's affections.)
- When someone dies, their loved ones mourn for them.
- People respond to tense situations with brave action.
- People are willing to battle physically or emotionally to get what they want.
- People with physical flaws try to impress others to avoid rejection.
- People are attracted first to external features.

WRITING PLAYS AND
CROSS-CURRICULAR COLLABORATIONS

Middle school students learn well when they see a link to other topics or subjects they are studying in other classes. Collaborating teachers who take time to create such lessons tend to have more success in getting their students to engage. One activity that lends itself well to cross-curricular collaboration is playwriting. For example, in many schools eighth graders study physical science, which includes units on geology, weather, and the planets. Many eighth-grade literature lists include legends and myths. What a wonderful opportunity to write plays based on those myths that attempt to explain early man's rationale for the way the Earth was formed, what causes weather, how stars come to be arranged in particular patterns, and why the planets exist.

The same kind of teaming could work with colleagues in the history or social studies department. Invite a teacher in the other department to work with you to design a joint assignment for which your students write a play set in the same historical period or that features the real people the students may be studying in one of those other classes. Think outside the box and consider working with a colleague in art or music, health or physical education.

Then, you can share the grading, using the features of the familiar Six Traits® rubric or one that teachers from both departments create together. For example, one of you could read the students' written plays for accuracy of facts and ideas, for voice and sentence fluency. The other could read for organization, word choice, and conventions of drama writing as well as for mechanics, usage, and grammar. Such sharing could halve the labor and double the pleasure of working together on a project that enhances authenticity of assessment in both areas of study.

Or, after studying a group of short stories, you may be ready to introduce students to playwriting instead of short story writing. Small groups could choose different short stories already studied and then create a script based on one of the short stories and incorporate the elements of drama they learn in this drama unit.[3] The students may find it helpful to use such questions as those that follow to self-check their progress in play writing on the topic you assign or they choose. See the companion website for ideas to a playwriting unit, http://teachingenglishlanguagearts.com/.

Play Writing Check–Up List

- Who are the two or three main characters in your play?
- What myth, short story, or incident is the basis for your play?

- What do you want the audience to think, feel and know as a result of reading or seeing your play?
- When does your play take place?
- Where does your play take place?
- Simple set requirements?
- Simple lighting required?
- Why are the characters in conflict? (universal issue)
- Parent child disagreement
- Sibling rivalry
- Desire for power or glory
- Peer pressure
- Boy meets girl
- Love triangle

If you begin planning early enough in the first semester, your drama teacher may have time to join forces with you and plan time for the drama classes in the second semester to perform selected dramas of your teen playwrights. You can imagine how gratifying it would be for these middle school authors to see their words come to life! Knowing their work is to be seen by their peers, families, and/or friends inspires the students to do a better job on the assignment. Win. Win. Win.

SUMMATIVE ASSESSMENTS

At the end of the unit, you know to assess student learning by having students demonstrate their understanding of relationships among the characters, or the author's use of literary devices and the newly taught elements of drama. You could include options for which they can choose to

- Summarize their learning by writing a poem about the play.
- Write an additional scene describing what happens next with characters who have survived.
- Write a one-act play with the same conflict set in a contemporary time or place.
- Take a test.
- Write a paper.
- Produce a video with live performers.
- Create an animated video to post on your class website.

CONCLUSION

The study of drama can be an enriching experience for students and teachers because it incorporates six language arts skills—reading, writing, speaking, listening, representing, viewing and using technology—and a reason to practice cooperative learning. Moreover, while reading drama, students get to see how earlier learned literary concepts are used in another genre of literature. Finally, drama is just fun because it appeals to a wide range of students across the range of multiple intelligences, especially those who like to talk, to watch, to move, and to act up. Who's left?

Yes, by the time you have completed a series of lessons with drama, you may find yourself quoting Cyrano's line, "I order you to be silent!" With your careful planning, your students become so excited about playing their parts that you may need to "write down their names" and they each will want to be "at the top of the list." When you issue the challenge to "Step forward, young heroes!" even the shyer students volunteer to be a part of the fun and be ready to "break a leg."

RECOMMENDED DRAMA

A Raisin in the Sun by Lorraine Hansberry: This Pulitzer Prize–winning drama is fully accessible to middle school students primarily because it tells a story with which many of them can identify—the struggle to improve the living conditions of a family.

Bull Run by Paul Fleischman: Northerners, Southerners, generals, couriers, dreaming boys, and worried sisters describe the glory, the horror, the thrill, and the disillusionment of the first battle of the Civil War.

The Mousetrap by Agatha Christie: This murder mystery about a couple who starts up a new hotel and is soon snowed in with five guests had the longest initial run of any play in the world, perhaps because of the twist ending.

The Diary of Anne Frank by Frances Goodrich and Albert Hackett: Set in Holland during World War II, this perennial favorite is a dramatization of a real young girl based on a diary her father found at the end of the war.

The Monsters Are Due on Maple Street by Rod Serling: This dark tale begins innocently with what appears to be the passing of a meteor that causes a power outage. This television script of an episode from *The Twilight Zone* series includes camera cues and lots of stage directions.

These Shoes of Mine by Gary Soto: This short play is about Manuel, a young man who resents the too-large shoes his mother has bought for him at the thrift shop. Spanish dialogue is translated, making it accessible to all readers.

Trifles by Susan Glaspell: This short mystery play explores gender differences in a way that amuses middle school students and leads to lively discussion.

Witness by Karen Hesse: In this play, a series of poems expresses the views of various people in a small Vermont town, including a young black girl and a young Jewish girl, during the early 1920s when the Ku Klux Klan is trying to infiltrate the town.

NOTES

Epigraph: Edmond Rostand, *Cyrano de Bergerac,* trans. Lowell Blair, *World Literature* (Lake Forest: Macmillan/McGraw-Hill, 1991), 472.

1. *Core Standards*, 2011, www.corestandards.org/assets/CCSSI_ELA%20Standards.pdf (accessed May 17, 2012).

2. *Cyrano de Bergerac* (with English subtitles), starring Gérard Depardieu and Anne Brochet, director: Jean-Paul Rappeneau, format: Color, NTSC Rated: PG. Studio: MGM/UA Studios, video release date: February 21, 2000.

3. You may wish to see the website accompanying this book for my *California English* article "An Audience of One's Peers" that describes in more detail writing a myth play, and then decide what kind of play would be best to assign to your class. An extended assignment handout also is there. The play in the article is written in response to a workshop presented by Playwrights Project, a nonprofit arts education organization in San Diego, for its approach to teaching playwriting in schools. Students and teachers at the Bishop's School worked with Playwrights Project for years (www.playwrightsproject.org). The organization's basic curriculum, written by founder Deborah Salzer, is available as Stage Write, published by Interact (www.catalog.socialstudies.com).

Afterword

Bon Voyage—Acknowledge the Challenge and Maximize the Opportunity

> Ideal teachers are those who use themselves as bridges over which they invite their students to cross, then having facilitated their crossing, joyfully collapse, encouraging them to create bridges of their own.
>
> —Nikos Kazantzakis

Be honest. Are you planning to teach in middle school because or until? Over my years of experience across the nation, I have noticed that many new-to-middle-school teachers accept a position not because it is the fulfillment of a lifelong dream to teach preteenagers but because they plan simply to settle in middle school until an elementary or high school position opens. At this time, it really doesn't matter your reason. If you conscientiously apply what you are learning in this book, you can be a successful educator wherever you are assigned.

Whether you are beginning your first, second, seventh, or seventeenth year of teaching middle school, you are set to embark on a trip of a lifetime. Each year of teaching can be different, unique, and surprisingly very much the same—an opportunity to learn and to inspire learning.

If you choose to remain as a language arts teacher in middle school, you will come to recognize that teaching young adolescents can be pure joy. You will realize that you are in the prime place, at a pivotal time in the lives of your students, a time when they either develop a healthy respect or a deep resentment for school. You will discover the satisfaction in helping the youngsters discover how they learn while they are acquiring skills and consuming information.

Language arts is the one course students take nearly every year they are in school. Those who teach them well come to appreciate the time and flexibility to adjust instruction in ways that enhance student learning across the curriculum and thus increase student enjoyment of schooling in general.

The core components of the language arts curriculum—reading, writing, speaking, and listening—are skills that form the foundation for learning in all other academic courses. Now with the onset of the Common Core State Standards for College and Career Readiness, proficiency in these areas is expected when these youngsters enter their middle school social studies, science, and math classes. When such aptitude is missing or deficient, language arts teachers usually are called on the carpet to explain why they are not doing their job. How should you respond? What can you do to reduce the angst when accused of being an ineffective educator?

First, acknowledge the challenge of teaching young adolescents. Yes, most of them come to middle school in the throes of puberty, dealing with raging hormones and startling physical changes or lack thereof; on distressing emotional roller coasters; and stymied with uncertainty trying to figure out what all these different teachers want from them! For the first time, some middle school students have multiple teachers daily—not just one teacher who knows what Gabrielle likes and dislikes and how she learns best; a teacher who makes allowances for Sydney when he's just moved from living with Dad for six months into the house with Mom, her current husband, and new baby; or one teacher who understands Juanita freezes when asked to read out loud without having time to practice. And these students may have to learn their way around a larger school building and find a place to eat lunch with people they don't even know. How can they attend to class work?

All this may seem just too much for some of these early teens. Add to it learning parts of speech and elements of fiction; how to research a contemporary topic; the best way to write a persuasive essay on a controversial issue with correctly formatted endnotes and then to present the report out loud to the class with visual aids in a PowerPoint presentation! It is overwhelming to be expected to know which teachers will make Lailani work in small groups with Duong, the guy she has a crush on, and with Shakira, the girl she had a fight with during soccer practice. Anyway, Andrew's teacher last year didn't teach him how to use a wiki and all the rest of the students in the class seem to know what the teacher's talking about. It's just too embarrassing and why did Mom and Dad make Kwami come to this school anyway?

At the same time, the language arts teachers have a curriculum to cover, a set of Common Core Standards for English Language Arts, to see that each student reaches, and parents who expect the teachers to do what parents may not be able to do—keep Sally and Salvador happy. How can teachers of young adolescents be professionally effective and personally satisfied enough to feel successful in middle school?

Maximize the opportunity. Students in middle school want to learn and they thrive with educators willing to learn how to teach such youngsters as individuals, not as receptacles of information. Research in the past 20 years has revealed what experienced teachers have suspected: Their classes reflect multiple intelligences and students who learn in different ways; culture makes a difference; and males learn better in certain settings than females do. The researchers urge teachers to adapt instruction to boost all learning. No, this does not mean creating individualized educational plans for every student you teach. It does mean designing lessons that teach the same lesson in a variety of ways and that offer students choices in how they show what they know.

You are not alone on this journey even within your classroom. Your students are there to help. They may know the school, the community, and neighborhood better than you, so let them teach you the ropes, but keep in mind that you are a professional. You are the adult hired to see that you all have safe passage through the sometimes tumultuous sea that is a year in the life of teenagers. Keep your eyes on the goal and, using your peripheral vision, keep your adolescents in view, too. They are who you are teaching. Yes, you are teaching kids, not just content. And with patience and persistence, you all can reach the shore safely, secure in the knowledge you have gained and the skills you have honed. How can you be assured that you can reach the shore intact?

- By carefully planning lessons based on what you know about the curriculum and what you learn about your students each school year
- By observing and documenting what goes on in your classes
- By varying the kinds of performance and product assessments you assign
- By being willing to modify your lessons to meet the needs and interests of your students
- By being firm but fair in your interactions with students, colleagues, parents, and guardians
- By recognizing that help is available—right in this book and right in your classroom and from your students, your fellow travelers on this journey
- By taking time each week to refresh yourself, spending time with family and friends or reading a good book
- By attending, every year, at least one conference, seminar, or workshop for professional and personal enrichment
- By believing that associating with excited, enthusiastic, and experienced educators is the best way to maintain your passion for the profession

Know that as you teach your young students to understand and use the language arts to receive knowledge and to express themselves, you are giving them the golden tickets to academic success and personal satisfaction. You, their language arts teacher, have the privilege of guiding, coaching, and accompanying young adolescents along the journey. You, who provide the balance between dependable discipline and appropriate play in a safe, supportive environment, can help raise their self-esteem and increase their confidence and competence in communicating.

What does this look like in the real world? For some classes, it means incorporating more technology in your teaching but recognizing that students come to you with access to a range of technology. It is your job to help them understand educational applications and encourage them to use what they know to learn what you teach so they ultimately are prepared for careers or colleges, wherever the next leg of their journey takes them.

So, whether you are teaching middle school language arts because it is your dream job or until you get an assignment teaching high school, do what you can to make these crucial years for young adolescents ones during which they learn to love learning because you have recognized the challenge and are maximizing the opportunity to enjoy and teach each student as a unique individual.

Each time you design flexible lessons permeated with rich experiences for exploring fiction and nonfiction in the print and electronic media, of writing in a range of modes for a variety of authentic purposes, by talking and listening to you, their peers and those they encounter face-to-face and online, and learning to critically view and use available technology, you are cultivating in them vital skills for growth. With diligence on your part and assiduousness on theirs, you all will complete a school year inspired by the success of the current year and eager to move on to the challenges of the next. So, bon voyage! Enjoy the journey!

NOTES

Epigraph: Nikos Kazantzakis, "Quotes by Nikos Kazantzakis," *Goodreads,* 2011, www.goodreads.com/quotes/show/301968 (accessed April 5, 2012).

Figure 9.1.   Careful planning leads to smoother sailing.

Appendix

Teacher Resources

TEACHER RESOURCE A: COLLAGE ASSIGNMENT— *THE CIRCUIT* BY FRANCISCO JIMÉNEZ

Task

As an introduction to the study of literature this school year, you are to work with a group of your peers to present your impressions of ways Francisco Jiménez uses various elements of the narrative—point of view, setting, characterization, conflict, symbolism, and figurative language—to create a story that is engaging, meaningful, and stylistically unique and effective.

Using whatever posterboard, cardboard, paper, fabric, electronic slide template, or similar tool that your group chooses, create a collage that depicts the aspect of the story that your group has been assigned. The completed collages are to be no larger than 11 × 14 inches or no more than six slides. In addition to pictures and drawings, the collage or slide presentation should include words and quotations from the story. All group members must participate in a presentation of the collage to the class. Your group also may create a digital collage using a PowerPoint, Prezi, or Animoto program.

Preparation and Organization

With your group members, review the story and brainstorm about the people, place(s), events, and images that come to mind as you think about your group's focus. At home, hunt through magazines, newspapers, or online graphics and bring to class four or five pictures, words, and direct quotations from the story that can best illustrate your group's focus area. Bring your materials to class. As a group, decide which quotations, pictures, and so forth can best illustrate the aspect of the novel your collage is to represent. Make the collage; then decide how your group can present the collage to the class. See "Presentation" below.

Options: Review the options below in preparation for being assigned in class to a collage group.

- *Setting*: Choose five or six significant settings. Represent the settings in terms of the impact each has on Panchito (the main character); consider also the connection of the various settings with the title of the story. In your presentation to the class, be prepared to explain the reasons for your choices.
- *Characters*: Choose five or six important characters. Present or depict them in terms of their relationship with Panchito and the significance of their influence upon him. In your presentation to the class, be prepared to explain the reasons for your choices.
- *Conflicts*: Choose five or six memorable conflicts in the story. Depict the characters involved in each conflict as well as the effect the conflict has on Panchito. (Note: He may have been an observer of the conflict and not necessarily directly involved.) In your presentation to the class, be prepared to explain the reasons for your choices.
- *Symbolism and Figurative Language*: Select examples of five or six particularly effective devices (symbols, images, metaphors, figures of speech) that Jiménez uses to illustrate character, conflict, or theme or to unify the story. In your presentation to the class, be prepared to explain the reasons for your choices.
- *Lessons Learned*: Put yourselves in Panchito's shoes. Identify three or four of the most important lessons that you think Panchito learns and, perhaps, benefits from his experiences growing up in a migrant family. These lessons may be supported by any of the previous elements: setting, characterization, conflict, use of symbolism, and figurative language. In your presentation to the class, be prepared to explain the reasons for your choices.

The Presentation

Plan a six- to seven-minute presentation during which you display and explain your collage. All group members should speak about an equal amount of time. Plan the order each member is to speak. Feel free to use notes, but please do not read them word for word. Decide where each group member should stand so that the whole class can see the collage as you make your presentation. Practice what you plan to say, then you can establish and maintain eye contact with members of the audience. If your group makes a digital collage, be sure to save and send a copy to the teacher the evening before your presentation day.

TEACHER RESOURCE B:
BOOK REPORT #1—MAKING CONNECTIONS

Step 1—Select and read a novel.
Step 2—Create a diagram of the plot.
Step 3—Write a summary of your novel.
Step 4—Decide whether to use Option A or Option B and write a meaty P.I.E. paragraph response.
Step 5—Share your report with your classmates on the due date _____.

Part I

One side of a 12 × 9" sheet of construction paper or one digital slide:

1. Draw a plotline that shows how the events in your story progressed. If you have a longer exposition than resolution, have the length of the lines reflect that. If you have a shorter rising action than falling action, let your plot line show that.
2. Show the following in words and drawings, computer graphics, or magazine cutouts.

   • Main characters
   • Setting
   • Conflict
   • Complications/obstacles in rising action
   • Climax
   • Falling action/dénouement
   • Resolution

Part II

On the reverse side of the same construction paper or second digital slide, word-process your paragraph, print it, and then glue it on.

Write a half-page summary of your book that includes the title, author, main characters, and the characterization the author uses; the setting, both time and place; the conflict and the specific kind(s); and the point of view. *Use the literary terms we've been learning.* Paste this summary on the left side of the back page.

Part III

Write a half-page paragraph response to Option A or Option B. Decide which questions best fit your book. (Consider them all, and then write about

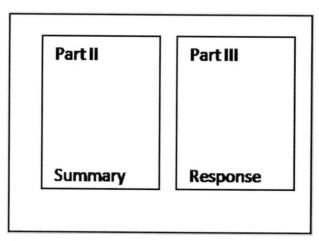

Figure TR1. Making Connections.

three or four of them.) Organize your responses so that your paragraph flows smoothly from one idea to the next. Word-process your paragraph, print it out, and then glue it onto the reverse side of the poster on the right side of the back page or on a separate digital slide.

Option A—My Response to This Book

First, answer these questions about your book, decide which are more significant to you, and then pull your responses together into a paragraph that is a unified whole. For example: qualities of character, connection to character, opinions expressed, expectations, and so forth.

1. What did you like best about the person you read about? Why?
2. What did you like least about the person you read about? Why?
3. Does this person remind you of yourself? Explain
4. What is the most difficult moment for this person? What does she or he learn from it?
5. What is the best moment for this person? What does she or he learn from it?
6. Which qualities of this person have that you want to develop within yourself?
7. Why would you like to develop these qualities?
8. Do any of the ideas, incidents, or actions in this book remind you of your own life or of something that has happened to you?
9. Do you feel that there is an opinion expressed by the author in this book? What is it? Why do you think this is an opinion? Do you agree with the opinion? Why or why not?

10. In what point of view is the book written? How would the book be different if it were written from a different point of view? Which one?

11. When you picked the book, what kind of book did you think it would be? Why? Was it the type of book you thought it would be? If not, did you like it anyway?

Option B—This Book Made Me . . .

Complete each of these eight ideas with material coming from the book you read.

This book made me:

- wish that . . .
- realize that . . .
- decide that . . .
- wonder about . . .
- see that . . .
- believe that . . .
- feel that . . .
- and hope that . . .

Now, decide which are more significant to you and then write a paragraph that pulls these together into a unified whole. Remember, to write P.I.E. paragraph: make your point, illustrate it with details from your book, and explain to show connection between illustration and point.

TEACHER RESOURCE C:
PREWRITING PROMPTS FOR TELLING T.I.M.E.

Telling the T.I.M.E. for (title) _____

T = Title, Thought, and Theme

- Who could be the speaker?
- Who could be the audience?
- What is a message, in your opinion?

I = Imagery and Figurative Language

- What kind(s) of imagery are used?
- What words or lines from the poem support your answer?

M = Music and Sound

- If there is a rhythm pattern, mark the poem: use stressed "/" and unstressed "u" marks to show the rhythm pattern.
- What kind of rhythm pattern is in this poem?
- On the poem, use "abc's" to show rhyme scheme.
- What special kinds of words or techniques does the author use to create sound for effect in this poem?
- What words prove your answer?

E = Emotion (Expressed/Experienced)

- What emotion is expressed by the poet in this poem?
- What words or lines support your answer?
- What emotion do you experience as the reader of this poem?
- What words, phrases, or lines evoke this emotional response for you?
- How well does this poem reflect our definition of poetry? (See notebook for exact wording.)

TEACHER RESOURCE D:
PERUSING, PICKING, PRESENTING,
AND PERFORMING POETRY

Spend some time reading poetry and decide which poem you like well enough to share with the class. (Please select a new poem; one not done for previous assignments or projects.)

Steps to Selection

1. Select a collection of poems (a collection by the same or by different authors).
2. Start with the first poem in the book. Read the first four lines, and then decide if you understand them.
3. If you also enjoy the poem you understand, stop, and go on to preparing your class presentation.
4. If not, read the next, continuing by reading the first four lines of each successive poem until you find one you understand and enjoy enough to share with the class.
5. Keep a record of the number of poems you read before selecting one to share in class.

Preparation for Presentation: Written and Visual

1. In your own words, tell what the poem seems to be saying.
2. Tell why you enjoyed the poem. What about the poem got your attention?
3. Copy out your favorite line from the poem, and tell why it is your favorite.
4. Tell what you noticed about the way the poet wrote the poem—the special way she or he used words, lines, stanzas, sounds, ideas, and comparisons. If you can use the language of poetry analysis, do so.
5. Pattern this poem by writing one of your own using some strategies used by your poet.
6. Photocopy or word-process the poems or write them in calligraphy or other attractive print.
7. Mount and illustrate, or select an appropriate border for them.
8. Bring your poem to class the day you are to present your poem. We plan to make an anthology of favorite poems.
9. Memorize the original poem.

Presentation Day

1. Recite the memorized poem dramatically. You can recite it twice. Once at the beginning of your presentation, and again at the end.
2. Your presentation should be about three minutes. During this sharing time, state the title and author of your poem, relate some of the information from your writing about the poem, and perhaps play some music in the background. (Let me know ahead of time so I'll have equipment in the classroom to play your music.)
3. Let me know if you wish to bring "neat to eat treats" on presentation day.
4. Turn in your illustrated poem and your writing about the poem.

ENJOY!!

TEACHER RESOURCE E: IN-CLASS PEER FEEDBACK

It is effective use of time to have students respond in class to the writing of their peers. Here's a structure that works well for a 50–60-minute class meeting. Keep in mind, it may take three tries doing it before students feel comfortable with the process.

Seven Values for This Use of Class Time

Value #1

Students get feedback on their drafts from at least three peers. Each reader focuses on one portion of the draft.

- Classmate A—*CONTENT* sufficient to meet requirements of assignment
- Classmate B—*STRUCTURE* of essay, of paragraphs, of sentences
- Classmate C—*LANGUAGE, QUALITY OF RESOURCES or EVIDENCE, MUGS* (mechanics, usage, grammar, spelling), and so on.

Sometimes, it would be better to use a version of the **Six-Traits Writing**© rubric and organize responses where students respond to

- Classmate A—Traits 1 and 4
- Classmate B—Traits 2 and 5
- Classmate C—Traits 3 and 6

Value #2

Students get to read ways their classmates respond to the assignment and have a sense of the pool in which their paper will be graded. They can see how strong or weak their writing may seem when read before or after that of their classmates.

Value #3

Students get to see what works and what doesn't work in the writing, and maybe even see ways to improve their own work as they use the same rubric or grading guidelines as the teacher will use to evaluate their writing.

Value #4

Students receive feedback from three different readers who will have given specific commendations and recommendations the writers can take into consideration during the revision stage.

Value #5

Teacher does not have to spend hours reading and responding to drafts when she or he can teach students to do the work.

Value #6

Teachers can scan the drafts and responses posted online and be prepared to tailor lessons for the next class meeting that include commendations on what already is well written and recommendations to help students during the revision step.

Value #7

Teachers receive empathy from students who see how long it could take to read and respond succinctly to a whole set of papers. Students may be a little more patient when it takes a teacher longer than 24 hours to return graded assignments.

Bibliography

"Adolescent Brain Development." *Act for Youth.* 2002. A collaboration of Cornell University, University of Rochester, and the NYS Center for School Safety. www .actforyouth.net/resources/rf/rf_brain_0502.pdf (accessed May 13, 2013).

Advanced Dictionary. Sunnyvale, Calif.: Thorndike-Barnhart Series, 1988.

"Artemisia Gentileschi and Elisabetta Sirani—Two women of the Italian baroque." http://newexpressionist.blogspot.com/2009/03/artemisia-gentileschiand-elisabetta .html (accessed April 3, 2012).

Asian Pacific Economic Cooperation. "21st-century competencies." http://hrd.apec wiki.org/index.php/21st_Century_Competencies (accessed March 16, 2012).

Assembly on Literature for Adolescents. "ALAN online: The official site of the Assembly on Literature for Adolescents." www.ncte.org/adlit (accessed March 16, 2012).

Bacon, Francis. "Essays of Francis Bacon—Of studies." *Authorama Public Domain Books.* www.authorama.com/essays-of-francis-bacon-50.html (accessed March 8, 2012).

Baines, Lawrence. "Cool books for tough guys: 50 books out of the mainstream of adolescent literature that will appeal to males who do not enjoy reading." *Alan Review* 22, no. 1 (1994).

Blau, Sheridan D. *The Literature Workshop: Teaching Texts and Their Readers.* Portsmouth, N.H.: Heinemann, 2003.

Bransford, John D., Ann L. Brown, and Rodney R. Cockin. *How People Learn: Brain, Mind, Experience, and School.* Washington, D.C.: National Academy Press, 2000.

Burke, Edmund. "Quotes and sayings about books and reading." *Quote Garden.* www.quotegarden.com/books.html (accessed September 7, 2009).

Carrasquillo, Angela. *Beyond the Beginnings: Literacy Interventions for Upper Elementary English Language Learners.* Clevedon, U.K.: Multilingual Matters, 2004.

Claggett, Fran, and Joan Brown. *Drawing Your Own Conclusions: Graphic Strategies for Reading, Writing, and Thinking.* Portsmouth, N.H.: Heinemann, 1992.

Claggett, Fran, Louann Reid, and Ruth Vinz. *Daybook of Critical Reading and Writing: World Literature.* Wilmington, Mass.: Great Source Education Group, 2008.

———. *Daybook of Critical Reading and Writing.* Wilmington, Mass.: Great Source Education Group, 1998.

Coffey, Heather. "Code-Switching." *UNC School of Education.* www.learnnc.org/lp/pages/4558 (accessed March 16, 2012).

"Common Core Standards for English Language Arts." *Common Core State Standards Initiative.* 2012. www.corestandards.org/ (accessed March 8, 2012).

Common Core State Standards for English Language Arts & Literacy in History/Social Studies, Science, and Technical Subjects. www.corestandards.org/ELA-Literacy/RST/introduction (accessed May 14, 2013).

CRLP participants. *Literature for All Students: A Sourcebook for Teachers* (Sacramento: California Department of Education, 1985).

Dickens, Charles. *A Christmas Carol.* New York: Viking, 2000.

Daniels, Harvey, and Steven Zememan. "Conferences: The core of the workshop." In *Teaching the Best Practice Way: Methods That Matter, K–12,* ed. Harvey Daniels and Marilyn Bazaar. Portland, Me.: Stenhouse Press, 2005. www.stenhouse.com.

"Education: The What, why, and how of 21st century teaching & learning." www.pearltrees.com/#/N-p=34752422&N-play=1&N-u=1_494424&N-fa=4099999&N-s=1_4100175&N-f=1_4100175 (September 19, 2013).

"English Language Arts Standards 'Anchor Standards' College and Career Readiness Anchor Standards for Language." *Common Core State Standards Initiative.* 2011. www.corestandards.org/the-standards/english-language-arts-standards/anchor-standards-6-12/college-and-career-readiness-anchor-standards-for-language/ (accessed March 16, 2012).

Estrada, Ignacio. *Think Exist.* http://thinkexist.com/quotes/ignacio_estrada/ (accessed March 2012).

"found poem." www.sdcoe.k12.ca.us/score/actbank/sfound.htm (accessed September 7, 2009).

Genevieve, Nancy. *Daughter of Chaos.* Eureka, Ill.: Nox Press, 2002.

———. *NYX: Mother of Light.* Eureka, Ill.: NOX Press, 2001; *ELM* 5, no. 2 (Spring 1997).

———. *American Religion and Literature Society Newsletter,* ed. Deshae Lott (Spring 2007).American Religion and Literature Society, 2007.

Gossard, Jenee. "Using read-around groups to establish criteria for good writing." In *Practical Ideas for Teaching Writing As a Process,* ed. Carol B. Olson. Sacramento: California Department of Education, 1987.

Gutièrrez, Kris. "Teaching and learning in the 21st century." *English Education* 32, no. 4 (2000): 290–98. http://centerk.gseis.ucla.edu/teaching_in_the_21st_century.pdf (accessed March 16, 2012).

Hazell, Ed. "21st-century teaching." *Access Learning* (March 2005): 8–9.

Hendrix, Sybylla Y. "Why our students study literature." *Gustavus Adolphus College.* http://gustavus.edu/academics/english/whystudyliterature.php.

Houghton Mifflin College Dictionary. Boston: Houghton Mifflin, 1986.

Jackson, Anthony, Gayle A. Davis, Maud Abeel, and Anne A. Bordonero. *Turning Points 2000: Educating Adolescents in the 21st Century.* New York: Teacher College Press, 2000.

Jago, Carol. *With Rigor for All: Teaching the Classics to Contemporary Students.* New York: Calendar Islands, 2000.

Jones, David K. *Online Teen Dangers: The Five Greatest Internet Dangers Teenagers Face and What You Can Do to Protect Them.* Scotts Valley, Calif.: Create Space, 2008.

Kazantzakis, Nikos. "Quotes by Nikos Kazantzakis." *Goodreads*, 2011. www.good reads.com/quotes/show/301968 (accessed April 5, 2012).

Koriyama, Naoshi. "Unfolding Bud." In *Inner Chimes: Poems on Poetry,* ed. Bobbye S. Goldstein and J. B. Zalben. Honesdale, Pa.: Mills Press, 1992.

León, Vicki. *Outrageous Women of the Renaissance.* New York: John Wiley, 1999.

Literature for All Students: A Sourcebook for Teachers. Sacramento: California State Department of Education, 1985.

Macmillan Open Dictionary. s.v. pecha-kucha. May 20, 20111. www.macmillandictionary.com/open-dictionary/entries/Pecha-Kucha.htm (accessed May 13, 2013).

Manguel, Alberto. *A History of Reading.* New York: Viking, 1996.

Mission, Ray, and Wendy Morgan. *Critical Literacy and the Aesthetic: Transforming the English Classroom.* Urbana, Ill.: National Council of Teachers of English, 2006.

Mulligan, Arlene. "Opening doors: Drama with second-language learners." In *Promising Practices: Unbearably Good, Teacher Tested Ideas*, ed. Linda Scott. San Diego: Greater San Diego Council of Teachers of English, 1996.

Northwest Regional Educational Laboratory. "Six Traits rubric writing scoring continuum." www.thetraits.org/pdfRubrics/6plus1traits.pdf (accessed March 16, 2012).

Notes in *Great Expectations.* Adapted by Brigit Viney and script by Jen Green. United Kingdom: Heinle, Cengage Learning EMEA, 2010.

"Outrageous women of the Renaissance." www.education-world.com/a_books/books126.shtml (accessed March 16, 2012).

Partnership for 21st-Century Skills. "21st-century skills map: English." www.p21.org/storage/documents/21st_century_skills_english_map.pdf (accessed March 16, 2012).

Peacock, Molly, Elise Paschen, and Neil Neches. *Poetry in Motion: 100 Poems from Subways and Buses.* New York: W. W. Norton, 1996.

Peck, Robert N. *A Day No Pigs Would Die.* New York: Alfred A. Knopf, 1972.

Professional Development for 21st-Century Education. "English Language Arts (ages 11 to 15) literacy to learn standards for students and teachers." www.usdlc-l2l.org/ela_mid.pdf (accessed March 16, 2012).

Reutzel, D. Ray, and Robert B. Cooter. *Strategies for Reading Assessment and Instruction: Helping Every Child Succeed.* Upper Saddle River, N.J.: Pearson/Merrill Prentice Hall, 2006.

Rostand, Edmond. *Cyrano de Bergerac.* Trans. Lowell Blair. In *World Literature.* Lake Forest, Ill.: Glencoe Macmillan/McGraw Hill, 1992.

RubiStar. "Create websites for your project based learning activities." http://rubistar.4teachers.org/index.php (accessed March 16, 2012).

Sandel, L. "Literature for the 21st century: A balanced approach." *Childhood Education* (Winter 1998).

Scales, Pat. "Winning back your reluctant readers." *Random House.* www.random-house.com/highschool/RHI_magazine/pdf/scales.pdf (accessed March 16, 2012).

Shafer, Gregory. "Standard English and the migrant community." *English Journal* 90, no. 4 (2001): 37–43. www.ncte.org/library/NCTEFiles/Resources/Journals/ EJ/0904-march01/EJ0904Standard.pdf (accessed March 16, 2012).

Smith, David I., and Barbara M. Carvill. *The Gift of the Stranger: Faith, Hospitality, and Foreign Language Learning*. Grand Rapids, Mich.: William B. Eerdmans, 2000.

Standards for English Language Arts. Urbana, Ill.: National Council of Teachers of English, 1996.

Starr, Linda S, "Outrageous women of the Renaissance: Warriors, artists, rulers, and thieves." *Education World*. www.education-world.com/a_books/books126.shtml (accessed March 16, 2012).

Stevenson, Chris. "Curriculum that is challenging, integrative, and exploratory." *In This We Believe—and Now We Must Act*, ed. Thomas O. Erb. Westerville, Oh.: National Middle School Association, 2001.

Stone, Linda. "Continuous partial attention." *Linda Stone*. www.lindastone.net (accessed March 16, 2012).

Tapscott, Don. *Growing Up Digital: The Rise of the Net Generation*. New York: McGraw Hill, 1998.

The Free Dictionary. s.v. code switch. http://encyclopedia.thefreedictionary.com/ Code%20switch (accessed March 16, 2012).

The Learning Record. "Royce Sadler: Conversations about the Learning Record." www.learningrecord.org/sadler.html (accessed March 16, 2012).

"The NCTE definition of 21st-century literacies." *National Council of Teachers of English*. 2013. www.ncte.org/positions/statements/21stcentdefinition (accessed May 13, 2013).

The Story of English. DVD. USA: Home Video, 2001.

"Top 15 educational tools/sites for middle school language arts." http://theit classroom.blogspot.com/2008/01/top-15-educational-toolssites-for.html (accessed March 16, 2012).

Treviño, Elizabeth Borton de, *I, Juan de Pareja*. Toronto, Canada: HarperCollins, 1993.

Troupe, Quincy. "My poems have holes sewn into them." In *Transcircularities: New and Selected Poems*, 98–99. Minneapolis: Coffee House Press, 2002.

Tuckman, Bruce W. "Developmental sequence in small groups." *Psychological Bulletin*. http://aneesha.ceit.uq.edu.au/drupal/sites/default/files/Tuckman%201965.pdf (accessed March 16, 2012).

"21st-century skills." *Thinkfinity/Verizon Foundation*. www.thinkfinity.org/21st-century-skills (accessed March 16, 2012).

Twain, Mark. *The Adventures of Huckleberry Finn*.

Vincent, Tony. "Learning in hand." http://learninginhand.com/blog/ (accessed March 16, 2012).

Ward, William Arthur. "Quotes about teaching." *National Education Association*. 2012. www.nea.org/grants/17417.htm (accessed March 8, 2012).

What's Your Learning Style? Edutopia. 2012. www.edutopia.org/multiple-intelli gences-learning-styles-quiz (accessed April 17, 2012).

Wiesel, Elie. *Night*. New York: Bantam, 1982.

Williams, Raymond. *Keywords: A Vocabulary of Culture and Society*. New York: Oxford University Press, 1976.

Williams, Terry, and Jenny Williams. "Image, word, poem: Visual literacy and the writing process." Workshop for National Council of Teachers of English at Detroit Institute of Art, 1997.

Woessner, Patrick. "21st-century literacy: Basic literacy." *Technology in the Middle* .http://pwoessner.com/2008/11/29/21st-century-literacy-basic-literacy/ (accessed March 16, 2012).

Wolterstorff, Nicholas. *Works and Worlds of Art*. New York: Oxford University Press, 1980.

Word Net Search. Princeton, N.J.: Princeton University, http://wordnetweb.princeton. edu/perl/webwn?s=renaissance (accessed March 16, 2012).

Wordle. www.wordle.net/ (accessed March 16, 2012).

Zenkel, Suzanne S., ed. *For My Teacher*. White Plains, N.Y.: Peter Pauper, 1994.

Zimmermann, Susan, and Chryse Hutchins. *Seven Keys to Comprehension: How to Help Your Kids Read It and Get It*. New York: Three Rivers Press, 2003.

Index

acting: drama, 181, 184; like a coach, 48; silly, 157; tableaux, *see* tableaux

active learning: 25, 29, 33, 60, 76, 86, 91, 136, 180

activities: drama art, acting, *see* drama; drawing and playing with childhood toys, 182; drawing and thinking, 56; geography and map study, 137; literature circles, 95; making video, *see* digital devices and uses; mask making, 181; oral presentations, *see* presentations, student(s); professional health, 35; sound effects, to plotline, 55; *see* group(s), grouping students

admit slip: 114–15

adolescents: affirming, 60, 76, 168; brain development, 23, 51; confidence, 79, 103; confused, 76; earn trust, 34, 94; emotional issues, 134; fairness, 183; fragile egos, 119; getting to know, *see* chapter 2 "Networking Socially at the Start of a School Year," 37; interdisciplinary success, 128; joy to teach, 191; learning styles, *see* multiplei ntelligence(s)/learning styles; matters of love, 185, 192; mischievous, 18; prior knowledge, 153; read aloud to, 84; social development, 101; squirmy, 169; trust choices, 29; trust, 29, 34, 94

analyze, analysis: character motivation, 26, 43; classic literature, 81; compare texts, 173; critical thinking skill, 24, 30, 98, 117, 120, 183; of test results, 102–3; poetry, 148–49, 170; T.I.M.E. strategy, 154; using literary language, 203

anthology: class created, 203; defining poetry, 152; first time, 38; graphic diagrams, 54; illustrations, 80; literary terms, 177; poetry collection, 153, 164, 168; quizzes, 63; resource, 47, 66; scavenger hunt, 37, 45; student choices, 61; student survey, 48; text features, 46; text structure, 87

appropriate: arts, 38; assessments, *see* assessments; attire, 177; balance of texts, 108; behavior, 17, 34; books, texts, 76, 84, 148; costumes, props, toys, 95, 181; differentiation, 61; drama, 175; for aural learners, 84; gestures, 184; grouping, *see* groups, grouping students; library materials, 19; music, songs, 100, 153, 168; online resources, 119; pacing lessons, 79; poems, 168; repetition and review, 53; sound effects, 55;